PROCESS DETOX

Rehab for business processes

Dr Brad Poulson

tbp the bradley partnership

Published by The Bradley Partnership

British Library cataloguing in Publication Data.
A Catalogue record for this book is available from the British Library.

ISBN: 978-0-9930577-0-0

To Nellie Hudson, Brian Hudson, Audrey and Jack Poulson; sadly you weren't here to see this but influenced it immeasurably – thank you!

CONTENTS

FIGURES

TABLES

CASE STUDY COMPANIES

Case	Company/Example	Sector	Region	
T1	Santander	Banking	Europe	Large
T2	BBC (Children in need)	Media	UK	Large
	O2	Telecoms	Europe	Large
	Diamond Jubilee Concert	Media	UK	Medium
	London 2012 Olympics	Sports	UK	Medium
	BBC Radio events	Media	UK	Large
T3	Majestic Cafe	Hospitality	Portugal	Small
T4	Highways Agency	Gov. Agency	UK	Medium
	Amazon	Retail	Global	Large
	Travelex	Travel	Global	Large
	Pink Elephant Business Parking	Travel	UK	Medium
	Visa	Finance	Global	Large
T6	BT	Telecoms	Global	Large
T7	Driver Vehicle Licencing Agency	Gov. Agency	UK	Medium
	Motor Insurance Bureau	Insurance	UK	Medium
T8	Her Majesties Revenue & Customs	Gov. Agency	UK	Large
C1	Thames Valley Police	Police	UK	Large
	Nottinghamshire Police	Police	UK	Large
	E-sure Insurance	Insurance	UK	Large
C2	Birmingham Social Services Department	Local Auth.	UK	Medium
	Severn Trent	Water utility	UK	Large
	Solicitors	Legal	UK	Small
	E.On	Power utility	Europe	Large
	Southern Electric	Power utility	UK	Large
	EDF	Power utility	Europe	Large
	Doorstep salespeople	Sales	UK	Small
	Doctors & Healthcare	Healthcare	UK	Medium
	Lloyds TSB	Banking	Europe	Large
C3	NCP	Car Parks	UK	Medium
	GNER (Now East Coast Mainline)	Transport	UK	Large

Case	Company/Example	Sector	Region	Size
C5	E.On	Utility	Europe	Large
	BT	Telecoms	Global	Large
	O2	Telecoms	Europe	Large
	British Gas	Utility	Europe	Large
	HSBC	Banking	Global	Large
C6	Virgin Media	Media	Global	Medium
C7	Bradshaws Solicitors	Legal	UK	Small
	Legal Complaints Service	Legal	UK	Small
	Solicitors Regulation Authority	Legal	UK	Small
B1	Sainsbury's	Retail	UK	Large
B3	Independent Police Complaints Commission	Agency	UK	Small
	Financial Ombudsman Service	Agency	UK	Small
B4	East Coast Mainline	Transport	UK	Large
	Mercedes Benz	Motor	Global	Large
	Prescription Prepayment Certificate	NHS	UK	Small
	Costa Coffee	Hospitality	Europe	Large
B5	British Airways	Airlines	Global	Large

ABOUT THE AUTHOR

Dr Brad Poulson is Head of Innovation & Systems at Central College Nottingham and Honorary Associate Professor at Nottingham University Business School. He is a highly skilled CIO who works with organisations at the intersection of Information Systems and Operations Management and Organisational Behaviour and Change to develop their process capability through the strategic application of Information Systems.

The Bradley Partnership Limited was established in 2007 and combines industry knowledge and experience in the fields of Human Resources, Workplace Mediation, and Consultancy.

PREFACE

I don't believe organisations set out to do processes badly, but in many cases that is exactly what they do, especially when technology is involved. So this book is a practical guide aimed at informing practitioners to help them tackle the everyday processes of their businesses and industries they work within to influence a better outcome for both their customers and their shareholders. It's based on the experience of over 35 years of working at the intersection of Information Systems, Operations Management, and Change Management.

During the mid-nineties I was intrigued by the inexorable growth of ERP (Enterprise Resource & Planning) systems from companies such as SAP and Oracle, and the emergent philosophy that 'best practice' processes were embedded within these systems. The challenge for organisations was to adopt those embedded processes and change the way they operate to make this so. Observing that many organisations find this difficult to do (if not impossible), and the increasing number of abandoned ERP implementations, set me on a course of asking "why would businesses hand over the design (i.e. architecture) of their business to systems developers of the ERP packages", and given that the traditional skills of O&M etc. had long since become unfashionable and scarce within organisations, then who was it that now architects the business?

This line of enquiry subsequently shaped my PhD research which examined something I labelled as 'The commodity adoption paradox', that is, if a process is truly a commodity (i.e. it has no special value to an organisation) then why doesn't that organisation adopt it? This highlights the practical difficulties of how organisations understand what they do and how they do it; it challenged concepts of core competencies and through the use of actor network theory the impact of employees (people) to influence and determine how organisations work.

In 2004 I made the switch from being on the inside of organisations helping them to deliver their products and services how they would want to, to being on the outside looking-in, working in turn for three of the world's largest IT services providers (IBM, Fujitsu, and Wipro Technologies) working with client organisations across Europe, The Nordics, Australia and South Africa, as well as North America. Largely unencumbered by the politics of being 'within' the organisation, although replaced with a completely different set of politics, the perspective looking in from the outside is liberating and encourages a different approach and vision. The benefit of seeing how many different organisations go about their business, in the most intimate of detail, is hugely educational and provides a wealth of relevant benchmarks and comparisons to draw upon.

One example in particular; I developed and ran for a while IBM's Retail

Industry Solution Centre in La Gaude, a location in the hills above Nice on the Cote d'Azur. This Executive Briefing Centre was the venue for a constant stream of 'C' level visitors who were interested in understanding how they could develop their businesses and solve their business problems by utilising the products and services we had to offer, working with them at their most vulnerable, and, in an intimate way, was a fabulous opportunity.

There is a subtlety to an underlying shift in emphasis here over the years from the obsessive focus on how the organisation performs internally i.e. its productivity, efficiency, effectiveness, cost control, economies of scale, labour utilisation, technology adoption and utilisation, all concentrating on 'itself' and how it performs; to that of how it performs for its customers, and how what the organisation does is focussed on what its customers require (or even demand) of it. This is true also of my own focus, which today is equally concerned with what the end consumer / customer experiences informed by the internal method of operation, clearly recognising how closely coupled these two objectives really are.

I'm intrigued by how organisations operate in the way that they do and how they present themselves to their customers through the 'customer experience' they provide (or not)! To this end I have captured numerous examples of everyday transactions, be they associated with products or services, as they have happened to me, and made observations of the root causes of these process failures.

My broad experience gives me a wider perspective when designing and ensuring end-user experience, be it customers (in a retail environment), travellers (in the rail industry), investors (in Financial Services organisations), guests (in the hospitality industry), students (in Executive Education and University Business School environments), ensuring that we can include the best and latest thinking and not just replicate what has always been provided in Academia. When combined with my practical application of the techniques it gives me a balanced and rounded perspective.

About this book

I have recorded some of my new thinking about the subjects covered in this book in a number of articles, blogs, and publications. It seemed to me to be time to pull it all together in one place. It's not just a collection of previously published articles but a number of new ideas have been put forward here for the first time. I have updated a number of them and expanded where appropriate.

Dr Brad Poulson.
November 2014.
Owthorpe, Vale of Belvoir, Nottinghamshire

ACKNOWLEDGEMENTS

There are numerous people who have in some way (large or small) contributed to this book and many without really knowing but special mention must go to:

Professor Richard Ormerod for being an important influence in my academic life, where his insightful approach galvanised something within me to explore, research, and write. A true mentor and friend.

Professor Nigel Slack for what we referred to as 'fish & chip summits' when we would meet in the Cotswolds over lunch to discuss research and writing. Nigel would give me sound advice and practical feedback. I hope I listened to his advice and that he can see that from what has been produced here.

Dr Jimmy Huang for keeping me in touch with academia through our collaboration at Warwick Business School and for keeping me grounded in our friendship outside of it.

My thanks to all those who helped with production be it proofreading and editing, cover design, typesetting and indexing, especially Linda Poulson, Patrick Armstrong Book Production Services, and North Staffs Press Limited.

Finally to my wife Adele, who has a remarkable capacity to understand and join me in my obsessive interest in business processes. It has been of immense benefit to share and discuss the finer points of processes with someone who truly understands the subject, and of whom I can say with no hesitation is 'Process Smart'.

Thank you.

CHAPTER ONE: **Introduction**

1.1 Introduction

From banks to box offices; cafés to call centres; and healthcare to HMRC, we can't escape the fact that we are all subjected to processes in our everyday lives, be they processes of our own making or those more generally the domain of our families, employers, service providers, and ultimately national and local Governments. The role information technology plays in processes and the impact it now has upon our behaviours, our decision making, and the services we receive as consumers is reaching a new level of maturity and complexity, and everyone has a responsibility to understand what this means for our current and future technology enabled process design.

Processes at their simplest are a few connected activities and tasks that fit together in a logical sequence facilitating a desired outcome; and at their most complex a vast interconnection of associated sub activities and tasks, potentially under someone else's direction and control, with a huge degree of inter-dependency most of which the individual can't influence or manage. As the pervasive adoption of Information Technology makes so many more things possible we pay the price by increasing the complexity, dependency, and inter-connectedness of what we do. Even the relatively simple retail shopping experience is now a multi-channel minefield and relies on a plethora of underlying processes and data to support a seamless customer experience, and consider how disappointed you feel when your now heightened expectations of a sophisticated shopping process aren't met.

I have long been fascinated with the organisation of work, i.e. how businesses organise themselves, in particular how they recognise and organise processes. From this has stemmed various avenues of research and enquiry for me about this relationship, in particular:

- how businesses make decisions about processes, specifically the software they choose to support those processes;
- our relationship with technology and processes, i.e. how our behaviours change because of it;
- how we compare processes with other organisations (Process benchmarking);

- the people we select to design and change our processes (Process Smart);
- How the processes affect us as end users and customers, and
- How the adoption of core competencies competes with the adoption of commodity processes.

There has been a change in emphasis in the organisation of work in recent years from *'do it all'*, to *'do parts of it'*, largely attributed to technological advances and the ability to 'outsource' tasks, activities, and more recently business processes to third party organisations. Therefore you would want to believe that these changes are as a result of well thought through and executed plans but invariably, as this research will show, the decisions taken about how businesses organise their work, in particular with regard to business processes, are rarely as logical as you might think and the resultant processes are often poorer than expected. The addition of information systems to support those disparate and complex processes has added yet another layer of complexity, sometimes elevating the complexity well beyond that of the original problem it is intended to address, and I observe that our everyday lives are becoming increasingly 'challenged' by those processes and it isn't trending in a positive direction.

Today my interest in this is twofold and comes from directly opposing standpoints: firstly from what has been described by some as an 'inside-out' perspective[i] observing how organisations, and that really means the people (actors) within organisations, make decisions about how to organise work (i.e. specifically their business processes) especially where information technology (which is now ubiquitous) is involved; and secondly an 'outside-in' approach looking through the lens of the end customer / consumer / service user to examine how processes are received and to observe how the technology, and the behaviour of people engaged in those processes, affects the outcome.

This book addresses some of those issues and is made up principally of three parts (which are described in more detail later in this introductory chapter): *Part one* tackles one of the 'inside-out' issues that of the willingness and ability of organisations to adopt commodity business processes, and documents in great detail a research project I conducted examining how organisations go about this; *part two* looks through the lens of the end consumer in an 'outside-in' mode and explores how the business processes deployed by organisations actually operate and challenges some of our behaviour and issues emerging from our evolving relationship with information technology; and *part three* brings together the findings, conclusions and contributions from the previous parts to provide insight for those of us who enable organisations with information technology to better equip ourselves to ensure that both sides of the 'inside-out' and 'outside-in' dilemmas are addressed and ensure that information technology is truly enabling both business process design for the business and the end consumer.

1.2 Historical context of the organisation of work

"Paradise regained in Turner's rural idyll". This headline from an article in 'The Times' from August 1998 describes how the Derwent Valley at Swalwell near Gateshead, England, has been restored to its former beauty, as once painted by Turner, after it had been laid to waste by generations of industrial pollution. The article goes on to describe how Iron had been worked nearby since 1690, when Sir Ambrose Crowley set up his Winlaton Ironworks, Europe's first integrated manufacturing plant, pioneering the idea of putting raw materials in one end and taking finished goods from the other, an operation that had been in existence for 150 years. In fact, this degree of vertical integration was described as remarkable[ii], especially as a lack of integration was characteristic of the eighteenth century iron industry. The business embraced a wide range of processes and services, and included in their employee lists are references to clerks, coopers, carters, wallers, farmers, seamen, warehousemen and Thames watermen in addition to the usual iron workers. Crowley developed what was described as an "administrative framework" that enabled this integrated ironworks to be operated simply and efficiently by post from his London home. This framework existed in the form of a Law Book, which provided a codification of the rules and regulations and acted as a precise guide for employee behaviour.

Since the days of Ambrose Crowley there have been many significant developments. It was Adam Smith during the eighteenth century who championed the 'factory system' making work more efficient by specialisation and the division of labour comprising: development of skills, saving of time, and the use of specialised tools. Following the War of Independence, Eli Whitley capitalised on the shortage of muskets and subsequently pioneered the concept of designing and using interchangeable parts for production. This led to concepts of tooling-up, quality control, production standards, work-study and incentives.

F.W. Taylor built on much of the work that had gone before and formalised it into the 'Principles of Scientific Management' (1929). This introduced work design, work-measurement and production control. He specialised in 'fitting the task to the worker', and his research on the use of appropriate tools for the job and rates of work led to concepts such as method study and piece rate systems on the shop floor. From this time there were rapid developments in machinery. Towards the end of the nineteenth century the internal combustion engine was invented, leading to the development of the motorcar. Henry Ford embraced the modern assembly-line techniques reducing the time it took to assemble a car from twelve and a half hours for one man, to ninety-three minutes. Two world wars played a large part in speeding-up the rate of output. Forecasting became a problem and this led to the introduction of techniques such as statistical quality control and work sampling, and operational research was established within the armed forces. As organisations grew, improvements came from management and clerical work as much as from direct work. This led to the establishment of the Organisation & Methods (O&M) discipline.

Post-Industrial Age

Building on the work of Adam Smith (pin factory) through to Frederick Taylor (Bethlehem Steel Works), the underlying assumption is that industrial work benefits from being broken down into the smallest and most basic tasks. This relies on hierarchical, command and control structures. Functionally based structures became the norm, with all the associated problems of repeated and manual processing of information. Today enterprises are moving to a new organisational model, from a focus on 'functions', to one focused on "business processes". Technology Foresight (1995), asserts that "firms must learn that changes which optimise processes rather than functions can take them to world class performance". In many industries it is becoming more important to develop new products effectively than to produce old products efficiently[iii], however organisations hang on to their existing architecture long after it has ceased to be the best on offer to perform the particular tasks required of it[iv]. Now organisations are moving into a new 'post-industrial' age, powered by information technology, and as a result many firms are moving toward a 'combination' not 'division' of labour. New entrants pose a threat to existing organisations by 'adopting radically different modes of operation'. As Drucker[v] points out: "In 1880, about 9 out of 10 workers made things; today that is down to one out of five. The other 4 out of 5 are "knowledge people - or "service workers".

Population ecology perspective argues that change comes about because the existing mode of operation loses its legitimacy, rather than the cost and benefit argument[vi]. For example, the traditional way of operating loses its legitimacy when respected competitors adopt new organisational practices. More recently Information Technology (IT) has been revolutionary in the way it has co-ordinated and controlled production processes, the way it has enabled unprecedented cost reductions, and the way it distances workers (both blue and white collar) from the elements of labour. IT has been a vehicle for change in firms, especially when coupled with other technologies. It has made the co-ordination of the enterprise easier in three ways:

the ability to collapse time and distance, the ability to substitute generalised for highly specific tasks and processes, and the ability to capture and use organisational memory.

Business Process Reengineering (BPR) brought together three critical components: the ability of technology to change the way work was done in addition to improving effectiveness; the concept of observing activity across functional boundaries (a concept borrowed from the quality movement); and applying this to a clean-sheet-of-paper and not being constrained by the legacy of the past. The appearance of articles such as 'Reengineering work: Don't automate, obliterate'[vii], and 'The new Industrial Engineering: Information Technology and Business Process Redesign'[viii] brought these concepts of reengineering business processes to a wide audience. But as Davenport[ix] subsequently concluded *"the most profound lesson of business process reengineering was never reengineering, but business processes. Processes are how we work. Any company that ignores its business processes or fails to improve them risks its future"*. The three most influential process movements TQM, Learning Organisation, and BPR share a cross-functional orientation; TQM favours incremental change by continuous improvement based on existing processes, while BPR encourages radical change, reengineering everything from a 'clean slate'.

Miles and Snow[x] describe how efficient organisations constantly modify their structure, roles, relationships and management processes employed to run their businesses. This is a complex task requiring many inter-related decisions and they have developed a framework, the "Adaptive cycle", which describes three key problems senior management must solve. These are the entrepreneurial problem, engineering problem and the administrative problem. The entrepreneurial problem addresses the products, services and target markets. The engineering problem is concerned with the "operations management" aspects such as, appropriate production and distribution technology for its chosen products and services. The administrative problem addresses the structure and processes. It is a process of rationalisation, "stabilising those activities which successfully solved problems faced by the organisation during the entrepreneurial and engineering phases". This does however include a delicate balancing act between, what is described as, lagging and leading variables in the process, which will enable the organisation to continue to evolve. However, it is possible for the administrative problem to be resolved so "tightly" that whilst it adequately manages its current activities, it would jeopardise any future innovations.

Today, some three hundred years after Ambrose Crowley, "popular English has become coated with a managerial varnish"[xi], the emphasis being on 'tiered supply networks', outsourcing and assembly rather than manufacturing; working 'with' suppliers rather than vertically integrating the company; and on business processes, "a set of logically related tasks performed to achieve a defined business outcome"[xii]. More recent management prophets such as Handy[xiii] promote "upside down thinking", by describing the concept of the appropriately named "shamrock organisation" (the organisation structure it depicts resembles a three leaved shamrock connected only at the centre). The leaves represent the professional hub but with outsourced and partner associations to undertake the work.

What is a business process?

There is no shortage of popular definitions for business processes as can be seen from the selection that follows:

> A process is *"a structured, measured set of activities designed to produce a specified output for a particular customer or market. It implies a strong emphasis on how work is done within an organisation".* [xiv]
>
> *"A series of logically related activities that combine to accomplish specific aims by transforming given inputs to desired outputs".* [xv]
>
> Core Business Process: *"A series of logically related activities that combine to produce the primary output(s) from a business organisation".* [xvi]
>
> Business processes: *"a set of logically related tasks performed to achieve a defined business outcome".* [xvii]
>
> *Processes: Collections of tasks and activities that together, and only together, transform inputs into outputs.* [xviii]
>
> *"A process is thus a specific ordering of work activities across time and place, with a beginning, an end, and clearly defined inputs and outputs: a structure for action".* [xix]
>
> *"Process: Any activity or group of activities that takes input, adds value to it, and provides output, to an internal or external customer".* [xx]
>
> *"The direction and frequency of work and information flows linking differentiated roles within and between departments of complex organisation".* [xxi]
>
> *"A collection of activities that takes one or more kind of inputs and creates an output that is of value to the customer".* [xxii]
>
> *"A process is a set of linked activities that take an input and transform it to an output"* [xxii]
>
> *"A business process is most broadly defined as an activity that carries out a series of steps, which produces a specific result or a related series of results".* [xxiv]

Despite the variety of definitions of 'processes' in common use, when the components are compared (Table 1.1), there is a reasonable degree of consistency that generally includes a description of how they are made up from activities and tasks; discussion about the connectedness of activities and tasks through being logically related, structured, and combined also features prominently in the literature. Clearly defined inputs, outputs, start and end points are also common.

WHAT IT IS	WHAT IT DOES	HOW ACCOMPLISHED (APPROACH)	FOR WHOM	COMMENTS
a structured, measured set of activities	designed to produce a specified output		for a particular customer or market	It implies a strong emphasis on how work is done within an organisation
A series of logically related activities	by transforming given inputs to desired outputs	that combine to accomplish specific aims		
a set of logically related tasks	performed to achieve a defined business outcome			
Collections of tasks and activities	transform inputs into outputs	that together, and only together		
work activities across time and place	A beginning, and end, and closely defined inputs	a specific ordering of		
the direction and frequency of work and information flows	linking differentiated roles within and between departments of complex organisation			
a collection of activities	that takes one or more kind of inputs and creates an output		that is of value to the customer	
an activity	which produces a specific result or a related series of results	that carries out a series of steps		

Any activity or group of activities	Take input, add value to it, provide output		To an internal or external customer	
A set of linked activities	Take an input and transform it to an output			
An activity which carries out a number of steps	Specific result or series of results			

Table 1.1: Business process definition analysis

Their applicability to both internal and external customers, and they cross organisational boundaries[xxv], i.e., they occur across or between organisational sub-units, can take place between organisational entities, and can result in the manipulation of objects, both physical and informational. Typical examples of business process definitions are: developing a new product; ordering goods from a supplier; creating a marketing plan; and, processing and paying an insurance claim.

Why business processes are an important unit of analysis

Processes are a sensible unit of analysis as they look across a number of areas. Garvin[xxvi] cites two very important reasons for using the 'process' as a *"powerful lens for understanding organisations, and management"*. Firstly, using the metaphor of 'forests and trees' he describes how a process view ensures that both individual tasks or actions (the trees), and the organisation as a whole (the forest) are given the needed integration, ensuring *that "the realities of work practice are linked explicitly to the firms overall functioning"*. Secondly, this approach emphasises the links among activities, as part of an *'unfolding sequence'*, rather than seemingly unrelated tasks.

1.3 How the book is organised

As mentioned earlier this book brings together in one place research and subsequent writing undertaken over an extended period so it makes sense that it presents things in the order as they happened. Part one and part two can be read independently and neither relies on content from the other part to make sense of what is written. However in part three the conclusions and contributions build upon what has appeared in the previous parts, and in particular the terms used in the analysis of part one are more coherent for having first read the descriptions of the techniques within that part (although not essential).

Quite deliberately it leaves unaltered most of the text as it appeared at the time of writing in order to preserve the context, but where clarity can be improved then I have made comments and additions which hopefully help with the readers understanding. The names of individuals where included have been changed to protect the innocent, however organisations that appear central in the case studies in part two are as shown.

I have taken the findings, conclusions and contributions from each of the works to create a unified approach in response to the challenges business processes present us when faced with the task of technology enabled design for the end customer. Following on from this introduction (read in conjunction with Fig 1.1 below):

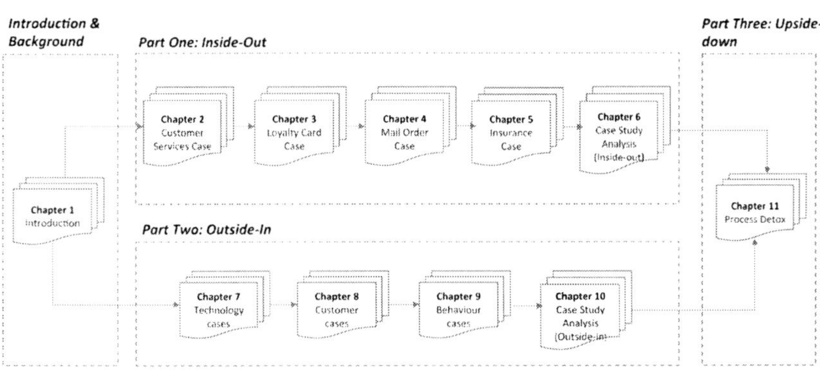

Fig 1.1: Chapter layout schematic.

Part One is taken up with original research conducted as part of my PhD research which examined the ability and willingness of organisations to adopt commodity business processes. The issue here being if a process is truly a commodity then why do organisations find it difficult to adopt it? The research defines three 'logics' (Process, Decision, and Alignment) that apply to organisations when making these decisions. The output is a framework that helps organisations understand the dynamics at play here and how they can be practically evaluated. This section comprises:

Chapters Two, Three, Four and Five: Commodity adoption paradox

An in-depth description of the four principal case studies referred to as the Customer Service case (CS), Loyalty Card case (LC), Mail Order case (MO), and the Insurance case (INS). Despite the similarity of all cases requiring call centre capability at the heart of the operation, the contexts and situations differ considerably, and were chosen for their contrasting approaches to the business problem. The research follows each of the initiatives in turn paying particular attention to the call centre process in use. Each case concludes with a longitudinal view using evidence of what actually happened to review the long-term development of each case over a five-year period.

Chapter Six: Case Study Analysis (Inside – Out)

This chapter analyses in detail the findings from the four case studies and applies a series of techniques to each case in turn which allows for a rich analysis of the individual situations.

In contrast to part one which concentrates on the internal focus organisations have had traditionally with regard to the provision of business processes, part two comprises a series of case studies that are based on direct observation as a customer, consumer, or service user of organisations, and how in our everyday lives those business processes good or bad actually perform when played out for real, and also how we perform within them. All of the case examples were directly observed by the author and were naturally occurring over a period of approximately five years (from 2008 to 2013), and that these things should naturally happen in the normal course of my life means that their relevance is equally valid to others and were preferred in favour of a collection of random anecdotes from other observers. Their volume, diversity, and interconnectedness is intriguing, and that I had the opportunity to not only experience them first-hand but observe them 'live' as they were unfolding was a distinct bonus.

The cases include many well-known high street names, are wide in scope, and unearth some disturbing behaviour and characteristics from organisations and institutions we would want to believe perform better than recorded herein. The cases have naturally coalesced around three themes these being: (i) Our relationship with technology and the impact it has on processes; (ii) how processes aren't always designed with the end user or customer in mind, and (iii) the behaviours exhibited by people (actors) within processes. Many of the characteristics observed appear in cases across all three themes.

Chapter Seven: the Technology cases

The technology cases are all underpinned by information technology and examine how that technology influences our behaviours as users especially when it goes wrong; it highlights how our dependency on technology can aggravate situations; and explores the way we use and adopt the technology embedded within processes.

Chapter Eight: The customer focus cases

The **'customer focus'** grouping is centred on process failures (be it design etc.) that mean that processes don't end up performing how they should when viewed from the end consumer (as the recipient of the processes). Why is this, who cares, and what is being done to avoid this? I had previously captured a whole series of cases for a blog called 'Thinking Aloud' which chronicles everyday activity that is unsupported by fit for purpose processes and some are included here. However most significantly is the case study of care services that emphasises the rather worrying breakdown of processes that care for the elderly and how most organisations, utilities providers, and banks are not geared-up for any deviation in processes when the elderly can't follow them. I use a personal example of how a family member (named here as 'John') struggled to cope.

Chapter Nine: Behaviours in processes

Behaviour in processes: the nature of people (actors) is explored to try and understand why people behave as they do in processes and the inability of people to 'adhere' to processes. It looks at how denial, instinct, perception, and learned behaviours affect what we do, especially when facing a process for the first time. It takes an extended look at complaints processes and what you have to do to complain when the complaints process breaks down. But also the 'meta processes' (i.e. the processes about processes), and the behaviours of the actors involved, all of which are at work for both organisations and consumers alike.

Chapter Ten: Case study Analysis (Inside – Out)

The purpose of this chapter is to analyse in detail the findings from each of the twenty case studies individually and collectively using cross-case analysis. The cases are arranged into logical groupings to aid analysis and causal conditions emerging from the cases are identified and discussed.

Part Three brings together the disparate themes and findings and tries to make sense of what has been observed in order to build on the body of knowledge in this area.

Chapter Eleven: Process Detox

This final chapter starts by building on the work described in part one which concludes with what I have described as the *'seven characteristics of commodity process adoption'*. Despite the original focus of the research being to assess commodity process adoption the findings are equally applicable to all process change activity especially with the 'inside-out' focus. This is supplemented with some practical insights gained from this study that could inform the way managers and practitioners might approach similar situations.

It then builds on the case studies from part two where the technology, behaviour and customer focus issues were examined. This results in the development of what I have labelled as the 'Process A.C.T.I.O.N Framework'.

I then go on to introduce the new concept of 'Process Smart' building on the work of Dr Howard Gardner, which looks at the skills and capabilities required of practitioners who work with business processes and is the subject of ongoing research. Methodological contributions are documented and the chapter closes with some final conclusions.

1.4 Who should use this book?

This book is intended to provide insight into business processes and how they might be effectively enabled by information technology, and is equally applicable to novices and experts alike who wish to understand more about how organisations deploy business processes from an 'inside-out' perspective, and also how those very same processes are received by the customer/consumer taking an 'outside-in' approach.

- *Operations Managers* – this is a practical guide for practitioners to help recognise and identify the symptoms and sources of poor business processes. It describes some of the identified problems so you know what they look like when you see them in contrast to starting with Operations Management theory and projecting forward.
- *IT Managers* – the insight gained from understanding how actors in organisations make decisions about their business processes and subse-

quent IT deployment will help inform their approaches to analysing situations and to make sense of the outputs.

- *Organisations* – can learn that how they operate and how their approach to their own business can be misleading and counter-productive, and to consider different approaches going forward.
- *Professional Services organisations* - it provides some useful insight into the behaviour of organisations when considering the application of technology. It challenges the core competency versus commodity process debate and offers new alternatives. It should provide the foundations for new and more informed consultancy methodologies and techniques.
- *Researchers* – it documents in detail the research undertaken and describes the use of SCA as a research instrument. It also suggests further subject areas for potential research activity.

Notes on Chapter

i PRICE, R and BRODIE, R.J., 2001. Transforming a Public Service Organisation from Inside Out to Outside In', Journal of Service Research 4 (1) 50-59.

ii FLINN, M.W., (Ed.) 1957. *The Law Book of the Crowley Ironworks.* Durham: The Surtees Society, Andrews & Co., Quaritch.

iii MACINTOSH, R., and FRANCIS, A., 1997. The Market, Technological and Industry Context of Business Process Re-engineering in the UK. *International Journal of Operations and Production Management,* No 17 pp344-364.

iv FRANCIS, A., and SOUTHERN, G.,1995. Epochs and institutions: contextualizing business process re-engineering. *New Technology, work and employment.* 10, 2.

v DRUCKER, P.F., 1993 "Professionals Productivity", *Across The Board.* November - December, V.3 No.1, 1996, pp31-41.

vi HANNAN, M.T., and FREEMAN, J., 1989. Organisational Ecology. Cambridge, MASS: Harvard University Press.

vii HAMMER, M., 1990. Reengineering Work: don't automate, obliterate. *Harvard Business Review,* July-August, 104-112.

viii DAVENPORT, T.H. and SHORT J.E., 1990. The New Industrial Engineering: Information Technology and Business Process Redesign. *Sloan Management Review,* 11-27.

ix DAVENPORT, T.H., 1996. Why Re-engineering Failed: the fad that forgot people. *Fast Company, Premier Issue, 70-74.*

x MILES, R.E., SNOW, C.C., MEYER. A. and COLEMAN. H., 1978. Organisational Strategy, Structure and Process. *Academy of Management Review.* 3. 546-562.

xi PETTIGREW, A. and WHIPP, R., 1991. *Managing change for competitive success.* London, Blackwell.

xii DAVENPORT, T.H. and SHORT J.E., 1990. The New Industrial Engineering:

Information Technology and Business Process Redesign. *Sloan Management Review*, 11-27.
xiii HANDY, C., 1989. *The Age of Unreason*. London: Century Business.
xiv DAVENPORT, T.H., 1993. *Process Innovation: Reengineering work through Information Technology*. Boston: Harvard Business School Press.
xv PATCHING, D., 1995. *Business Process Reengineering: Getting to the heart of the matter*. Essex: SSETS.
xvi PATCHING, D., 1995. *Business Process Reengineering: Getting to the heart of the matter*. Essex: SSETS.
xvii DAVENPORT, T.H. and SHORT J.E., 1990. The New Industrial Engineering: Information Technology and Business Process Redesign. *Sloan Management Review*, 11-27.
xviii GARVIN, D. A., 1998. The Processes of Organisation and Management. *Sloan Management Review, Summer*, 33-50.
xix DAVENPORT, T.H., 1993. *Process Innovation: Reengineering work through Information Technology*. Boston: Harvard Business School Press.
xx HARRINGTON, H.J., 1991. *Business Process Improvement*. New York: McGraw-Hill.
xxi GALBRAITH J.R. and KAZANJIAN, R.K., 1986. *Strategy Implementation: Structure, systems and process*. St. Paul, Minnesota: West.
xxii HAMMER, M. and CHAMPY, J., 1993. *Reengineering the corporation: A manifesto for Business Revolution*. London: Nicholas Brearley.
xxiii JOHANSON, J.H., McHUGH, P., PENDLEBURY A.J., and WHEELER III, W.A., 1993. *Business Process Reengineering: breakpoint strategies for market dominance*. New York: John Wiley & Sons
xxiv MORRIS, D. and BRANDON, J., 1993. *Reengineering your business*. New York: McGraw-Hill.
xxv DAVENPORT, T.H. and SHORT J.E., 1990. The New Industrial Engineering: Information Technology and Business Process Redesign. *Sloan Management Review*, 11-27.
xxvi GARVIN, D. A., 1998. The Processes of Organisation and Management. *Sloan Management Review, Summer*, 33-50.

PART ONE:
‘Inside-out’

INTRODUCTION: PART ONE

This section describes the approach and outcomes of a research project that originally started in 1996 and finished in 2002 with the intention to examine in detail the ability of organisations to adopt commodity work business processes. The study investigated the process logic, decision logic, and alignment logic in four internal corporate initiatives within one major UK retailer (The BeingWell Company Limited) where each initiative required a call centre at the heart of its operation. The goal was to develop insights into the development of new business processes and thereby understand what approach would be required in order to adopt commodity work business processes. The key questions were to discover:

- How key architecture decisions are taken?
- What are the conditions under which commodity adoption takes place?
- What is the influence of commodity work business processes in that decision-making?

The term 'architecture' is used in this context to mean the way organisations choose to design their processes and procedures, and not the internal organisation of computers components, or that of a systems network.

Following on from this introduction **chapters two, three, four and five** develop the four principal case studies referred to as the Customer Service case (CS), Loyalty Card case (LC), Mail Order case (MO), and the Insurance case (INS). Despite the similarity of all cases requiring call centre capability at the heart of their operation, the contexts and situations differ considerably, and were chosen for their contrasting approaches to the business problem. The first of these, Customer Service, is a redesigned internal venture that developed and implemented a new in-house call centre capability. The second case, Loyalty Card, was a completely new venture that started with an outsourced call centre, which was later brought in-house. The third case, Mail Order, was another new venture but with a completely outsourced call centre. Finally, the Insurance case is a new joint venture with the call centre operated by the partner organisation involved. In each venture the call centre represented a significant and fundamental part of the business operation. The research follows each of the initiatives in turn paying particular attention to the call centre process in use. While the initiatives were initially completely unrelated to each other and each had a large amount of autonomy, the research does attempt to highlight any impact that they might have had on each other, particularly as all four were introduced within a thirteen month period and evolved over a relatively short yet similar time period.

Limiting the investigation to a single business process (call handling) eliminates many of the extraneous variables that might otherwise be present if looking across a number of disparate business processes, and restricting the case studies to one organisation limits the organisational variables. This approach was quite deliberate to concentrate on the 'decision-making' characteristics rather than the organisational or business process ones. **Chapter six** analyses in detail the findings from each of the four case studies both individually and collectively using cross-case analysis, looking at in turn the *process logic; decision logic;* and the *alignment logic*. Three concepts from actor network theory: *inscription, translation,* and *irreversibility* are also utilised. It uses the inscription/specialisation analysis framework to help understand these concepts and concludes by discussing the 'patterns of activity' identified and the integration of the three logics using a conceptual model of commodity business process adoption.

Research techniques

The initial approach was to gain an understanding of each case individually before attempting any cross case comparisons. In addition to the rich textual case description three techniques have been used as frameworks, thereby improving validity, to structure the data and then used as a lens through which to understand the data. The three techniques are (i) Activity Records, (ii) Strategic Choice Approach, and (iii) an Inscription/Specialisation framework. The analysis that follows uses much of the language of the three techniques so in order to make sense of that analysis the three techniques are described here in more detail as follows:

Activity Record

The Activity Record technique as devised by Werner and Schoepfle[i], is used in this research to compare the work content of the business processes under review in the four case studies. An advantage of using this technique is that all parts of the process are described with clear beginnings and endings (breakpoints), and the hierarchical nature makes each activity within the process visible. In addition it highlights processual context, and defines activities and their sub-activities. Figure I.1 gives an example of an Activity Record.

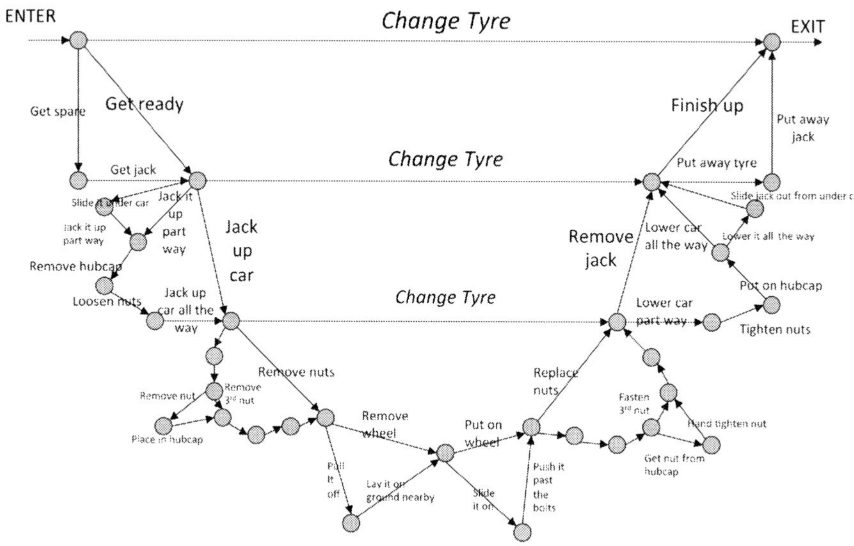

Figure I.1: Activity Record example (Werner and Schoepfle 1987)

The arrow represents an activity that is named, with the node representing the relation "and then...". Thus in the accompanying example you "get spare" and then "get jack", and then "jack it up part way", the hierarchy being clearly demonstrated that you need to "jack up the car" before you can "change the tyre". This makes this technique very explicit showing the time boundaries and sequential/hierarchical structure of the process.

Strategic Choice Approach

The second technique, Strategic Choice Approach (SCA), is an approach to decision making developed from research conducted at the Tavistock Institute and based on the findings from two seminal projects, one in the construction industry[ii], and the other in city government[iii]. The approach deals primarily with the interconnectedness of decision-making by building incremental progress towards a final decision by examining alternative ways of managing uncertainty. It is important to emphasise that the term 'Strategic Choice' is not a reflection that the problem in focus has to be a high level strategic one, but that the decision is approached in a 'strategic way'.

Described by Friend and Hickling[iv] as *'Planning under Pressure'*, SCA is used when people are faced with a number of complex decisions and dilemmas and need to decide between factors like current commitment versus future flexibility, or who should be involved, all overlaid with real-time pressures. Although both of the seminal projects typically have widely diffused powers of decision making, the approach can, and does, transfer into other organisational settings, whatever the management and planning context. SCA was not used originally in any of the cases under investigation, but is used in this research to 'articulate', in a more explicit way, the decision-making processes taking place. This approach recognises three types of uncertainty each requiring a different approach. These are:

1 Where the consequences of moving forward are difficult to predict and not enough is known about the circumstances i.e. the working environment surrounding the decision. Undertaking surveys, investigation costing and data gathering can generally resolve them. These are uncertainties about the working environment, labelled **UE**.

2 The second uncertainty arises where there is a lack of clarity regarding priorities, interests or objectives, and additional information is required regarding the guiding values. They can be resolved by consulting those affected, relevant interest groups, or evaluation of alternative proposals. These are uncertainties about the guiding values, labelled **UV**.

3 The final uncertainty relates to problems of restricted scope, where it might be unreasonable to take decisions without reference to other related decisions. These can be resolved by collaboration with other decision makers, by taking a broader planning approach, or to consider more linked decisions. These are uncertainties about related decision fields, labelled **UR**.

This approach recognises the real and practical choices decision makers face when confronting uncertainty and assumes not only scarce resources (the timely availability of money and people), but also the demands of time pressures and any delays. Frameworks of structured techniques are offered for use when working in any one of the four proposed modes for decision-making, these modes are: shaping, designing, comparing, and choosing. To take each one in order:

- *Shaping:* addresses the structure of the decision problem to understand if it should be linked to any other decisions. The decision graph technique of mapping related (and unrelated) decision areas is proposed. *Designing*: addresses the concerns about the possible courses of action, their implications and possible constraints and policy issues. Here AIDA - Analysis of interconnected Decision Areas[v] is the predominant approach.

- *Comparing*: addresses the range of approaches available from detailed analysis through to a simple evaluation of 'pros' and 'cons'. Using such concepts as *comparison area, relative assessment, advantage comparison,* and *working shortlists,* and finally

- *Choosing*: addresses the management of uncertainty and the development through time.

Practical implications of using SCA as a research instrument

Strategic Choice Approach was used to record the decision-making processes applied when faced with the problem of providing call centre capability for an internal business venture. Retrospectively applying SCA as a research instrument some years after the event, rather than using it as part of the decision making process at the time the decisions were being made, highlighted a number of issues as follows:

- SCA provides a systematic approach to decision making, so when using SCA to simulate the events, decisions, uncertainties and possible outcomes of a previous decision making occasion it is likely to identify new schemes or options that were not identified at that time. Care must be taken to ensure that the options being developed are those that could have been suggested at the time of the original analysis and decision-making and aren't as a result of new information or with the benefit of hindsight.

- The actual feasible option schemes chosen within the case studies would not necessarily be the scheme of choice when using the output from SCA today. It can appear that the scheme chosen at that time was inappropriate when compared with its alternatives. However, the techniques in use at that time might mean that the alternatives would not have been identified or viewed positively at that time.

- In some of the cases the decision scheme that best matched the criteria and appeared most suited to the situation was not that chosen in the case study. Where this occurred SCA highlighted the variance between the 'ideal' outcomes and that of the outcome chosen at that time. This is particularly relevant to the Mail Order case where the 'real-life' choice would not have been progressed through to analysis. Whenever this situation occurred the SCA choice was used as a comparison with the actual choice.

- SCA works best in a workshop environment so the opportunity to recreate the original decision making activity comprising the key participants and decision makers in the cases to simulate the decision-making processes would have been preferable. However, many of the original participants had moved to new positions within the organisation, and some to new organisations therefore the requirement to get enough of the right people to make it a worthwhile exercise was not practical.

- Doing the 'within-case' analysis on each case separately meant that some of the terms and abbreviated names were re-used in different cases. When it came to the cross-case analysis this repeating of abbreviated names was confusing, so some of the options and actions were renamed to avoid confusion.

- The iterative nature of SCA ensures that you capture as many issues, uncertainties and options as possible. However, its 'additive' nature means that should you uncover new evidence then it has to be re-worked into the analysis from the start, which subsequently means that all the analysis that follows has to be re worked. This can be quite a lengthy and time-consuming process.

- With some of the events happening up to five years prior to the research, the accuracy of what is recorded is always open to interpretation. With the benefit of hindsight participants might now have a view on the relative importance of issues and uncertainties that is different from that held at the actual time of decision-making. Clearly this is an issue arising from the adoption of longitudinal research that relies on participants and informants memories over an extended period of time, rather than an issue because SCA was chosen.

- The natural 'bracketing' of the SCA does not always fit the natural 'brackets' within the case studies. For example, the approach can be used to work through the stages to reach a decision point having considered all of the evidence and analysis. In practice, decisions were being made at each leg of the decision making process rather than as a holistic decision at the end. SCA does accommodate such decision-making profiles but would, if being used as the decision tool rather than as a research instrument be reworked at each stage. This would be confusing to the reader if all the reworking was to be portrayed in this way.

- When formulating a working shortlist comparison measures were used that were indicative of those expressed by those interviewed and are intended to reflect the requirements as defined.

- The complete end-to-end nature of SCA addresses the 'chain of evidence' issue.

Inscription/Specialisation

Introduction

The third analytical framework borrows techniques and concepts from Actor Network Theory (ANT) in order to help in the detailed understanding of the relationships between the actors and the decisions surrounding commodity process adoption. ANT is most prominently associated with the French sociologists Bruno Latour and Michel Callon. The actor network is used to represent the influence of a wide range of surrounding factors when going about doing your business. An actor network, then, *is "the act linked together with all of its influencing factors (which again are linked), producing a network"* [vi]. One way of putting this is that the actor network spells out the contents of the context or situatedness of an action[vii]. Actors are *"entities that do things"* [viii]. Networks are *a "group of unspecified relationships among entities of which the nature itself is undetermined"*[ix].

Latour[x] describes three common misunderstandings when working with actor networks as being:

- The misuse of the technical network metaphor to describe and understand actor-networks. He suggests *that "an actor-network may lack all the characteristics of a technical network: it may be local, it may have no compulsory paths, no strategically positioned nodes".*

- Unlike social networks, actor network theory does not limit itself to human individual actors but extends the word 'actor' (or actant) to non-human, non-individual entities.

- Finally, he describes how networks enable us to remove *"the tyranny of distance"*, giving examples of how proximity doesn't ensure connectedness and that distance doesn't conversely mean disconnectedness.

Three concepts from ANT are of particular relevance for this research, they are (i) Inscription, (ii) Translation, and (iii) Irreversibility. Each concept is now taken in order.

Inscription

"The notion of inscription refers to the way technical artefacts embody patterns of use"[xi]. *"Technical objects thus simultaneously embody and measure a set of relations between heterogeneous elements"*[xii]. Hanseth and Monteiro[xiii] have identified four key aspects of inscription:

- The identification of explicit anticipations (or scenarios) of use held by the various actors during design (that is standardisation),
- How these anticipations are translated and inscribed into the standards (that is, the materials of the inscriptions),
- Who inscribes them, and
- The strength of those inscriptions, that is, the effort it takes to oppose or work around them.

Translation

The concept of a translation is succinctly described by Somerville[xiv]:

"Translation rests on the idea that actors within a network will try to enrol (manipulate or force) the other actors into positions which suit their purposes. When an actor's strategy is successful and it has organised other actors for its own benefit it can be said to have translated them".

Translations are *"embodied in texts, machines, bodily skills which become their support, their more or less faithful executive"*[xv]. Translate: *"That is, re-interpret, re-present or appropriate, others interests to one's own"*[xvi]. Latour[xvii] describes an interesting example of translation and inscription by a hotel wanting to encourage guests to leave their room key when departing the hotel. He describes a progression of inscriptions from signage behind the reception desk, security staff on the hotel exit (both unsuccessful), and finally through to a bulky key fob which had its weight increased to the point at which guests would prefer to leave the key rather than taking it with them. Thus the hotels interest was finally inscribed into a network strong enough to impose the desired behaviour on the hotels guests.

Irreversibility

Irreversibility represents the strength of inscriptions, whether they must be followed or avoided, and depends on the irreversibility of the actor-network they are inscribed into. For example the strength of an inscription, say a work routine, could be reinforced by training. If this was too weak then being embedded in textual description within a manual could reinforce the inscription. If this was still too weak then supporting them with information systems could reinforce the routines. The cumulative effect of superimposing these inscriptions increases strength and promoted irreversibility.

Inscription/Specialisation analysis framework

In order to assist with the analysis the following conceptual framework was devised to analyse two critical dimensions that capture the characteristics of work business processes, and the components that make up those processes, these are: *the degree of specialisation, and the degree of inscription.* The two dimensions can be plotted on a graph as shown in Figure I.2.

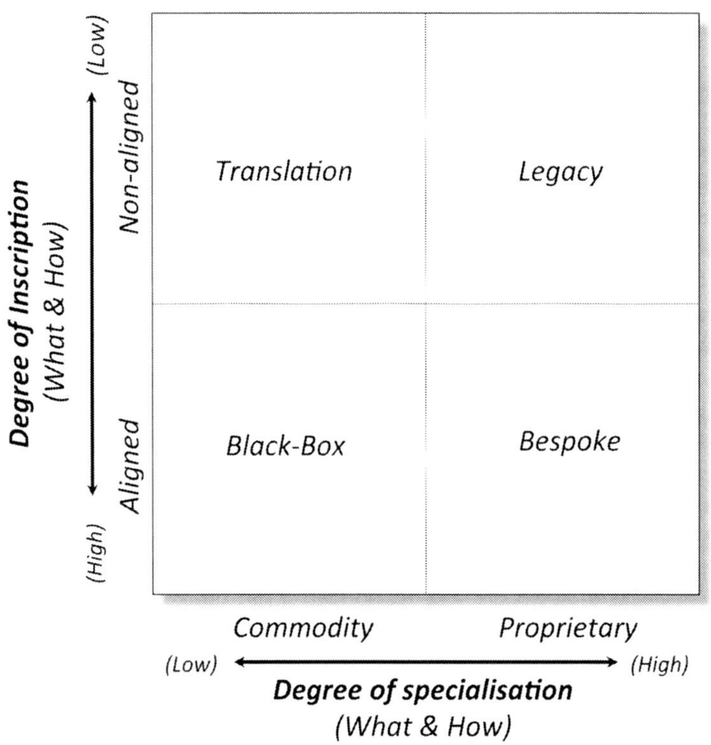

Figure I.2: Inscription/specialisation analysis framework

Degree of Specialisation

The degree of specialisation (X axis) focuses principally on 'what' is done within a process, and to a lesser degree 'how' it is done. Work business processes with a low degree of specialisation will comprise standard tasks, activities and routines that are shared by many companies. They will not normally be the source of differentiation in their own right, and provide no real competitive advantage from what is undertaken. Typically they will contain commodified components, be self-contained and modular. In contrast, a process with a high degree of specialisation will be tailored to the specific and non-standard needs of a business, which contains tasks, activities and routines that are likely to be unique to that business. This specialism will almost certainly be a source of differentiation and is likely to generate significant competitive advantage. The components of the process will be integral to the offer, and they are likely to be proprietary.

Degree of inscription

The degree of inscription (Y axis) principally focuses on the alignment of the interests of actors in the network. A high degree of inscription would characterise a situation where the potentially diverse set of interests of actors in the network are highly aligned, i.e. consensus on how things are done would be evident, and there would be general agreement as to how to proceed. This alignment would be embodied in the computer systems, procedures adopted, the training provided, and in the tasks and activities that make up the process. Where the degree of inscription is low, then this would characterise a situation where the diverse interests of the actors in the network are not aligned, consensus would not be evident, and there would be attempts to 'translate' other actors to their inscribed view. There would be no agreement as to how to proceed and the systems, procedures and training would not be embodied with a common alignment. The strength of the inscription, that is whether it must be followed or can be avoided, would be determined by the 'irreversibility' of the actor-network they are inscribed to.

Patterns of activity

This gives rise to four patterns of activity:

(i) *High-inscription/low-specialisation (Aligned-commodity) or 'Black-box'*
The 'aligned-commodity' space represents those process components

where 'what' is undertaken is highly routine, standard and non-specific to a particular business, and where both 'what' and 'how' it is undertaken is fully aligned with the interests of the actors involved. Their content, i.e. the way it works, is considered a black box, i.e. *"It contains that which no longer needs to be considered, those things whose contents have become a matter of indifference"*.[xviii]. Callon[xix] observed that, *"To construct a market transaction (that is to say to transform something into a commodity), it is necessary to cut the ties between this thing and other objects or human beings one by one. It must be decontextualised, dissociated, and detached"*.

(ii) Low-inscription/low-specialisation (Non-aligned commodity) or 'transformation'

The 'non-aligned commodity' space represents those process components where 'what' is undertaken, and or 'how' it is undertaken, is highly routine, standard and non-specific to a particular business, however this is not fully aligned with the interests of the actors involved. This non-alignment is likely to promote translation activity hence resulting in transformations taking place. The propensity for translation is further increased where, due to a market transaction (i.e. where a product or service has been purchased), the relationship with the supplier is maintained. This continued relationship allows the supplier to be part of the network and can therefore attempt to align the interests of its customers to their own interests. For example, the ongoing relationship with a telephony rental company allows that company to influence its customers through the products and services it offers, its pricing structure, its attitudes, culture and behaviour, its union agreements, and its general ethos.

(iii) High-inscription/high-specialisation (Aligned-proprietary) or 'bespoke'

The 'aligned-proprietary' space represents those process components where both 'what' is undertaken, and 'how' it is undertaken, is non-routine, non-standard and highly specific to a particular business, and is fully aligned with the interests of the actors involved. The business process is likely to be unique to this situation only, and be provided through components that are bespoke and non-standard.

(iv) Low-inscription/high-specialisation (Non aligned-proprietary) or 'Legacy'

The 'non aligned-proprietary' space represents those process components where 'what' is undertaken, and or 'how' it is undertaken, is non-routine, non-standard and highly specific to a particular business, and at the same time is not aligned with the interests of the actors involved. The absence of clear actor alignment encourages translation and a high degree of ambiguity, coupled with the highly customised and specialised tasks and activities of a unique process, makes the ensuing process instantaneously a legacy, i.e. in the form of an inheritance of future development and maintenance difficulties.

Summary

This section introduces the four case studies and provides an overview of the research techniques used throughout all the case studies that appear in part one. The techniques are repeated deliberately within each case to ensure consistency and make comparison more effective.

Notes on Chapter

i WERNER, O. and SCHOEPFLE, G.M., 1987. Systematic fieldwork: Vol.2. Ethnographic analysis and data management. Newbury Park, CA: Sage.

ii CRICHTON, C., (Ed.) 1966. *Interdependence and Uncertainty: a Study of the Building Industry*. Tavistock: London.

iii FRIEND, J.K. and JESSOP, W.N., 1977. *Local Government and Strategic Choice*. 2nd edition. Oxford: Pergamon.

iv FRIEND, J.K. and HICKLING, A., 1987. *Planning under pressure: the Strategic Choice Approach*. Oxford: Pergamon.

v LUCKMAN, J., 1967. An approach to the management of design. *Operational Research Quarterly*, 18, 345-58.

vi HANSETH, O, and MONTEIRO, E., 1998. *Understanding Information Infrastructure, Manuscript 27, August 1998*. Available from: http://www.ifi.uio.no/~oleha/Publications/bok.html

vii SUCHMAN, L., 1987. *Plans and situated actions: The problems of Human-Machine Communication*. Cambridge: Cambridge University Press.

viii LATOUR, B., 1992. "Where Are the Missing Masses? The Sociology of a Few Mundane Artifacts" In: W. E. BIJKER, & J. LAW eds. *Shaping Technology / Building Society*. Cambridge, Mass: MIT Press p241.

ix CALLON, M., 1993. Variety and Irreversibility in networks of Technique conception and adoption. *In:* D. FORAY AND C. FREEMAN, eds. *Technology and the Wealth of nations: Dynamics of Constructed Advantage*. London: Pinter. 232-268.

x LATOUR, B. 1997. The trouble with Actor-Network Theory, in: OLSEN, F., 1997. *"Om aktor-netvaerksteroi. Nogle fa afklaringer og mere end nogle fa forvikinger", Philsophia* (Danish philosophy journal), vol. 25, n3 et 4, 47-64.

xi HANSETH, O, and MONTEIRO, E., 1998. *Understanding Information Infrastructure, Manuscript 27, August 1998*. Available from: http://www.ifi.uio.no/~oleha/Publications/bok.html

xii AKRICH, M., 1992. The de-scription of technical objects. In: BIJKER, W. and LAW, J. (eds.) *Shaping Technology / Building Society: Studies in Sociotechnical*

Change. London: MIT Press. 205-224.

xiii HANSETH, O, and MONTEIRO, E., 1998. *Understanding Information Infrastructure, Manuscript 27, August 1998*. Available from: http://www.ifi.uio.no/~oleha/Publications/bok.html

xiv SOMMERVILLE, I. 1998. Actor-Network Theory: A useful paradigm for the analysis of the UK cable/on-line socio-technical ensemble? Department of Communication and Information Studies, Queen Margaret College, Edinburgh, Scotland

xv CALLON, M., 1991. Techno-economic networks and irreversibility. In J. LAW ed. *A sociology of monsters. Essays on power, technology and domination*. London: Routledge. p 132-161.

xvi HANSETH, O, and MONTEIRO, E., 1998. *Understanding Information Infrastructure, Manuscript 27, August 1998*. Available from: http://www.ifi.uio.no/~oleha/Publications/bok.html

xvii LATOUR, B., 1991. Technology is society made durable. In: J. LAW (ed*). A Sociology of Monsters. Essays on Power, Technology and Domination*. London: Routledge pp. 103-131.

xviii CALLON, M., and LATOUR, B., 1981. Unscrewing the big Leviathan: how actors macro-structure reality and how sociologists help them to do so. In K. KNORR-CETINA and A. V. CICOUREL, eds. *Towards an Integration of Micro- and Macro-Sociologies*. Routledge & Kegan Paul. p 259-276.

xix CALLON, M., 1999. Actor-network theory – the market test. *In:* J. LAW AND J. HASSARD, eds. *Actor Network Theory and After*. Oxford: Blackwell and Sociological Review, 181.

CHAPTER TWO
Case Study One – BeingWell Customer Service

2.1 Introduction

The BeingWell Company (BW) Customer Service function is a centralised facility which handles approximately one thousand telephone calls, and five hundred letters, faxes and e-mails daily from customers and stores about the products and services BeingWell provides. Based in the Corporate Head Office, Advisors handle a wide range of enquiries and complaints ranging from the straightforward, such as store opening times, product availability queries, or product specific enquiries such as the use of hair colourants and skin preparations; through to complaints as diverse as the service quality received in any of the 1500 stores, nudity in television adverts, the grammar used in literature and promotional material, and product recalls. However this has not always been the case, and the 'Customer Service Complaint Handling Review' stated that the strategic intent for Customer Service is: *'to maximise customer relationship opportunities thereby driving customer loyalty and increasing sales and profit'*. This to be achieved through two phases:

1 Effective management of customer complaint handling within BW, and
2 The development and execution of a customer relationship strategy to include care lines, expert help lines, and Loyalty Card customer contact handling.

The effective management of complaint handling within BW is intended to "act as a springboard" for the development and execution of a customer relationship strategy. The complaint handling objectives were described as:

- Prompt and effective resolution of complaints,
- Consistency of delivery in performance and communication,
- Information feedback contributing to increased sales and profit, and
- Protection and enhancement of BW's reputation.

However, the Customer Services Manager described customer service above all as: *"A necessity, you have to recognise that customers want to contact you"*.

At the time of the above review, the methods, processes and systems used to handle complaints did not support the strategic intent, and BeingWell competitors had been investing heavily to improve the perception of their customer service. Providing the customer with positive personal service and good after sales service is perceived by BeingWell as being critical to differentiation. Comparisons with other retailers such as Marks & Spencer, Sainsbury and Safeway revealed that the productivity of handling written complaints was half that of the worst in the comparable group, and only 20% of the best. This did not reflect its mid-table ranking for investment in customer service. Complaints were running at approximately 65,000 per year, with the majority (86%) being merchandise related, while the remaining 14% comprised service, pricing value, professional services and miscellaneous categories. The ratio of complaints to enquiries was 1:1. BeingWell has a diverse inventory of about 55,000 lines (approximately 30% own brand), most of which are available through the stores channel (however not all lines are available at all stores).

The 'decentralised' Customer Service units at that time did little more than respond to paper generated complaints, which led to inconsistencies in quality and content of correspondence, a random mix of formal and informal tones, different service levels for turnaround of responses, and even differing remedies to problems. Staff, who were not necessarily selected for their customer service skills, operated the units, and their approach was characterised as *"anything for a quiet life"*.

When customers contacted BeingWell by telephone this was via the head office switchboard, which often led to the caller being forwarded to an inappropriate department or person. For example, a Product Supply Manager would not be well equipped to handle a supply enquiry from a customer concerning the stock level of a specific hair shampoo, at a specific store, at a specific time. In much the same way, a customer complaining about being trapped in an elevator in a store would thoughtlessly be put through to a building engineer. As a Group Telecommunications Client Manager explained:

"Customer Service was born out of a need to gather together in one place the complaints that were received via the switchboard, which was inconvenient for them and the caller. We also lost lots of information. Switchboards are about 'speed' and 'volume' and passing on the call as speedily as possible. It's not necessarily about chatting with the customer. The principle of taking a call live and dealing with it at the first attempt, then that's the most productive way of dealing with any complaint or problem".

The present day department was formed five years earlier from the disparate 'complaint handling' units which were located within the then separate Business Centre structure[1]. Customer Service is an amalgam of

1. The Marketing function at that time comprised five Business Units, each dedicated to a specific product category range. For example: Health, Baby, Photographic, Leisure, and Beauty Personal Care.

those original units, now located together in one location, ensuring that a consistent approach to handling customer enquiries and complaints is given, and that all calls are logged, and that the resolution of any problems is as professional as any customer of BeingWell would expect, ensuring that: *"It matches the experience you get in a BeingWell store"*, which incidentally was very good.

The structure of the case studies

In this case, and the three cases that follow, three sections in turn examine: (i) the detail of the process under review, i.e. how the process was constructed at the time of its implementation, labelled *'process logic'*, and presents the activities and tasks that make up that process; (ii) the approach taken by the actors in the case to decision-making, labelled the *'decision logic'*, including a detailed account of the decision making process; and (iii) using concepts from Actor Network Theory an understanding of the alignment of the actors in the network, labelled *'alignment logic'*. Each of the four cases is presented in an identical style, although each was researched independently. The case studies conclude with a summary of the key themes. Recorded semi-structured interviews were conducted in this case with John Eddington – Customer Services Manager, and Murray Newham – Director of Corporate Development, as well as actors from the business units involved in each of the case studies, department representatives from internal functions such as Information Systems (IS) and Group Telecommunications (GT), suppliers representatives, telephony vendors, and members of the BW Executive. Archive material such as call logging records and service level agreements were also used.

2.2 The customer service process in focus (Process logic)

Introduction

This first section examines the Customer Service work business process under review as it operated at that time and presents the five prime activities and tasks that make up that process, namely: (i) Receive the 'inbound' calls; (ii) Identify the customer & information; (iii) Handle the complaint or enquiry; (iv) Initiate other processes; and (v) Close the call. It is not the intention to include all the activities that go to make up the complete end-to-end Customer Service process, only those that relate to the call centre process.

The process starts with an inbound call from a customer, and ends when the dialogue, and all the associated components of the interaction (letters of apology, credit notes etc.) are complete for despatch. Figure 2.1 below shows an Activity Record of the call centre process as utilised for Customer Service.

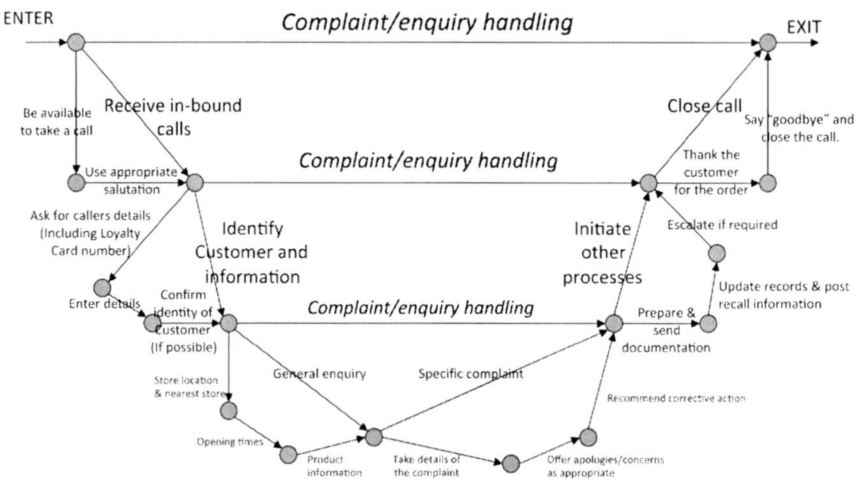

Figure 2.1: An Activity Record of the Customer Service process

Each of the activities is described in full as follows:

Activity One: Receive 'inbound' calls

The process starts with an 'inbound' call from a customer using the customer service contact number which is included on most product information and increasingly on packaging, literature, and in-store material. The call centre is manned six days a week from 0800 to 1800 Monday to Friday and 0800 to 1700 on Saturdays. At all other times key customer services staff are contactable by mobile phone in case of emergencies. Over forty Advisors with specific knowledge of the products they had previously been associated with make up this new function. Similarly, a new management structure was established which reflected the desire to divide the department into small teams (maximum 8 people), in order to maintain a manageable and 'human' environment.

Office accommodation is 'open plan', a structure that suits the interchange of information between Advisors and creates a mutually supportive environment. It can help to lessen the boredom when call rates and energy are low. Access to the building is round the clock, seven days per week, which also included 'out-of-hours facilities.

At that time a local cable network television company were using Automatic Call Distribution (ACD)[2] telephony technology for their own purposes, and it was relatively easy for BW to utilise some of their capacity, paid for on a 'per-user' basis. A low entry-level cost was achieved by limiting capital investment to the purchase of consumables such as operators' headsets, and to upgrade the line capacity between the Head Office building and that of the cable company, where the telephony equipment was housed. Risk was limited through a one-year contract just in case the customer service concept didn't take off. Implementation of the managed service while not without technical problems was relatively easy and straightforward. Although the service was 'basic' it benefited from detailed call logging data, which had previously been unavailable. From this it was possible to gauge the daily call profile and subsequently from this the staffing levels and coverage required. The data on 'peaks' of activity and average call lengths, abandoned calls and out of hour's activity was invaluable, and has subsequently benefited others in their project work by being able to compare and challenge metrics and forecasts.

The reasons for a call to Customer Service can be wide ranging, from a general enquiry as to the location and opening times of the nearest store, right through to a complaint about a product or service which could, ultimately, have caused death or serious injury. This requires that Advisors are professional, patient, courteous and knowledgeable about the products and services BeingWell provides.

Activity Two: Identify customer and information

The transaction with a customer might well require an exchange of personal and product information, which is captured as part of the enquiry / complaint process and retained for subsequent problem resolution, product design, and marketing initiatives. Customers are asked to identify themselves if a Loyalty Card holder by quoting their membership number. Customer Service Advisors use a system called 'ENQUIRY Q' which is designed for internal customer contact centres and help desks, and is produced and distributed by a third party software vendor. It captures, stores and retrieves critical information instantly through an interface, and accesses information from multiple knowledge bases. When first launched 50% of the calls received were from stores, which highlighted two key

2. ACD - Automatic Call Distribution system is an intelligent switchboard, or PABX. It monitors traffic, routes calls automatically and provides performance analysis. More advanced systems have links to voice or touch tone response systems, and ACD's can also be linked in a network.

issues: firstly that stores will take the easy option and call someone else for a resolution to a problem rather than solve it themselves, and secondly, that there was a need to satisfy those requests where help was genuinely needed. Today this has reduced to around 10% of calls, and these will normally involve the customer being present in store at the time the call is made.

Advisors have access to other BW systems such as the 'Store Directory', which includes details of the opening hours of stores, their locations, the Loyalty Scheme Operating System (LSOS) to assist in the answer of Loyalty Card queries, and office automation software for answering letters scanned into the system. Electronic Mail (e-mail) enables Advisors to communicate with each other, within their teams, and with the rest of the organisation.

Product recall or product information can be posted onto an electronic notice board and an upgraded version of ENQUIRY Q was later installed to rectify some of the initial problems associated with the earlier version. Correspondence is scanned into the system and read 'on-screen'. Standard letters are generated in a semi-automated way and will shortly be connected to ENQUIRY Q.

Activity Three: Handle the complaint or enquiry

At this stage the call will fall in to two broad categories: (i) a general enquiry, or (ii) a specific complaint. General enquiries will typically require the Customer Service Advisor to obtain information from a related system such as a database or a store directory, and then relay this information to the customer. The most frequent questions relate to store opening times, the nearest store to a specific location, or whether a store stocks a particular product. Most enquiries of this nature are easily answered to the customer's satisfaction and no further action is required.

Alternatively, if the call relates to a complaint then the Advisor will obtain the customers details along with the nature of the complaint. Typically the customer wants to demonstrate their annoyance, anger and disappointment, while gaining some recognition and understanding of how this issue will be avoided in future. They will also expect, and will always be offered, an apology. Within pre-defined limits the Advisors can (and do) suggest corrective action such as replacing faulty or defective goods, a full refund, credit notes, or BeingWell gift vouchers as a goodwill gesture. However, on occasions, either due to the severity or nature of the complaint, or at the customers' insistence, the call can be escalated to a more senior and experienced Advisor.

Activity Four: Initiate other processes

If the complaint cannot be resolved to the customers' satisfaction, or the severity requires that a more experienced Advisor be consulted, then the complaint will be escalated to a senior person. Typically this is done as part of the original call however it might be beneficial to return the customers call. The call details are documented, and pre-briefing the senior Advisor prior to handing over the call usually is sufficient. For less serious cases Advisors will produce any associated documentation such as letters of apology, gift vouchers, refunds, or make arrangements for product recalls.

Activity Five: Close the call

On conclusion of the telephone call the Advisor will thank the customer for their enquiry / complaint and close the call. The associated documentation is produced automatically where applicable, any notes about that particular call are logged, and product information added to the appropriate database.

2.3 The approach taken to the business problem (Decision logic)

Introduction

This second section provides a detailed account of how the Customer Service call centre process was approached and managed, in particular what decisions were considered and the outcome of those decisions. The senior management team within the Customer Service function, i.e. the Director of Customer Service and other senior managers, assumed ownership for this business problem and for the most part managed the process. Interviews were conducted with members of the senior management team, plus representatives from Information Systems (IS), Group Telecommunications (GT), as well as having unrestricted access to internally published reports and data. The opportunity to listen-in on live calls from customers was also taken. Strategic Choice Approach (SCA) was used as a research framework to reconstruct the decision logic used within this case with hindsight, as told to the author by those involved. This section has therefore been split into the four logical sections used by SCA and describes each of them in turn, namely: (i) *'Shaping'* i.e. the judgements about possible connections between one field of choice and another, (ii) *'Designing'* the possible courses of action, (iii) *'Comparing'* those possible courses in the light of what the consequences might be, and finally (iv) *'Choosing'* mode, where commitments for action through time are formulated.

Step one: Shaping of problems

This first step examines the judgements about possible connections between one field of choice and another. The Decision Graph, as shown in Figure 2.2, depicts those decisions seen by the actors in this case to be key to the outcome of the project. Those decisions shown within the boundary of the problem focus were given prominence over those outside the boundary, however it is realised that all the decisions shown are closely related.

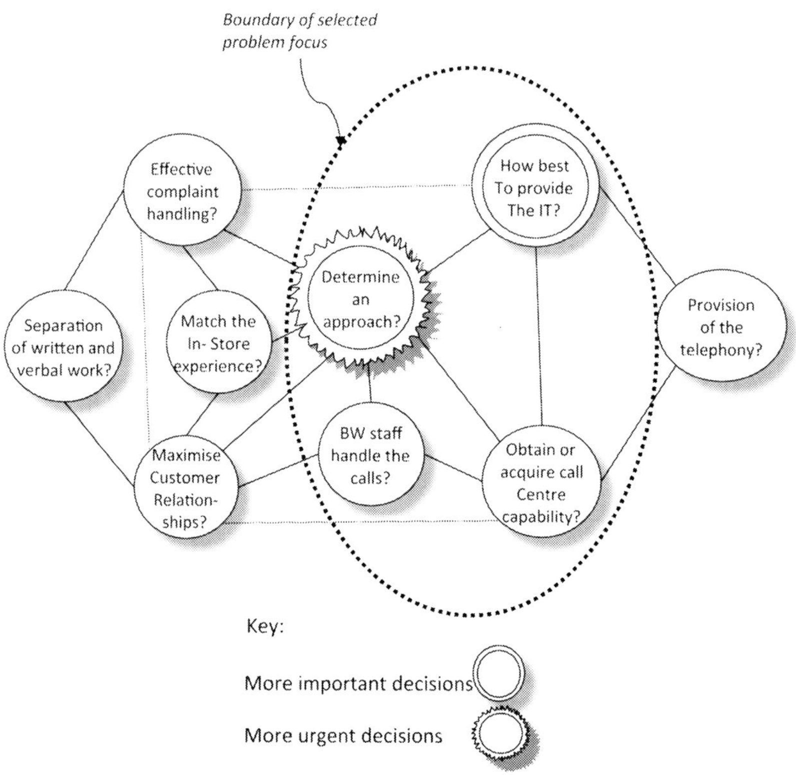

Figure 2.2: A Decision Graph of the key case decisions

The four key decisions within the boundary of the problem focus are (i) Determine an approach, (ii) How best to provide the IT, (iii) Obtain or acquire call centre capability, and (iv) BeingWell staff handle the calls. To take each decision in order:

Determine an approach?

The project team considered three possible options:

- Current structure and resource is retained within each Business Centre, i.e. do nothing,
- Current structure and resource is retained within each Business Centre but with central management of the teams, and
- Centralisation: All resource is brought together within a common management structure.

Some initial analysis comprised process flows, financial appraisal, risk analysis, internal opinion gathering, and external visits.

How best to provide the IT?

This was largely a choice between developing a bespoke application and utilising an existing packaged product. The principle requirement of the information technology is to capture the details of the complaint or query as it is received in real time and enter it directly into a customer service system. The Customer Service management team were already aware of a preferred product known as 'ENQUIRY Q'. The early versions of 'ENQUIRY Q' were neither intuitive nor interactive and were designed principally around taking information from correspondence, which didn't allow for the easy capture of information during telephone calls.

Obtain or acquire call centre capability?

At the time of setting up the centralised Customer Service function BW had no in-house call centre capability. However, as a Telecommunications Account Manager observed:

"At that point there were no call centres in the company as such, although we did have a number of 'help-desks'. Why do we differentiate between a 'help-desk' and a

call centre? I believe we have dozens of call centres going on here. If you define a call centre as a number of people within a close geographical proximity (although the technology means they don't even have to be seated together), taking and making telephone calls on a limited range of issues or questions, then we have dozens of them. Any one of a number of 'help-desks' is doing exactly that".

No facility currently existed within Customer Service to handle financial transactions via the telephone (i.e. to take payments for goods and services, refunds, or deposits), and there was a perception that this would be something that was difficult to achieve. The options considered to be available to the team at that time were (a) to develop an in-house call centre capability, or (b) outsource to a third party.

BeingWell staff handle the calls?

An important principle of any new approach was *'Making people feel valued'*, and the demanding environment of taking calls directly from irate customers has been key in ensuring that Advisors are likely to be mature in years having developed 'life skills'. As the Customer Service Manager described it: *"A unique aspect is the quality of our people. You see people smiling, you see people crying, as that goes with the territory"*

The question was whether the call centre staff needed to be recruited from experienced BeingWell staff, who understand the products and service culture, or whether any suitably trained and motivated staff could perform the tasks in a way that was acceptable to BeingWell.

The key decisions considered to be outside the boundary of the problem focus were: (i) Effective complaint handling, (ii) Match the in-store experience, (iii) Maximise customer relationships, (iv) Separation of written and oral work, and (v) Provision of the telephony. To take each of those decisions in order:

Effective complaint handling?

It was a requirement of this project to improve the existing arrangements for complaint handling and by doing so it should also create opportunities to improve the customer contact experience so that it is at least as good as, but ideally superior to, its competitors. The decision is therefore whether to design a solution that maximises complaint handling, or to emphasise the related 'contact' issues.

Match the in-store experience?

Most BeingWell customers will have experienced the service a BeingWell store provides which has become a fundamental of the BeingWell brand. As far as is practicably possible the intention was to replicate the same level of service within the call centre. Therefore the decision options are (a) whether to establish service level agreements (SLA's) for call centre staff as in stores, and (b) whether to link the SLA's to the performance management scheme.

Maximise customer relationships?

The issue here was whether to simply deal with issues raised by the customer or whether to treat it as an opportunity to build the relationship with the customers. The majority of customer calls were initially treated as anonymous with the emphasis being placed on capturing the nature of the call, for example an enquiry about store opening times or the location of the nearest store to a specific location, rather than the personal details of the caller. However, this personal information is now considered useful in gauging effectiveness of advertising, understanding if special interest groups are adequately catered for, or even establishing if the customer already has a relationship with BeingWell. The customer details will now be captured on all occasions that contact is made with a customer.

Separation of written and oral work?

Traditionally the work had been split into two teams, those answering the calls and queries from customers using the telephone, and those responding to letters and emails. It was felt that this division of labour helped improve the productivity. Alternatively, keeping the two together would provide some variety for the teams, facilitate skills transfer, and create a more flexible workforce.

Provision of the telephony?

From a telephony perspective Customer Service was treated as a trial. The 'soft' nature of the benefits made them difficult to quantify, and there was a reluctance to invest in capital expenditure for something considered a trial. The number of operators envisaged at that time was roughly equivalent to the total number of staff engaged in the decentralised Customer Complaints units within the individual Business Units, at that time approximately 15-

25 people. Therefore opportunities existed to take advantage of a *'managed service'* from a local cable company, rental from existing mainstream telecommunications companies such as BT, or outright purchase of an in-house system.

Step Two: Designing the possible courses of action

This second step focuses on designing possible courses of action, and Table 2.1 summarises the key decisions to be taken along with the possible options under consideration. The 'option label' is an abbreviation used to represent that option in future tables and models.

DECISION AREA	OPTIONS	OPTION LABEL
Determine an approach?	- Do nothing - Centralisation of teams - Centralisation management of teams	- Nothing - Centralise teams - Centralise mgt.
BeingWell own staff to handle the enquiries or complaints?	- Yes - No	- Yes - No
How best to provide the Information Technology?	- Predominantly Bespoke - Predominantly Package	- Besp - Pack
Obtain or acquire call centre capability?	- Develop in-house - Outsource to third party	- In-house - Outsource - In-house - Outsource

Table 2.1: Options within the boundary of the decision area

A key feature of the decision making process is the interconnectedness of the decisions and the consequences of those decisions, and that the likely outcome will rely on a compromise between possible options. SCA utilises the Analysis of Interconnected Decision Areas approach (AIDA) to help in understanding the relatedness of these decisions and is useful here to understand how and what decisions have been made. Figure 2.3 shows the results from comparisons of options from each decision area, with the options from every other decision area. This pairing of options ensures that incompatible or doubtful combinations are highlighted and potentially excluded from future analysis.

		CALL CENTRE?	
		In-house	Out-Source
IT?	Besp	•	?
	Pack	•	•

		CALL CENTRE?	
		In-house	Out-Source
Approach?	Nothing	X	X
	Centralise teams	•	X
	Centralise mgt.	•	X

		IT?	
		Besp	Pack
Staff?	Yes	•	•
	No	•	•

		STAFF?	
		Yes	No
Approach?	Nothing	X	X
	Centralise teams	•	X
	Centralise mgt.	•	?

		IT?	
		Besp	Pack
Approach?	Nothing	X	X
	Centralise teams	•	•
	Centralise mgt.	•	•

		CALL CENTRE?	
		In-house	Out-Source
Staff?	Yes	•	?
	No	X	•

Key: · = Compatible combination X = Incompatible combination ? = Doubtful compatibility

Figure 2.3: Analysis of interconnected decision areas (AIDA)

The Option Graph in Figure 2.4 diagrammatically represents the outcome from AIDA. The convention used for Option Graphs is to show the decision areas as circles, the options as nodes within the circles, which are connected by solid lines where there is an incompatible option (option bar), or a broken line where a doubtful compatibility has been identified, i.e. requiring further analysis. For example, a solid bar joining for instance 'Package' and 'Nothing' indicates an incompatible combination. A dotted line, for instance, between 'Bespoke' and 'Outsource' indicates doubtful compatibility.

This is a key step that cuts down the potential decision schemes (a decision scheme represents a combination of options from each decision area) in this case from twenty-four to four. Two prominent options that create 'bars' are the do 'Nothing' and 'Outsource' options. Clearly the option to do 'nothing' if chosen would make any option it pairs with unacceptable, as do nothing while a valid option would not address the issues or meet the objectives. Any decision to 'outsource' the call centre was seen as incompat-

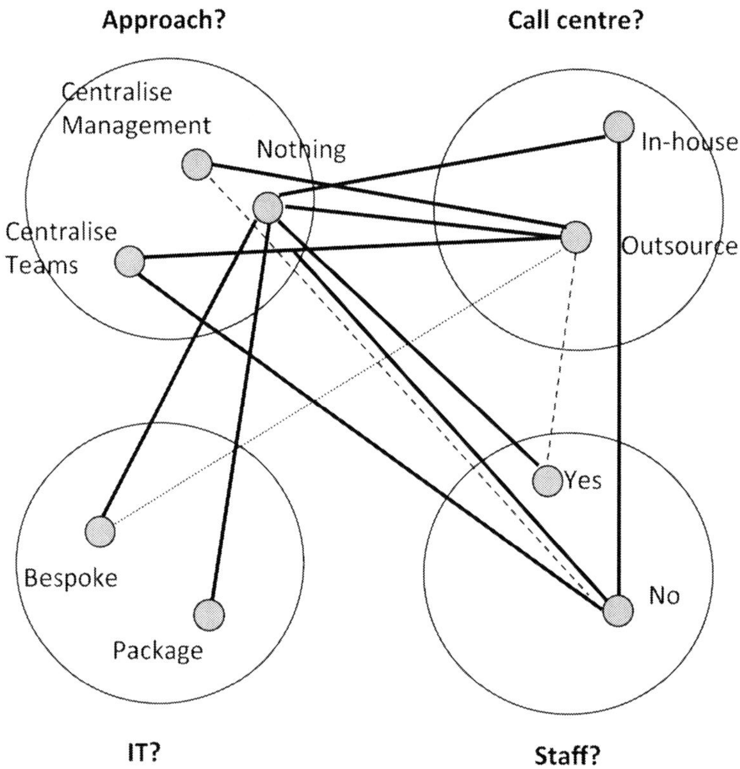

Figure 2.4: Option Graph – Customer Service

ible with a structure of centralised teams or management thereof, so these pairings were excluded. Having determined which options are compatible it is then possible to establish which combination of those options can be realistically crafted into a feasible decision scheme. A feasible decision scheme is one where it doesn't violate any of the incompatibilities established during earlier analysis, but their inclusion in the final solution is still not automatic. Using a diagram similar to a decision tree it is possible to map the possible decision schemes so that they can be logically assessed for future consideration.

Figure 2.5 shows that when the compatible options are re-presented to determine what feasible decision schemes are possible only four decision schemes emerge from the analysis, however none of these have any doubtful compatibilities that would need to be resolved in order to establish if they are truly feasible.

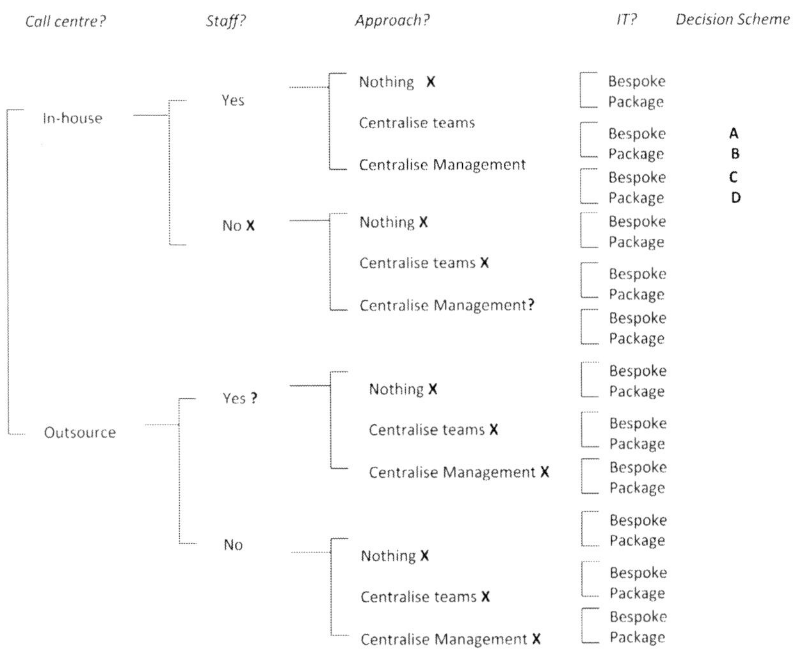

Figure 2.5: Feasible decision schemes for the Customer Service case

Step three: Comparing the possible courses of action

Having determined a list of feasible decision schemes the next step is to compare each of the schemes in light of what their consequences might be. Table 2.2 lists those comparison areas that emerged to be of importance to the actors in this case, and a comparative measure has been assigned to each comparison type.

A working shortlist can be developed from the feasible decision schemes identified earlier, by comparing each of them against what the project teams considered were the top three comparison areas in this case, namely: *'cost'*, *'maximise customer relationship opportunities'*, and *'consistency of delivery in performance and communications'*. Figure 2.6 shows the working shortlist along with the assessment of how each comparison area compared with the desired minimum ratings of at least 'medium' for both 'customer relationships' and 'consistent delivery', and a 'low' for cost.

COMPARISON AREA:	COMPARATIVE MEASURE:
Prompt and effective resolution of complaints: The ability to deal with any complaint efficiently and effectively that has a positive impact on the BeingWell brand.	Greater than 90% ↔ Less than 90%
Consistency of delivery in performance and communication: Coordinated approach across the disparate Business Centres.	High ↔ Medium ↔ Low
Opportunity for information feedback contributing to increased sales and profit: Good customer intelligence can greatly influence product development and customer service.	Yes ↔ No
Protection and enhancement of BW's reputation: With one of the most trusted brands on the high street BeingWell are extremely cautious about damaging the brand.	Good ↔ Poor
Maximise customer relationship opportunities:	High ↔ Medium ↔ Low
Driving customer loyalty and increasing sales and profit.	High ↔ Medium ↔ Low

Table 2.2: List of comparison areas

The outcome of the comparison ratings suggests that all four of the feasible decision schemes could form the working shortlist as they all met the minimum requirements for the comparison measure. However, according to the judgements included in Figure 2.6 decision scheme 'A' had marginally the most favourable comparison rating over decision scheme 'B'. The comparisons of each of the four key decision areas (Call centre, Staff, Approach, and IT) and the choices to be made are as follows:

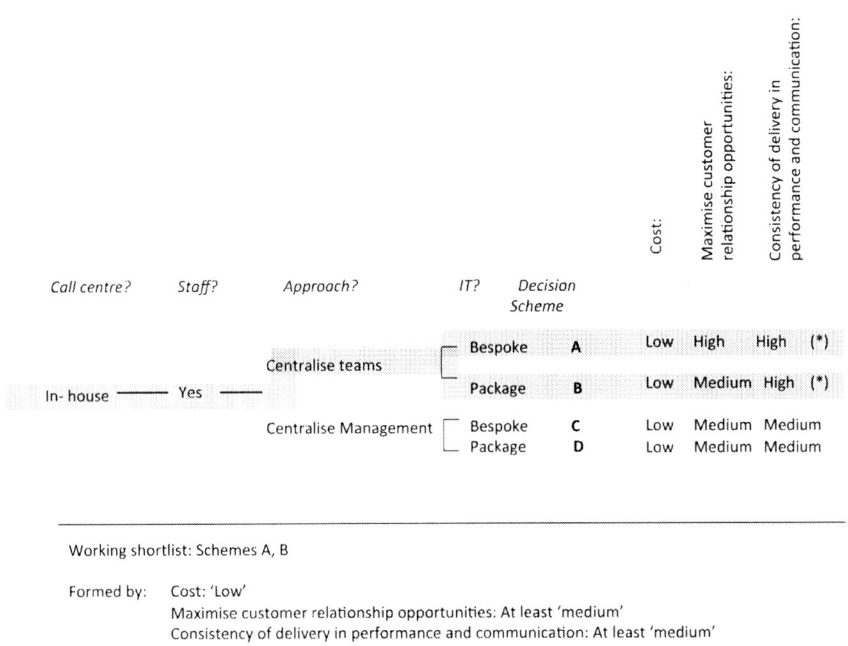

Figure 2.6: Forming a working shortlist – Customer Service

Call centre (*in-house versus outsource*)

The perceived relative high cost of outsourcing and the increase in risk to the BeingWell brand were central to the concerns of the actors in this case, having no internal experience at operating a call centre or any guarantee that the level of customer service would be improved by having a call centre. Looking back at this decision, one participant described amalgamating these functions as being:

> *"Bags of ignorance. We assumed it would be better, which it clearly is, but there was lots of pain in between. This was new territory and no-one had been there before".*

As the traditional approach had been a paper-based administrative function it was recognised that appropriate training and development was required for the staff, many of whom had never received Customer Services training or telephone skills training before. Similarly, appropriate systems training and support services and processes would need to be made available.

Staff *(BeingWell staff to handle calls 'Yes' versus 'No')*

The preference for an in-house approach was clear, and the following statement by the Customer Service Manager was typical of those interviewed:

> *"If we can't give you an answer we commit to come back to you with the answer. In contrast to outsourced call centres you are able to escalate the complaint, unlike call centres where you're not even talking to the people with whom you do the business. A third party hasn't got the incentive to do what we do"*

Considerable emphasis was placed on the importance of the BeingWell brand, the affection with which customers view BeingWell, and its standing as an established and cherished British retailer. The Customer Service Manager described this as follows:

> *"The Advisors are the voice of BeingWell, and customers look upon us as custodians of the nation's morals. We need to ensure that the 'music on hold' is sensible; that we adopt a semi-formal style; that correspondence is free of grammatical errors, and that adverts are free of naked ladies".*

The ready supply of experienced BeingWell Customer Service staff was also a contributory factor.

Approach (*Centralise teams versus centralise management*)

Consistency of delivery in performance and communication, and improved opportunity for information feedback contributing to increased sales and profit, were the two key reasons why the centralisation of teams was preferred to that of the centralisation of management. A centralised team makes rotation and management of staff easier and gives the Advisors variety and wider experience, while being more effective in delivering consistency in performance and communication. The results overwhelmingly favoured the centralisation option, some of the key conclusions being the commonality of processes across the business units. The Business General Managers although divided in their opinion over the proposals universally supported the concept of 'care lines'.

	A		B	
	In-house Yes Teams Bespoke	Call centre? Staff? Approach? IT?	In-house Yes Teams Package	
Comparison Area:			**Comparative comment:**	
Prompt and effective resolution of complaints: (Greater than 90% ↔ Less than 90%)	High	High	Both likely to be similar.	
Consistency of delivery in performance and communication: (High ↔ Medium ↔ Low)	High	High	Considered that centralisation would be more effective in delivering consistency in performance and communication.	
Opportunity for information feedback contributing to increased sales and profit: (Yes ↔ No)	Good	Good	A centralised team makes rotation and management of staff easier and gives the Advisors variety and wider experience.	
Protection and enhancement of BW's reputation: (Good ↔ Poor)	Good	Good	Both likely to be similar.	
Maximise customer relationship opportunities: (High ↔ Medium ↔ Low)	High	Medium	Bespoke software is more likely to be able to integrate with existing in-house and legacy systems enabling a 'single view of customer' in a much better way. Packages while offering speedy functionality can be harder to integrate.	
Cost: (High ↔ Medium ↔ Low)	Low	Low	In both schemes the relative costs are very similar and would not make a significant difference. However, it was assumed that in-house software development resource would be used if a bespoke development were undertaken.	

Table 2.3: Comparison under uncertainty

IT (*Bespoke versus package*)

Faced with limited knowledge of actually operating a customer service call centre, and the desire to manage costs and complexity, the added complication of designing and developing a bespoke customer Service IT application, albeit more functionally rich and tailored to BeingWell specific requirements, in addition to all the other development activity needed to support this project was seen as prohibitive. There was clearly a desire to benefit from the development work that others had invested in software products for this application, and an understanding that functionality could be compromised in favour of speed, a known and fixed implementation timetable, and a tried and tested product.

Comparisons under uncertainty

In Table 2.3, two of the four short-listed decision schemes (labelled 'A' and 'B') are compared against each other in terms of all six comparison areas listed earlier.

This provides further opportunity to make additional forms of comparison to the crude assessments that were made in earlier short-listing. The 'textual' rather than 'numeric' descriptions convey uncertainty, which is explored in the following section.

Step four: Choosing commitments for action through time

The final step is the formation of proposed commitments to action through time. Table 2.4 is a cumulative list of uncertainty areas identified by the actors and captured during the analysis, which have been categorised into one of the three uncertainty types, UE (uncertainties about the working environment), UV (uncertainties about the guiding values) or UR (uncertainties about related decision fields), along with an indicator to the salience of this uncertainty to the final decision. The two most salient uncertainties identified by the actors were the relative difficulty of integrating packaged software as opposed to bespoke software (?PACKINT), and the absence of customer service call centre experience (?EXPERT).

UNCERTAINTY AREA	LABEL:	TYPE:	SALIENCE:
From 'Managing customer relationships' comparison: ? That packaged software will be more difficult to integrate than bespoke software.	?PACKINT	UE	•••
From 'Cost' comparison: ? The assumption that in-house development resource will be available to bespoke an application.	?DEVSKILLS	UR	••
? The ability of an outsourced call centre to use 'company specific' bespoke software.	?BESPOUT	UE	•
? Availability of suitable office accommodation.	?ACCOM	UR	•
? No real 'Customer Service' call-centre experience.	?EXPERT	UE	•••
? Soft benefits are difficult to quantify.	?SOFTBEN	UV	••
? The uncertainty of the project being worth the investment in in-house telephony	?TELINVEST	UE	••
? Will a call centre improve customer service	?SERVPLUS	UE	••

Table 2.4: Comparing uncertainty areas

Figure 2.7 plots those uncertainties previously identified on an uncertainty graph for the Customer Service case, which clearly shows a concentration of uncertainties of the UE type. This diagram would help in determining which uncertainties will be most influential on the final outcome and which can be deferred for the moment. The two uncertainties that have been classified 'high' in salience (the absence of any call centre experience, and the integration of packaged software to existing systems) are therefore likely to have a significant influence on the final outcome. Indications of the options likely to resolve those uncertainties are also indicated.

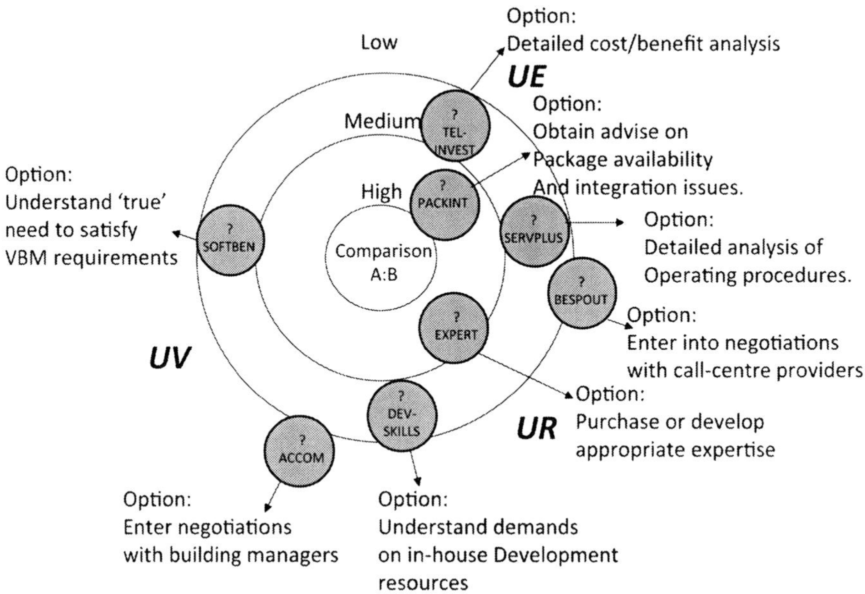

Figure 2.7: Uncertainty graph – Salience of uncertainty to this comparison

Commitment package

A judgment has to be made as to what decisions can be made now, how much exploration should take place in order to reduce uncertainty, and what arrangements can be made to defer decisions to a later date. SCA addresses this issue by rearranging the feasible action schemes so that the more 'urgent' decision areas can be brought forward to earlier branches of the decision tree and those that are less urgent can be deferred. An example of such a rearrangement for this case is shown in Figure 2.8. In practice when considering decision schemes 'A' or 'B', there was little choice in three of the four decision areas in this case, leaving outstanding the decision of how to provide the IT, which had no impact on the earlier decisions. Although the choice of approach had initially been seen as a more 'urgent' decision, when the decision schemes were compared in the context of the likely outcomes the actors in this case were prepared for this decision to be deferred.

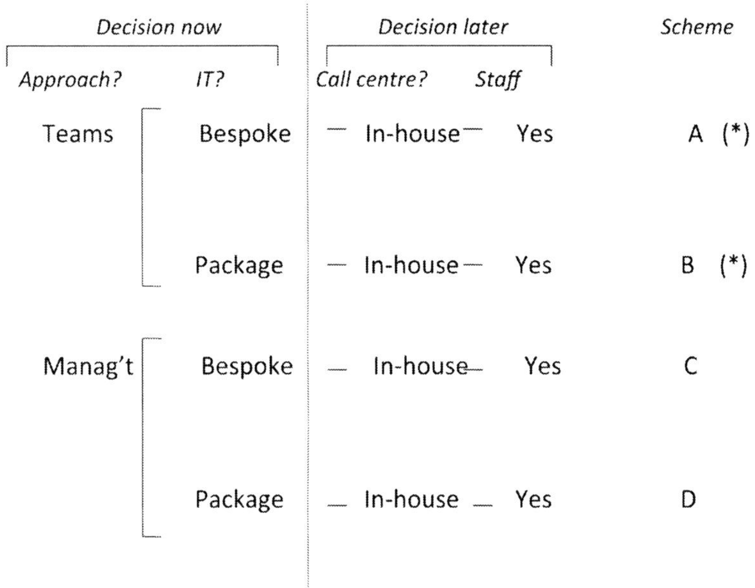

(*) Short listed decision schemes

Figure 2.8: A comparison of the feasible action schemes

Strategic Choice Approach uses the concept of the commitment package as the framework for determining those actions that have to be taken immediately, those actions that require further exploration to reduce the salience of areas of uncertainty, and finally the other arrangements that need to be made to enable actions to be deferred. Table 2.5 sets out the commitment package framework for this case and is a summary of the commitments and actual decisions taken in this case now, and those that were deferred to later.

The actual decision scheme chosen by BW (i.e. an *'in-house'* call centre, *'yes'* to their own staff, a *'centralised teams'* approach, and *'package'* systems) was labelled as decision scheme 'B'.

	DECISIONS NOW		**FUTURE DECISION**	
	Actions	Explorations	Deferred Choices	Contingency Planning
Call centre:	Operate an in-house call centre but rent the telephony from a local provider.		Consider the purchase of the appropriate telephony.	Limit rental contract to one year.
Staff:	BeingWell own staff to operate the call centre.			Outsource to a third party.
Approach:	Centralise the existing teams at Head Office.		Consider alternative location other than Head Office.	
IT:	Start by using a package application in order to gain experience and speed up implementation.		Consider alternative package and bespoke applications for future use.	

Table 2.5: Commitment package framework - Customer Service

2.4 The alignment of the Actors in the Network (*Alignment logic*)

Introduction

The third phase of the analysis uses concepts from Actor Network Theory to understand the alignment of the actors to the proposed approaches. If we plot the process components for the Customer Service case study on to a process inscription/specialisation framework, which represents the view as defined by the actors in the case study (Figure 2.9), the following can be observed.

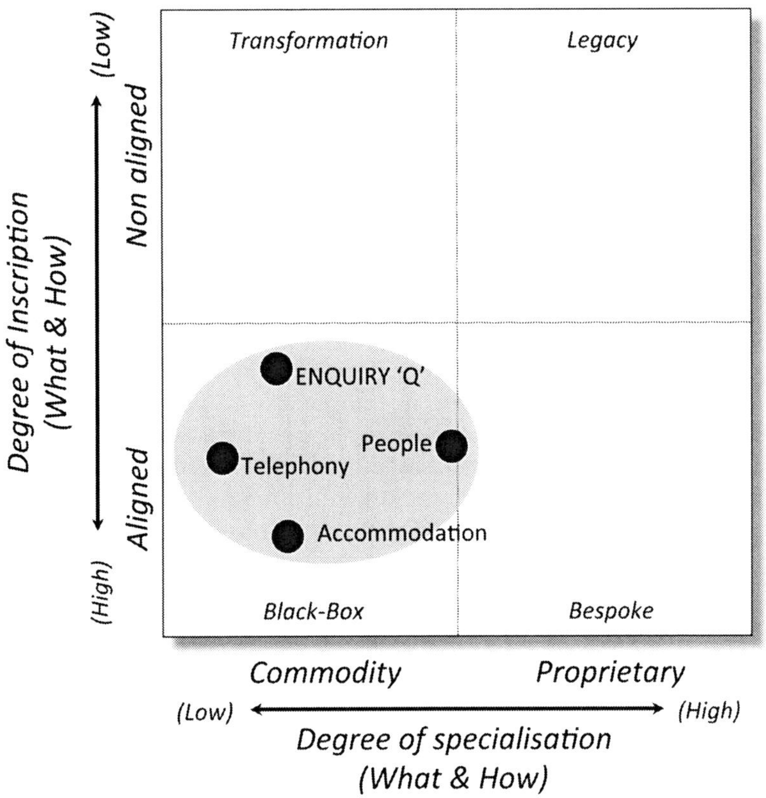

Figure 2.9: Customer Service process inscription/specialisation framework

In the Customer Service case the components of the process are concentrated in the 'aligned-commodity' space, which would suggest that not only are the components considered standard, routine and typical of those used by many companies i.e. low degree of specialisation, there is also broad alignment of the actors that they are of this type (in other words there is considerable agreement).

People – Customer Service Advisors

The Customer Service Advisors are considered by BeingWell to have BeingWell specific know-how hence the positioning of the 'people' component towards the proprietary sector however; their *tacit* knowledge could be made *explicit* by use of a knowledge base, software, or good documentation hence promoting movement back towards commodity. More importantly however when representing the company, especially when dealing with a complaint, it is considered very important by BeingWell that a customer should be able to talk with an employee of the company, rather than their agent, as they would be more likely to be empathetic, have a sense of ownership and pride in the company, and therefore represent it more accurately and favourably. This view was the aligned view of the internal stakeholders in the network.

ENQUIRY Q – Customer contact software

The use of 'Enquiry Q' software as the preferred choice reflected the views of the actors to limit complexity of the final solution, and to reduce cost by adopting industry standard protocols and approaches as inscribed within the software. This was a conscious and deliberate decision that acknowledges the likely limitations of integration with other in-house software, and therefore the ability to undertake all the customer services identified. It does however reflect their lack of experience to be able to articulate clearly what functionality might not be provided within such a package.

Telephony

Without exception, the project team were happy to accept that the telephony components should be industry standard and that they would work within the parameters of what could be provided at a cost that was affordable. Long term commitments to telephony vendors or transaction specific investments were actively avoided and future options kept open.

Accommodation

Most call centres operate in office environments that are typical of any modern office accommodation, and have minimal 'special needs' over and above those normally provided. This was also true in this case and standard office accommodation was made available and utilised.

2.5 A longitudinal view – BeingWell Customer Service

Introduction

Six years on from the original case BeingWell Customer Service function expanded into new and diverse areas of service provision. Despite what was initially only a basic knowledge of how to operate a Customer Service call centre, with most of the experience being product related and largely tacit due to the absence of any formal mechanisms to capture and disseminate what was learned, the call centre has established itself as an effective and efficient operation. It has achieved its primary objectives of improving customer contact through better complaint handling, consistency of delivery, protecting and enhancing the BeingWell brand and reputation, and the provision of feedback to help improve sales and therefore profit.

Development of the call centre process (TEAMS) (PACKAGE) (IN-HOUSE) (YES)

The formation of a single Customer Service unit (TEAMS) has enforced the discipline of accurate and complete recording of calls, which can be converted into customer and product intelligence. Accurate metrics regarding the cost of operating the call centre along with detailed breakdowns of the costs of escalating complaints, responding to correspondence, and the associated cost and structure of telephony services has been established enabling accurate cost comparisons to be made with third party suppliers.

The decision to purchase a packaged customer contact software product (PACKAGE) was at the time universally accepted as being the most appropriate decision when set in the context of all the other activity required to establish a call centre. ENQUIRY Q has been a stable and robust product, but increasingly this software is considered an inhibitor as the call centre develops into new areas of activity and a capability established. The inability to interface with existing legacy systems is also seen as an inhibitor, as the Call Centre Manager said, *"If only we had betters systems we could be far more efficient"*.

A much better understanding has now been gained of the telephony elements of operating a call centre (IN-HOUSE) and the appreciation that these are largely commodities has been reinforced. A *'managed service'* approach from a local cable network company was the preferred entry-level option. Alternatives from suppliers such as BT were initially found to be prohibitively expensive on a unit cost (per seat) basis, based on the number of operators currently engaged in the decentralised Customer Complaints functions within the individual Business Units, at that time approximately

15 - 25 people per function. However, in October 1999 Group Telecommunications (GT) purchased a 'Lucent Definity® ECS[3] Call Centre' system as a Group-wide asset. The growing trend in demand for call centre capability throughout the company is such that it will only become 'cheaper' to the Group over time, as once an investment has been made the equipment is there to be utilised. Sites are connected through a virtual private network (VPN) and Group companies are now recharged on a 'per-seat' and functionality basis. GT is effectively providing an internal 'managed service' to other Group companies.

Finally, the decision to use BeingWell own people (YES). Advisors are targeted to answer approximately 170 calls per day, which has been known to peak at around 250 calls per Advisor a day. As the Call Centre Manager commented: *"We don't want a 'battery hen' call centre, but when we are busy an Advisor can experience almost continuous calls"*. Problem calls are passed to 'Senior Advisors' and customers appear to be reassured by the escalation and both the implied and real increase in experience and expertise that goes with the senior role.

Support for new products and services

The Customer Service call centre has been actively involved in BeingWell's expansion into other healthcare services (Dentistry, Health & Beauty Centres), by being the main customer contact centre for these burgeoning businesses. Acting as the pre-launch contact centre, with a widely publicised telephone number on promotional literature and advertising hoardings, calls are received for new stores, dental practices and health centres before they open, in some cases being able to take bookings for treatment so that the new location can get off to a flying start. The Customer Service call centre is also the point of escalation for these new services along with 'BeingWell.com', 'Hearing Centres', 'Lazer eye treatment', and information portals, and more recently Health & Travel Insurance. BeingWell Opticians Limited (BOL) had traditionally operated its own Customer Service call centre, but as the following announcement (which appeared on the BeingWell Communications website) demonstrates, the bringing together of the BOL and BW Customer Service call centres have joined forces:

---

3. The DEFINITY® ECS Call Centre provides a powerful total solution for customers', sales and service needs. Building on the performance and flexibility of the DEFINITY ECS, you can select from a powerful assortment of features and capabilities, specially designed to enhance call centre operations. Features such as the patented Expected Wait Time and sophisticated routing algorithms make sure customers reach the appropriate destination and the agent best qualified to handle their call.

5th March 2001

BEINGWELL OPTICIANS CUSTOMER CONTACT INCORPORATED INTO BW CUSTOMER SERVICE

As a move towards a new BeingWell UK and Ireland structure is announced BeingWell Customer Service department will handle BeingWell Opticians Limited (BOL) customer contacts as well as those for BW. This will mean an additional 7,000 customer contacts will be handled by the multi-skilled team in BW Customer Services. This has been made possible by an investment in customer contact software and state of the art telephony.

John Eddington, BeingWell Customer Service Manager
Adele Flint, BeingWell Opticians Customer Service Manager.

Customer Relationship Management (CRM) trial

The Customer Service call centre participated in a CRM trial by receiving all calls from one local large BW store, which also incorporated a BOL implant. The trial was considered a great success with all calls being answered by the call centre in a professional and consistent way, enabling the store to concentrate on serving customers. A small number of calls were difficult to answer without reference to the store, for example the customer who had left her shopping in the store and was describing its location, over the phone, as she thought she was talking directly to store staff. As the trial was conducted without the necessary IT systems support then appointment booking for BOL patients was unsophisticated relying on fax copies of paper diary sheets being shared between the store and call centre, however it proved the concept could work if adequately supported. The success of the initial trial encouraged an extended trial incorporating a mix of four quite different and geographically spread stores (Leicester, Woking, Ripley, and West Bridgford), which mirrored the results from the original exercise.

While successful, any move to support c1500 stores in this way would required significant investment in information technology within the call centre, the appropriate telephony to be in place in all stores to enable call forwarding to the appropriate Advisor, and a significant increase in call centre staff which would fundamentally change the nature of the call centre and the type of work it conducts. Further trials are planned.

2.6 Summary

This case study describes the approach taken by BeingWell to establish a customer service call centre, with the objectives of ensuring consistency in the provision of prompt and effective complaint resolution and information feedback, all of which protects and enhances the BeingWell brand. The existing functionally located customer service units (which are predominately correspondence based) were not providing the service required, and a call centre approach was the desired outcome although it was not known how that was to be achieved. The case study examined in turn the detail of the process under review (process logic); the approach adopted to decision making (decision logic); and using concepts from Actor Network Theory an understanding of the alignment of the actors in the network (alignment logic). Activity Records are used to examine each of the five prime call centre activities, while the decision making process was re-created by means of SCA. Using the inscription/specialisation framework developed for this research by the author, the alignment of the actors in the network is captured for each of the call centre process components. The actual choice adopted by BW was decision scheme 'B' i.e. (TEAMS – PACKAGE - IN-HOUSE – YES), which was extremely close to the decision scheme labelled 'A' (TEAMS – BESPOKE – IN-HOUSE – YES), which emerged as the optimal choice from retrospectively applying SCA. The differences reflect a deliberate preference for packaged software chosen for reduced complexity, in preference to a bespoke solution and increased functionality. The process as determined in the Customer Service case comprises largely commodity components (telephony, software, and accommodation), and these are also seen to be commodities by the actors in the network. However, it was determined that the Customer Service Advisors despite having commodity skills must be BeingWell employees, a decision that was supported universally by the actors in the network. It later transpired that this was the only case where alignment supported a proprietary solution to manning call centres, and demonstrated the power and influence of an aligned view. The next chapter examines a call centre in a completely different business context.

CHAPTER THREE
Case Study Two - BeingWell Loyalty Card

3.1 Introduction

With over twelve million cardholders, and new applications running in excess of 40,000 per week, the BeingWell Loyalty Card was Europe's largest retail 'smart card' loyalty scheme in operation. Targeted heavily towards women in the 20-40 years age range, shoppers receive four points for every £1 spent on all purchases in store (with the exception of medicines, gift tokens and stamps), with one point being worth 1p. When enough points have been earned these can be used by the customer to 'treat' themselves from a selection of pampering or beauty products, or health & beauty treatments at nearby venues. In contrast to the vast majority of loyalty schemes the emphasis is on *'female self indulgent rewards'* for the cardholder, rather than a discount scheme on commodities, or a supplement for housekeeping. The vast majority of loyalty schemes are of the traditional credit card, airline, or petrol types, with a strong 'male' bias based on a proposition of rational discounted purchases. Some schemes offered by clothing and fashion retailers such as C&A and BHS do have more of a feminine bias but straddle the rational/discount and emotional/indulgent categories. However, the BeingWell Loyalty Card has a massively feminine bias (93% of cardholders are women), and the rewards are clearly emotional/indulgent in nature, targeted specifically at that group.

In addition, the customer can be made aware of exclusive offers on products of interest, information and advice, and access to 'in-store' events. Rated by 85% of cardholders as being *'excellent/good'*, consumers consider it to be *"more different, more generous and offering better rewards"* than comparable cards.

BeingWell see the Loyalty Card as having a role in its evolution from being *"Chemists to the nation"* to *"The place for products and services that help me look good and feel good"*. It will allow them to focus the customer offer and values according to the needs and behaviours of individual cardholders, and to enable and enhance new initiatives such as product development; non traditional retail products and services; store efficiency initiatives, and new retail services.

However, twelve million cardholders, (85% of them regular users) generate significant levels of ongoing administration, which broadly fall into two discrete categories:

Changes to personal details such as name, or change of address (typically women upon marriage); lost or stolen cards; progress chasing upon applying for a card; and

General enquiries about the Loyalty Card scheme (points balances, points earned) etc., including comments about how the scheme operates such as *"they think its sexist"*.

Most of this administration is handled by the 'Loyalty Card Call Centre', which at the time of the national launch was operated by T.COM on a wholly 'outsourced' basis. This call centre operated from 0800 - 1800 Mondays to Fridays, with IVR[4] out of hours. Although the store should be the first point at which customers raise queries, many find it much more convenient to telephone a call centre at a local rate call charge and speak to an experienced agent about their query. In addition, the centre also operated a store help line for use by store staff that had queries.

The approach taken to this case study

The approach taken here was the same as that described in the previous case. The case contains data from interviews conducted with Project Team members, Gerry McGovern the Loyalty Card Programme Manager, Business unit representatives, and members of the Loyalty Card Marketing team, Information Systems, Group Telecommunications, Implementation & Training Development, and Operations Improvement Department. Access to archive material such as call statistics, and findings from the regional trials, were freely available.

3.2 The Loyalty Card process in focus (*Process logic*)

Introduction

This first section examines the Loyalty Card work business process under review and presents the five prime activities and tasks that make up that process, namely: (i) Receive the 'inbound' calls; (ii) Identify the customer & information; (iii) Service the account; (iv) initiate other processes, and (v) Close the call. It is not the intention to discuss all the processes that go to make up the complete end-to-end Loyalty Card business however; card

4 IVR – Interactive Voice Recognition. Automated voice response and touch-tone prompting route calls and switch-on computer applications or scripts.

fulfilment, i.e. delivering the card to the cardholder, a process initiated from within this process, is discussed because of the closely coupled association with the process under investigation.

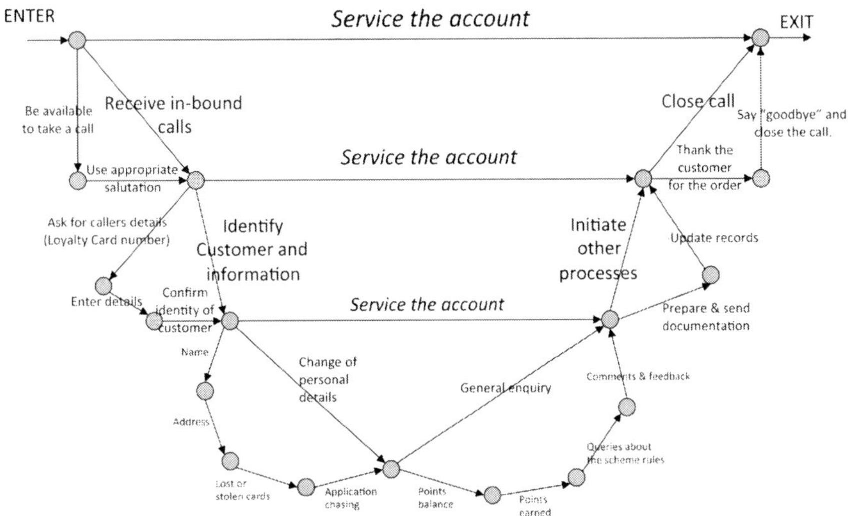

Figure: 3.1 An Activity Record of the Loyalty Card process.

The Process starts with an inbound call from a customer, and ends when the account details change or enquiry has been completed satisfactorily, and any correspondence sent to the customer. Figure 3.1 shows an Activity Record of the call centre process as utilised for the Loyalty Card. Each of the activities is described in full as follows:

Activity One: Receive 'inbound' calls

The process starts with an 'inbound' call from a customer. Calls generally follow a pattern of activity with Monday being the busiest (following on from Saturdays trading), with Friday being the next busiest. Daily patterns follow a mid-morning and post 4.30 PM peak. Mid-week activity is typically quiet[5]. Call volumes average at approximately 2,700 per day, rising to 4,000 at Christmas. Advisors are expected, somewhere during the conversation, to identify themselves, thank the customer for calling, and empathise and demonstrate active listening by confirming and acknowledging the facts.

5 This pre-dates widespread Sunday trading.

The Customer Service Manager commented:

"We do expect people to behave in a certain fashion during the call. We apply Being-Well rules, BeingWell empathy, and make the caller feel good about the transaction".

Average call duration is usually between 60 and 90 seconds and although the facilities are available, and there might be some opportunities to utilise them in future, CLI (Call Line Identification)[6] and CTI (Computer Telephone Integration)[7] are not currently used as the customer's telephone number is not captured on the Loyalty Card database, and customers tend to call from their workplace.

Activity Two: Identify customer and information

Approximately 10% of calls are received from BW stores, sometimes with the customer present. Stores use a national rate number, which allows the call centre to identify the call as coming from a store before it is answered. Customers use a local rate number (prefixed 0845), which appears on all of the literature but not on the Loyalty Card itself. Automatic Call Presentation (ACP)[8] has recently been introduced which 'forces' an available advisor to take an incoming call. Advisors have received this change positively as it makes the job easier, in addition they have also been given an extra paid break to recognise the increased call handling capability this technology has enabled, and the subsequent achievement of the published service levels.

Activity Three: Service the account

Servicing the Loyalty Card account normally comprises two main activities: (i) Changes to personal details such as name, address, or lost and stolen cards and sometimes progress chasing their card application; and (ii) General enquiries about the Loyalty Card scheme, for example points balances, redemption enquiries, and general comments about how the scheme operates. Both enquiry types will require access to the Loyalty Scheme Operating System (LSOS) in order to record the new customer details.

---

6 CLI - Call Line Identification detects and identifies the incoming telephone number.

7 CTI - Computer Telephone Integration provides integrated functionality to telephone and information systems users. A telephone call may be influenced by information from a computer or a computer may be directed to perform functions based on a call. The computer can also monitor a call and record additional data, such as the total time from the beginning of the telephone ringing to the end of the conversation, with outcome and process.

8 ACP - Automatic Call Presentation routes calls 'live' to an operator without them having to respond to a ring-tone.

Activity Four: Initiate other processes

Ancillary processes are largely confined to the preparation and sending of confirmatory documentation or chasing a card application that appears to have been 'lost' in the process. This might result in telephone calls being made to the card producer.

Activity Five: Close the call

On conclusion of the telephone call the operator will thank the customer for making contact and close the call. The associated documentation is produced and posted to the customer. The process ends.

3.3 The approach taken to the business problem (*Decision logic*)

Introduction

This second section provides a detailed account of how the Loyalty Card process was designed and managed, in particular what decisions were considered and the outcome of those decisions. Sponsored by the Director of Marketing, this high profile project was managed as a marketing initiative, and consequently the composition of the project team had a strong marketing bias. Unrestricted access to company confidential information was maintained throughout the research. This section documents the decision-making activity adopting the logical sequence of SCA.

Step one: Shaping of problems

This first step examines the judgements about possible connections between one field of choice and another. The Decision Graph, as shown in Figure 3.2, depicts those decisions seen by the actors in this case to be key to the outcome of the project. The decision graph shows two problem focus boundaries, one labelled *'original'*, and the other *'new'*. This study will focus on the events surrounding the original decision however; the subsequent decisions taken within the 'new' problem focus are material to this case and is discussed later. Clearly, in this case the initial decision to determine the overall approach was urgently required, as it would influence many of the associated decisions.

The four key decisions within the boundary of the original problem focus are (i) Determine the approach, (ii) Whether to utilise smart-card technology, (iii) How best to provide the technology, and (iv) Obtain or acquire call centre capability. To take each decision in order:

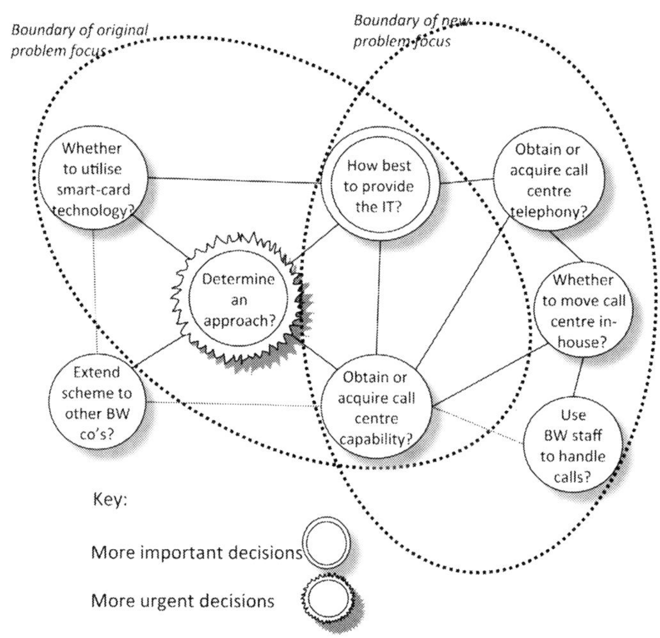

Figure.3.2: A decision graph of the key case decisions

Determine an approach?

Two controlled trial areas had previously been established in Norwich and South West, which incorporated 14 and 29 participating BW stores respectively. With a joint customer population in both areas totalling approximately 1.3 million, different reward levels were tested and valuable data on 'active' cardholders established. Early indications from the trials were that 35% of sales were linked to the card, and incremental sales running at 3.5%, but despite this there was still some anxiety by those involved of the true benefits of the scheme. The team were faced with the decisions to continue with a controlled trial or pilot in much the same way as in Norwich and South East, get a third party to administer the scheme, or administer the scheme in-house. Clearly this was the most urgent decision, as this one would influence many of the related decisions.

Whether to utilise smart-card technology?

The conventional approach to card based products was to hold information on the card using a magnetic stripe as most credit and bank cards did at that time. The magnetic stripe is capable of holding limited amounts of data that can be read and updated by machine. This technology although well established and widely accepted is quite old and has limited functionality. The development of memory and micro-processor chip cards was just emerging, and although the banks were actively supporting the benefits of cards that utilise chip rather than the magnetic stripe technology (due to improved options for security and fraud detection), loyalty schemes of the day were still using magnetic stripe, for example Sainsbury's 'Reward' card, and the Tesco 'Club card'. BeingWell envisaged the Loyalty Card as being the 'key' to a number of product and service related offerings to its customers, possibly incorporating sensitive medical records and prescription data of the cardholder, applications that would be ideally suited to a memory or micro-processor chip card. The magnetic stripe card could utilise standard in-store technology as all stores already have magnetic card readers, however the use of a chip card would require investment in approximately 15,000 chip card reader / writer devices (one at every point-of-sale position), and the development of the associated software interfaces.

How best to provide the IT?

The administration of a loyalty scheme requires a customer database that comprises the complete records for customers who have a Loyalty Card. As with the customer service case, this was largely a choice between purchasing an existing software application package (a number existed that were designed around conventional 'discount' Loyalty Card schemes using magnetic stripe technology), and developing a bespoke application that catered for the extensive vision BeingWell had for its Loyalty Card. Enhancements would also be required to existing systems (tills, card reader interfaces, and nominal ledgers) to facilitate a seamless transaction at the point of sale or service. This decision is closely related to the decision to use a chip card or not.

Obtain or acquire call centre capability?

During the Norwich and South West trials T.COM provided call centre capability on a temporary basis. However, it was clear that a dedicated call centre would be needed to handle the volume of calls anticipated should the customer take-up of cards be in line with the predictions following the trials. The Customer Service call centre had been established a few months earlier and was therefore included in the possible options. The Customer Service

Manager commented:

> *"At the time of the Loyalty Card launch we had the telephony capability and know-how. The critical issues were the people, where do we put them, especially as headcount numbers were under pressure? The Head Office building was being refurbished and a new annex being constructed which was very disruptive".*

Group Telecommunications supports and encourages the use of industry standard products and services and fosters relationships with the major telecommunications providers. The telephony industry is a standards-based one, a necessity to allow the connectivity of calls between systems around the world, and this has therefore helped in making the telephony components a commodity. At that time Nortel ACD Telephony was being rented from a cable company, therefore the options considered to be available to the team at that time were (a) utilise the existing internal Customer Service call centre, (b) outsource the call centre to a third party, or (c) set up a new internal call centre.

The four key decisions outside the boundary of the problem focus were: (i) Extend scheme to other BeingWell companies, (ii) obtain or acquire call centre capability, (iii) whether to move call centre in-house, and (iv) use BeingWell staff to handle calls. Decisions (ii), (iii), and (iv) were to take on a greater significance later on in the case. To take each of those decisions in order:

Extend scheme to other BeingWell companies?

Although restricted to use within BW only at the time of its launch, it was likely that the Loyalty Card could be extended to include the customers of other BeingWell Group companies for example BeingWell Opticians. Although no immediate resolution to this question was required the general approach should consider the wider implications of extending the scheme to other customers, such as deployment at the point of sale or service, confidentiality of data, and data protection regulations.

Obtain or acquire call centre telephony?

Group Telecommunications constantly survey the market to understand what is available in order to influence the strategic direction of the company. A Telecommunications Project Manager commented on the growing trend to rent managed services from third parties:

> *"It became clear that the functionality of the managed service was limited, and*

the supplier wasn't growing the service at the rate our demand for functionality was growing. Other Business Units such as BeingWell Opticians, BeingWell Healthcare International and more recently help-desks such as our own (Group Telecommunications) and Information Systems were taking up the service. There comes a point where you are paying 'n' times the rate the managed service are charging you, and you can do it for a similar price in-house".

This view placed the issues surrounding the use of third parties firmly on the corporate agenda, which meant that alternatives needed to be considered when considering telephony issues in future.

Whether to move call centre in-house?

The Loyalty Card call centre was launched with the help of T.COM, the contract with T.COM being signed just as Maureen Lilley (Director of Customer Service) was going through the final stages of submitting a business case for the Customer Service call centre, but she wasn't quite at a point where she could say that they could support the Loyalty Card initiative. The initial price per call basis for charging soon became prohibitive, with call rates rising sharply in line with the dramatic take up of Loyalty Cards. Similarly, service issues were also surfacing as T.COM changed ownership, and along with it their philosophy and approach. BeingWell were described by T.COM as being *"quite demanding and not an easy client"*. This pressure on cost and service was central to considering the decision to bring the Loyalty Card call centre back in-house.

Use BeingWell staff to handle calls?

BeingWell is very protective of the brand and generally prefers to use its own staff to interact with its customers. However, it was recognised that there is a difference between call centres that specialise in order fulfilment, advice lines, or in this case simple enquiries and data changes, and was likened by one project team member to a 'Tango' soft drinks campaign that required customers to contact a call centre that captured their name and address and in return sent them a 'money off' voucher. The decision therefore is whether BeingWell should use its own staff, or the staff of a third party.

Step two: Designing the possible courses of action

This second step focuses on designing possible courses of action, and Table 3.1 summarises the key decisions to be taken along with their possible outcomes under consideration.

DECISION AREA	OPTIONS	OPTION LABEL
Determine an approach?	- Controlled trial or pilot - Get a third party to administer the scheme - In-house administration	- Pilot - Outsource - In-house
Whether to utilise smart-card technology?	- Yes - No	- Yes - No
How best to provide the Information Technology?	- Predominantly Bespoke - Predominantly Package	- Besp - Pack
Obtain or acquire call centre capability?	- Utilise internal call centre - Outsource - Set-up new internal call centre	- Internal - Outsource - New

Table.3.1: Options within the boundary of the decision area

Figure 3.3 shows the results from comparisons of options in each decision area with every other option in each decision area (AIDA). This pairing ensures that incomparable or doubtful combinations are highlighted and potentially excluded from future analysis.

The Option Graph in Figure 3.4 diagrammatically represents the outcome from AIDA. This step cuts down the possibility of up to thirty-six decision schemes to twenty-one decision schemes, however unlike the preceding case the number of option bars is greatly reduced, with only three incompatible combinations, and four doubtful ones (but some of these doubtful combinations might be reversed with further work or analysis). Figures 3.4 demonstrates how it would be incompatible to elect to deploy smart-card technology and expect to utilise software packages to support the loyalty scheme, as there were no software packages to support a smart-card loyalty scheme at that time. This reduced number of doubtful or incompatible combinations improves the choice of decision schemes going forward.

Smart card?	CALL CENTRE? Internal	Outsource	New
Yes	•	•	•
No	•	•	•

Approach?	IT? Besp	Pack
Pilot	?	•
In-house	•	•
Outsource	•	•

Approach?	SMART CARD? Yes	No
Pilot	•	•
In-house	•	•
Outsource	•	•

IT?	SMART CARD? Yes	No
Besp	•	•
Pack	X	•

Call centre?	IT Besp	Pack
Internal	•	•
Outsource	•	•
New	•	•

Approach?	CALL CENTRE? Internal	Outsource	New
Pilot	•	•	?
In-house	•	?	?
Outsource	X	•	X

• = Compatible combination X = Incompatible combination ? = Doubtful compatibilit

Figure 3.3: Analysis of interconnected decision areas (AIDA)

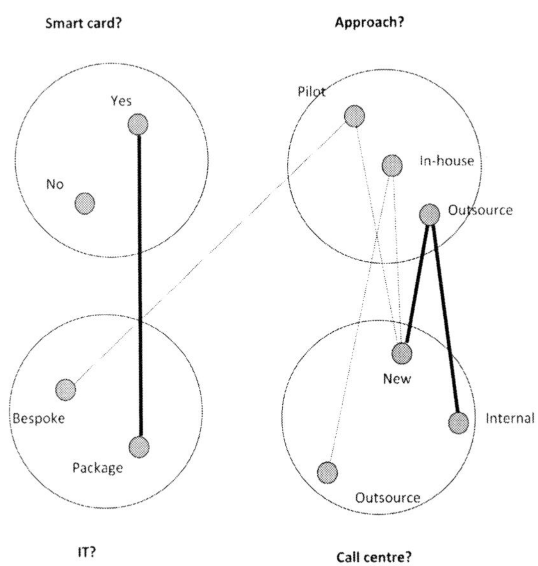

Figure 3.4: Option Graph – Loyalty Card

Having determined which options are compatible it is then possible to establish which combination of those options can be realistically crafted into a feasible decision scheme. A feasible decision scheme is one where it doesn't violate any of the incompatibilities established during earlier analysis, but their inclusion in the final solution is still not automatic. Figure 3.5 shows that when the compatible options are re-presented to determine what feasible decision schemes are possible twenty-one decision schemes emerge from the analysis, thirteen of those having doubtful compatibilities that would need to be resolved in order to establish if they are truly feasible.

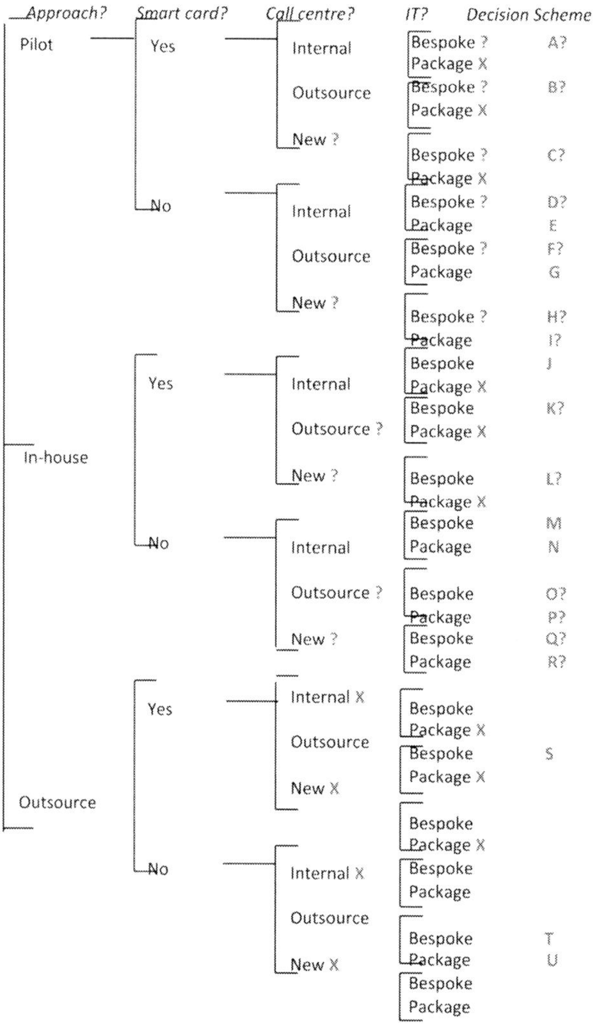

Fig.3.5: Feasible decision schemes for the Loyalty Card case

Step three: Comparing the possible courses of action

Having determined a list of feasible decision schemes the next step is to compare each of the schemes in light of what their consequences might be. Table 3.2 lists those comparison areas that emerged to be of importance to the actors in this case, and a comparative measure has been assigned to each comparison type. A working shortlist can be developed from the feasible decision schemes identified earlier, and compared against those considered by the project team to be the top three comparison areas in this case, namely: *'support for new products and services'*, *'cost effective administration'*, and *'flexibility to cope with high demand'*. Figure 3.6 shows this working shortlist along with the assessment of how each comparison area compared with the desired minimum ratings of at least 'average' for the support of new products and services, for cost effective administration to at least 'break even', and demonstrate at least 'medium' flexibility to cope with high demand.

COMPARISON AREA:	COMPARATIVE MEASURE:
The ability to enhance new initiatives: **A number of initiatives were being considered which utilised the Loyalty Card and the associated processes.**	Yes ↔ No
Cost effective administration: **The administration of the Loyalty Card is seen as a 'necessary evil' and a direct cost, with little or no value adding capability.**	Effective ↔ Break even ↔ Ineffective
Scalability to include other BeingWell Group companies: **Although restricted to BW at the time of its launch, it was expected that the Loyalty Card would be extended to include other BeingWell Group companies (e.g. BeingWell Opticians).**	High ↔ Medium ↔ Low
The ability to support new retail products and services: **The Loyalty Card is seen as being central to a number of related activities**	Good ↔ Average ↔ Poor
Flexibility to cope with high demand: **All the marketing predictions showed the potential for a massive take-up of the Loyalty Card.**	High ↔ Medium ↔ Low

Table.3.2: List of comparison areas

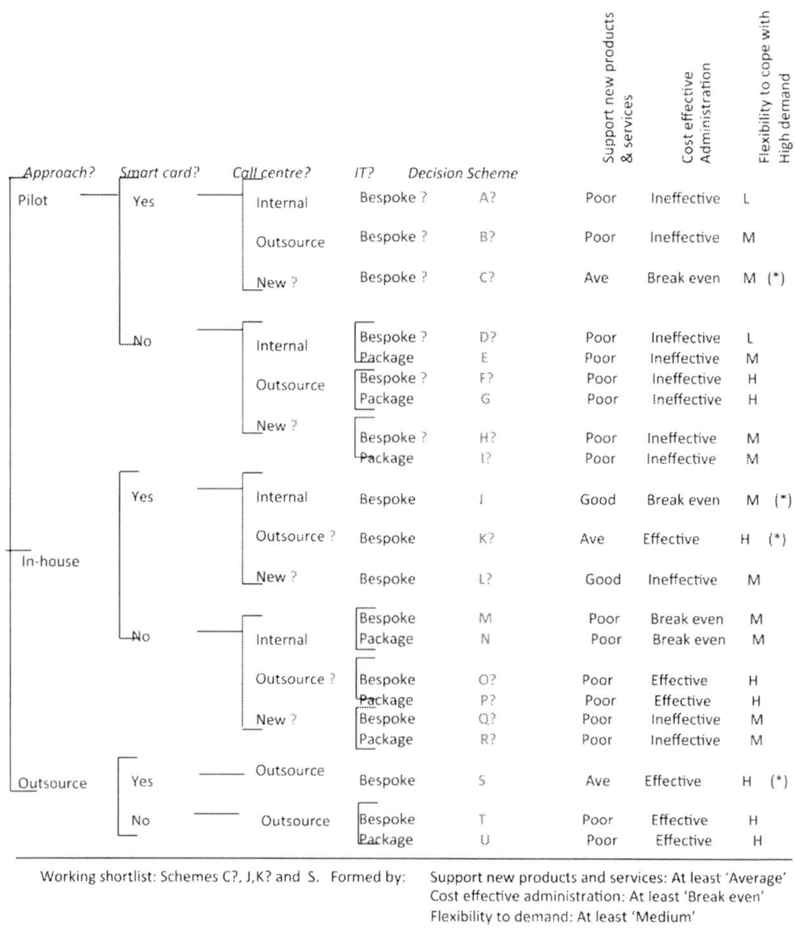

Figure 3.6: Forming a working shortlist – Loyalty Card

The outcome of the comparison ratings suggests that decision schemes 'C?', 'J', 'K?' and 'S' should form the working shortlist as all four options met at least the minimum requirements for the comparison measure. However, as schemes 'C?' and 'K?' had doubtful compatibility (signified by the question mark) they were removed from further analysis. The comparisons of each of the four key decision areas (Approach, Smart-card, Call Centre, and IT) and the choices to be made are as follows:

Approach (*In-house versus Outsource versus Pilot*)

The existence of two previous trials was enough to convince the project team that BeingWell customers would positively receive, and actively participate in, a Loyalty Card scheme. The administration of the scheme was considered a burden and therefore there was little appetite to actively take it on. The Customer Service call centre was in its infancy and not able at that time to accommodate the predicted levels of additional Loyalty Card work. Therefore the option to outsource to a third party, in this case T.COM was actively pursued.

Smart-card (*Yes versus No*)

Unique at the time of the launch was the decision that the card should contain a memory chip (often mistaken for a micro-processor chip), which unlike most other Loyalty Cards that used magnetic stripe technology did not rely on the concept of a 'home store'. This enabled customers to shop at the BeingWell stores of their choice, and points could be added or redeemed at any location as the crucial personal and point's details were held on the chip.

Call centre (*Internal versus Outsource versus New*)

Gerry McGovern the Loyalty Card Programme Manager said:

> *"The perception of the team is that the call centre was a cost with little or no value. Not that they dismissed its value, but more that it isn't value creating, unlike the investment in a database where you can see revenue streams or improvement in profit delivery arising from it. The Loyalty Card scheme had to be value creating, therefore everything that created it was a positive cost, the two items that weren't were points redemption (which is just pay-back), and call centres which are a necessary evil. Rightly or wrongly when you have to find ways of saving money, this great 'lump' [call centre] doesn't positively contribute anything, and if we can reduce that by reducing the number of calls we operate better. It wasn't a penalty for operating badly; it was a necessary cost of doing the business, just like ground rents are a necessary evil in running a store. People recognised that it was critically important but begrudged spending the money on it because it didn't contribute to a revenue stream".*

While in this frame of mind it would be difficult to support the provision of a new in -house call centre, or to burden the existing Customer Service call centre with the additional calls from the Loyalty Card. In keeping with the outsourcing of the administration it also follows that the call centre should also be outsourced.

IT (*Bespoke versus package*)

The absence of packaged software being readily available to administer a chip card based loyalty scheme led to a bespoke software development being commissioned. The deliverables being a Loyalty Scheme Operating System (LSOS), which contains details of customers personal details, card details such as points balance, card numbers, customer number (which is transparent to the customer), and an account number. In addition to LSOS a Customer Database Analytical System (CDAS) was implemented which has the ability to mine customer information to assess shopping habits. Item level transaction details are passed through CDAS to understand shopping habits. By virtue of size, LSOS has become the de facto Customer Database and is at the heart of any CRM activity. As the Programme manager explained:

> *"We considered the creation of an internal database but it wasn't followed through. The external option was preferred at the time as it was going to be tricky to tackle and would shy away from it ourselves, and we didn't have the resource for the call centre. We didn't have the will to impose a BeingWell solution. The quickest way to market is to have someone else drive it for you".*

Comparisons under uncertainty

In Table 3.3, two of the four short listed decision schemes (labelled 'J' and 'S') are compared against each other in terms of all five of the comparison areas listed earlier. This additional form of comparison provides another opportunity to make an assessment using the full range of comparisons identified. The comparisons include a mix of 'numeric' and 'textual' comparisons.

Step four: Choosing commitments for action through time

The final step is the formation of proposed commitments to action through time. Table 3.4 is a cumulative list of uncertainty areas identified and captured during the analysis, which have been categorised into one of the UE, UV or UR uncertainty types, along with an indication of the salience of this uncertainty to the final decision. The most salient uncertainty considered by the actors involved in this case is the uncertainty surrounding the true cost of outsourcing.

	J	S	
Approach? Smart Card? Call centre? IT?	In house Yes Internal Bespoke	Outsource Yes Outsource Bespoke	
Comparison Area:			**Comparative comment:**
The ability to enhance new initiatives: (Yes ↔ No)	Yes	Yes	No advantage lies with either scheme, as both are likely to enhance new initiatives.
Cost effective administration: (Effective ↔ Break even↔ Ineffective)	Break even	Effective	An assumption has been made that an outsourced call centre will be more cost effective than the in-house alternative, thereby increasing the efficiency.
Scalability to include other BeingWell Group companies: (High ↔ Medium ↔ Low)	Medium	Medium	No clear requirement for the use of the Loyalty Card exists within other Group companies at present, but neither scheme appears any more favourable than the other.
The ability to support new retail products and services: (Good ↔ Average ↔ Poor)	Good	Average	Scheme 'J' is totally within the control of the company therefore increasing the ability to support new products and services.
Flexibility to cope with high demand: (High ↔ Medium ↔ Low)	Medium	High	It is assumed that an outsourced call centre will be more flexible and able to cope with a rapid growth in demand.

Table 3.3: Comparison under uncertainty

UNCERTAINTY AREA	LABEL:	TYPE:	SALIENCE:
? The ability to cope with the rapid take-up as indicated by the trials.	?TAKE-UP	UE	••
? The true cost of outsourcing.	?OUTCOST	UE	•••
? The likelihood of setting-up a new internal call centre when one already exists for another service.	?NEWCALL	UR	••
From 'Scalability to include other BeingWell Group companies' comparison: ? The real likelihood that other Group companies will require the Loyalty Card.	?GROUP-CARD	UV	••
? The likelihood of outsourcing the call centre when an 'in-house' administration option has been chosen.	?IN-OUT	UR	••

Table 3.4: Comparing uncertainty areas

Figure 3.7 plots the uncertainties previously identified on an uncertainty graph for the Loyalty Card case. Clearly the uncertainty labelled '?OUTCOST' is likely to have a significant influence on the final outcome, and further explorations to reduce the uncertainty should be taken.

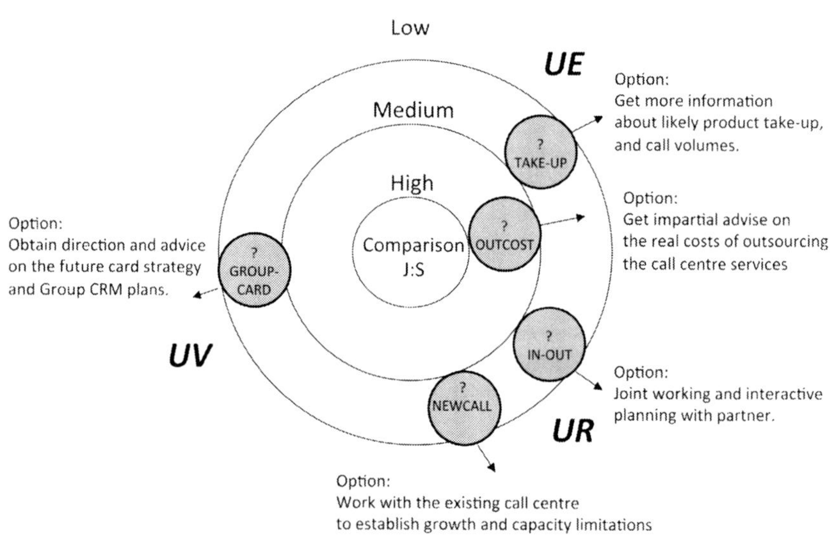

Figure 3.7: Uncertainty graph - salience of uncertainty to this comparison

Commitment package

In practice decisions can be made in sequence rather than at the same time, and deferring decisions can provide time to reduce uncertainty and bring forward any decisions that should be, or can be, made sooner. Figure 3.8 rearranges the feasible action schemes to reflect those decisions that can be taken sooner (i.e. there is little choice), but at the same time building flexibility by allowing those decisions where there is some choice to be taken later, perhaps when more information is known or uncertainty reduced. By adopting this strategy choice can be engineered when determining 'approach' and 'call centre' options.

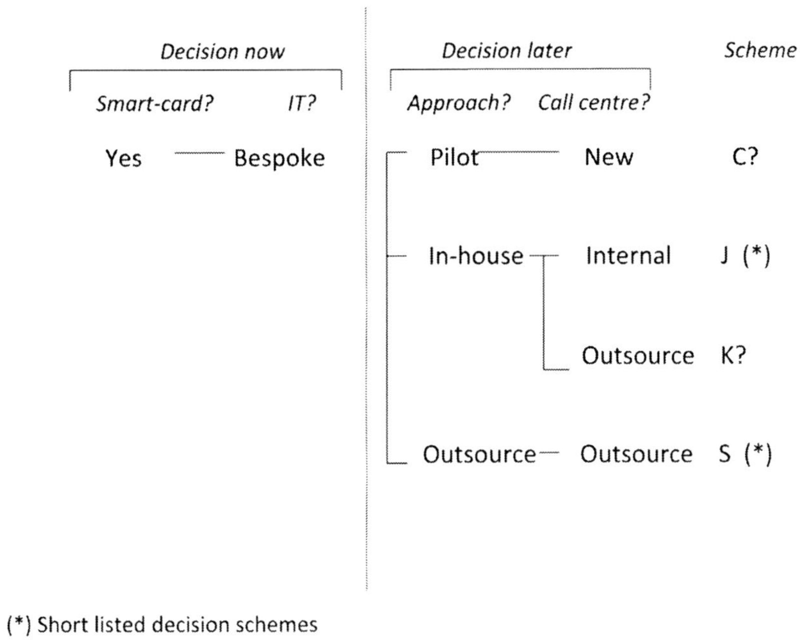

Figure 3.8: A comparison of the feasible action schemes

Figure 3.8 implies that the most urgent decision 'Approach' has, or could be, deferred. The reality is that 'Smart-card' and 'IT' have been moved forward, and as they feature in all four option schemes there is no reason to defer them, thus allowing time to investigate the other options in more detail.

The commitment package is the method Strategic Choice Approach uses to set-out the framework of the decisions to be made, and distinguishes between those actions that have to be taken immediately, those actions that require further exploration to reduce the salience of areas of uncertainty, and finally the other arrangements that need to be made to enable actions to be deferred. The commitment package in Table 3.5 is a summary of the actual decisions taken in this case and distinguishes between those decisions taken initially and those that were deferred.

	DECISIONS NOW			**FUTURE DECISION**	
	Actions	Explorations		Deferred Choices	Contingency Planning
Approach:	Outsource the administration of the scheme to a third-party.	Consider alternative administrative providers.			Limit contractual arrange-ments to increase flexibility.
Smart-card	Invest in chip card technology to maximise future exploitation of the card and data.	Investigate alternative card smart-card suppliers.		Consider amalgamated Credit/smart-card readers	
Call centre:	Outsource the call centre activity to T.COM.			Consider alternative providers to T.COM.	Limit contractual arrange-ments to increase flexibility.
IT:	Commission the development of a Loyalty Scheme operating system.	Might be developed by the in-house IT depart-ment.			

Table 3.5: Commitment package framework – Loyalty Card

The actual decision scheme chosen by BW i.e. (an *'outsource'* approach, *'yes'* to utilise a smart-card, to *'outsource'* the call centre, and to *'bespoke'* the IT) is represented by decision scheme 'S'.

3.4 The alignment of the actors in the network (Alignment logic)

Introduction

The third approach uses concepts from Actor Network Theory to understand the alignment of the actors to the proposed approaches. Plotting the process components on the inscription/specialisation framework the Loyalty Card case has different characteristics to those seen in the Customer Service case. Figure 3.9 shows the relatively tight grouping of the 'people', 'accommodation' and 'telephony' components all in the 'aligned-commodity' space, while the two systems CDAS and LSOS are positioned, quite separately, in the non aligned-proprietary space. So why is this?

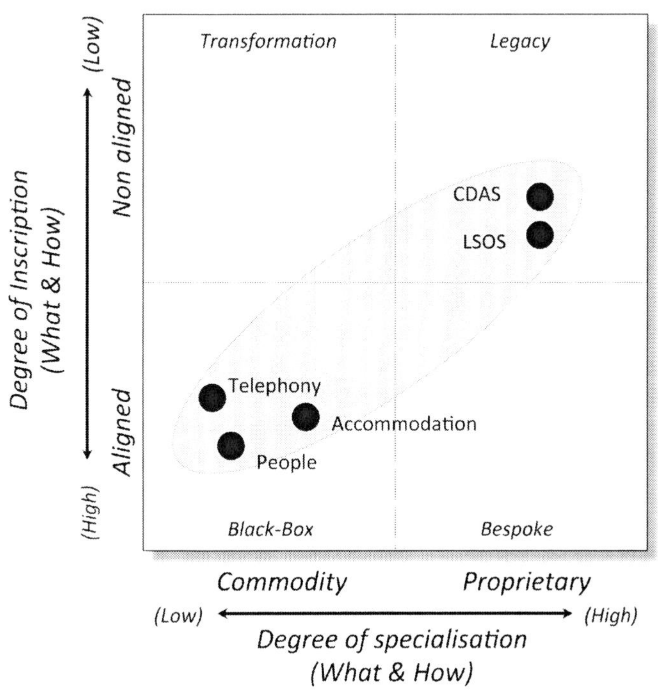

Figure 3.9: Loyalty Card process inscription/specialisation framework

Telephony and accommodation

Firstly, the positioning of 'telephony' and 'accommodation' components is consistent with the other cases and is considered 'black-box'. As with customer services, it was accepted that these components were standard, and that normal office accommodation and standard telephony features were perfectly acceptable in this case.

People

The role of the Advisors in this case is far more routine, non-specialist and consistent with what is provided in multi-customer call centres. The nature of the enquiries received is routine, and responses are well scripted thus ensuring a consistent approach. The systems support is sufficient to allow a novice to easily answer queries or make changes to the standing data. No special skills or BeingWell know-how is required to successfully handle the call. The high degree of inscription ensures that this remains the case with the actors being aligned to this view.

CDAS/LSOS Technology

There is evidence of *overflowing*[i] as far as the software products are concerned. 'Overflowing' refers to the impossibility of total framing, i.e. where framing is the ability to isolate or cut off a product, service, or actor from externalities. While rightly considered 'bespoke', the systems are operated and maintained by IBM and there is little alignment or agreement of the functionality required by these systems. For example, many consider that LSOS should be the engine for any CRM system, and others that as BeingWell has a well-established and mature in-house Information Systems capability, which is quite used to operating large mainframe-based applications that it should, and could, be operated in-house in a more cost effective way. At that time the immature market for smart-card loyalty scheme software inevitably resulted in a proprietary solution, while the reliance on a third party to operate the system added extra opportunity for translation activity.

3.5 A longitudinal view: Loyalty Card - BeingWell Loyalty Card

Introduction

Such was the success and subsequent take-up of the Loyalty Card (with applications running at 40,000 per day) it attracted five million users in its first sixteen weeks, and the associated card administration was also growing rapidly as: *"more cardholders means more calls"*. Monthly Call Centre costs quickly reached six figures. This massively exceeded the budget, drawing attention to the Call Centre and its operation. This prompted a number of reviews and close scrutiny of the arrangements with T.COM as it transpired that service level statistics were being 'massaged', the staffing levels previously agreed were not being honoured, and the service arrangements were inadequate. This coincided with the change in appointment of the BeingWell Director of Customer Services, who was both receptive and supportive of the proposals to bring the call centre in-house as part of the existing Customer Services call centre capability.

Developing the call centre process (OUTSOURCE)(YES)(OUTSOURCE)(BESPOKE)

The growing unease at the existing arrangements prompted a review of the outsourced call centre (OUTSOURCE), and the third-party administration of the loyalty scheme (OUTSOURCE), which coincided with an external consultancy review of call centre operations. The objectives, findings, and recommendations were as follows:

Spring 1999.

CALL CENTRE STRATEGY STUDY – EXTRACT FROM THE EXECUTIVE SUMMARY

Objectives:

- Develop a consensus of opinion across BW stakeholders on key call centre issues and priorities,
- Understand the impact of future IT and systems requirements, and
- Compare costs and benefits of three alternative models for implementation.

The key findings of the review were:

- That there were good foundations and base of expertise for bringing future call centres in-house
- Short contracts with outsourced companies allow flexibility - quick to set-up future services,
- Potential for breakdown in delivery of the 'BeingWell Experience' (through fragmented service offers)
- Threat of escalating costs (due to potential for diminishing control of outsourced activities)
- No definitive single view of any individual customer of customer transactions.

The recommendations were:

- Bring Loyalty Card call centre activities in-house (establishing a consolidated Customer Service group),
- Focus on developing consistency of customer service,
- Establish consolidated skill groups for 'Sales', 'Professional' help lines and 'Customer Services'.

(Source: Call Centre Strategy Study – Executive Summary).

Exiting the contractual arrangements with T.COM was not easy but close scrutiny of the contract revealed that a staged withdrawal was possible over a nine-month period, with store only calls coming in-house initially, third party and a small percentage of store calls in-house a few months later, and all calls totally in-house within 8 months. This was possible by firstly transferring the calls from stores to the centre while the appropriate people and skills were put in place. The Loyalty Card Programme Manager commented:

> *"There was a desire amongst Customer Service to take it on, and a recognition that the quality of call management was not at the level we would have liked it to be in external call centres. There was this tension between improving the quality of the call management but you pay a premium. For example, to answer every call within three rings will equate to additional staff. So we took a 'fit for*

purpose' approach, the majority of the calls weren't customer relationship threatening and so we went for the middle of the road response time in order to manage the cost".

"Customer Service agreed to take it on and could show clearly that they were going to be cheaper, clearly there was no third party margin involved. And the Marketing perspective of getting a better level of service for every pound you spend drove us to say we would do it internally, and it was just a matter of managing the terms of the contract".

The decision to use smart card functionality (YES) has not really leveraged the benefit as anticipated as new developments have been slower to materialise than originally predicted. BeingWell launched the Loyalty Card Organ Donor Scheme a joint initiative with the Department of Health. This initiative, the first of its kind in the UK, allows new and existing card holders to join the NHS Organ Donor Register and carry the NHS Organ Donor symbol on their Loyalty Card rather than having to carry a separate Donor card. The partnership with the NHS fits very strongly with BeingWell healthcare heritage and aims to build stronger relationships with customers and strengthen loyalty to the Loyalty Card. Six months later, 120,000 cardholders had joined the Organ Donor Register through the Loyalty Card initiative. Cardholders can now join the Organ Donor Register through the Loyalty Point[9]. This is the first initiative of its kind and removes the need for paper based application forms as customer details are automatically sent to the NHS for inclusion on the register. The Loyalty Card also evolved into a "loyalty credit card". This hybrid card functions like a normal Visa card and is administered by a third party banking group. Those cardholders that join the scheme accrue one loyalty point for every pound spent on the card, or five points per pound if the purchase is at BeingWell. APACS (The Association for Payment Clearing Services)[10] required that any new issue credit/debit card must now be a smart card (i.e. contain a memory chip), which forms part of the new banking standards.

Both CDAS and LSOS (BESPOKE) continue to be the main operational and analytical software systems to support the Loyalty Card. Richard Caines of Mintel cited an example from BeingWell of how to use the customer data (CDAS) as a useful planning tool:

---

9 Loyalty Point is a retail kiosk network which covers 75% of BW's transactions. 90% of all Loyalty Card customers can visit a Loyalty Point store within a 20-minute drive time.

10 APACS (The Association for Payment Clearing Services) was set up in 1985 as a non-statutory Association of major banks and building societies and has become the umbrella body at the heart of the UK payments industry. APACS provides the forum for banks and building societies to discuss non-competitive issues relating to money transmission).

> 11th May 2000
>
> "If a supermarket operates a loyalty scheme just to give away points, it's not good value. The value is in the data generated on shoppers' habits. If they use it for planning, then it's very useful".
>
> "They [BeingWell] analysed shopping patterns among its Loyalty Cardholders, it found a link between the purchase of baby products and photographic goods - when you have a baby, goes the logic, you want to send pictures to grandparents. The store now puts its camera films close to its nappies".
>
> Source: Richard Caines of Mintel. The Guardian Newspaper 11th May 2000.

As BeingWell becomes more involved in CRM activity there is pressure to develop LSOS (by adding functionality) to be the core of a CRM application, and concern has grown to such an extent that a strategically important system such as LSOS is administered by a third-party, that arrangements are in place to bring it in-house. This new arrangement (IN-HOUSE – YES – INTERNAL – BESPOKE) is the decision scheme labelled 'J' in the earlier analysis. The promise of cost effective administration was not realised, and greater flexibility of scheme 'S' not tested.

The amalgamation of Customer Service and Loyalty Card call centres

Although initially operated as two separate call centres, albeit operating in adjacent areas, the newly combined Customer Service and Loyalty Card call centre went on to handle approximately 20,000 customer contacts per week, comprising telephone calls (85%), correspondence (13%), and emails (2%). Loyalty Card scheme maintenance accounts for 54% of contacts, enquiries 25%, customer complaints 17%, support for stores colleagues 3%, and compliments 1%. Although Customer Service is still viewed as a *cost* rather than *profit* centre, people are valuing the work that is done by the department and are beginning to recognise the value adding activity of the gathering data cycle within the business, and the contribution it forces from suppliers. There is a cost advantage to BeingWell of operating this call centre in-house as the margin added on when a third party is involved is avoided. Gerry McGovern, the Loyalty Card Programme Manager commented:

"It was predicated by a belief that we should simply do it, and should not have a myriad of call centres supporting BW businesses. Risk of them exploding all over the place, there was the Asthma help-line, Loyalty Card, Customer Services etc.. Maureen Lilley (Customer Service Director) was inclined to amalgamate them all anyway, and her reasons were that she could guarantee a more standardised level of service, efficiencies and so forth, and the investment she wanted to put into the BeingWell 'start-up' call centre by putting more pieces of business its way, and to leverage the technology base with new screens etc.".

The combined call centre now employs approximately ninety Advisors (which peaks at one hundred during Christmas), who are arranged in five multi-skilled teams, and a dedicated escalations team, which now combine telephone, letter and email work. This is a change from the original postal/telephone arrangements. Skills' based routing[11] is used to automatically route specific calls to Advisors with the appropriate skills to answer that complaint or enquiry. This enables the Customer Services team to supplement the Loyalty Card team at peak or difficult times; it helps in the development of Loyalty Card Advisors in their move to handle the generally more complex calls associated with Customer Services. It gives Advisors variety and develops their general business know-how, which will make them more valuable to the business and gives them an opportunity to develop their career in other parts of the BW organisation. This investment in people has clearly paid off, as the area now experiences lower than average absence and attrition levels, vacancies are quickly filled, and the role of 'Customer Service Advisor' is seen as a role to which others aspire. Key performance indicators for the department reflect this approach and in addition to the traditional measures for call handling statistics also include metrics on internal and external promotions, and the number of days training received.

Working in conjunction with the Loyalty Card team, Loyalty Card points are now being given in lieu of customer payments (i.e. cash compensation for poor service or products). Utilising the 'pending points' facility, Customer Service Advisors can credit a customer's Loyalty Card account, which is automatically credited with the points at their next visit to an in-store Loyalty Card kiosk. This reduces the cost of administration, achieves footfall in store, and encourages the use of the kiosks while at the same time promoting the loyalty scheme.

---

11 Skills' based routing is a facility that enables inbound calls to be routed to an advisor with the appropriate skills. For example, simple name and address changes requiring basic telephone and systems know-how can be routed to a junior member of staff. More complex customer service enquiries or complaints can be routed to more experienced advisors.

3.6 Summary

This second case study describes the approach taken by the Loyalty Card project team within BeingWell, to establish the Loyalty Card call centre in order to handle the ever-growing administration associated with the Loyalty Card scheme. BeingWell envisaged the Loyalty Card as being the 'key' to a number of product and service related offerings to its customers, and fundamental in its evolution from *'chemists to the nation'* to *'the place for products and services that help me look good and feel good'*. As in the previous chapter the details of the process logic, decision logic, and alignment logic were examined using the tools and techniques as described in the introduction.

The actual choice adopted by the team was decision scheme 'S' i.e. (OUTSOURCE – YES – OUTSOURCE – BESPOKE). This choice was considered marginally better than its closest rival decision scheme 'J' (IN-HOUSE – YES – INTERNAL – BESPOKE), as at that time it was thought to have greater flexibility to respond to an as yet unknown demand, and be more cost effective. As with the Customer Service case telephony and accommodation components are considered commodities, but in complete contrast to the Customer Service case so were the people. The aligned view of the actors was that the role of the Advisors was routine, non-specialist, and consistent with what is provided by multi-customer call centres. The specialised nature of the software components forced a proprietary approach but that did introduce the possibility of 'overflowing' (i.e. the ability to isolate these systems from externalities). Fewer option bars existed in this case than in the Customer Service case, which subsequently generated more feasible action schemes and therefore choices in how to proceed.

The next chapter examines a call centre in a mail order environment.

Notes

i CALLON, M., 1999. Actor-network theory – the market test. In: J. LAW AND J. HASSARD, eds. *Actor Network Theory and After*. Oxford: Blackwell and Sociological Review, 181.

CHAPTER FOUR
Case Study Three – Mother & Baby Direct (Mail Order)

4.1 Introduction

Mother & Baby Direct (MABD) is a home shopping catalogue operated by BeingWell, with a range that includes over 1500 products, including maternity wear, larger and 'one-off' items such as pushchairs and cots, and regular but bulky baby care essentials for 0-2's such as disposable nappies. Nearly half the range is available only from the MABD catalogue. Calling a local rate order line can place orders, or alternatively, by completing an order form contained within the catalogue that can be either posted or faxed. Delivery is guaranteed within five working days direct to the customer's door (invariably the home), which is free from delivery charge when the value of the order is over fifty pounds.

Mother & Baby Direct was seen as a first phase in BW's plans to enter the national 'alternative shopping' arena, and an opportunity to gain understanding of the customer requirement and how alternative shopping can be leveraged. The *'pregnant women/new mother'* consumer had been identified as a profitable one with whom BW is advantaged, and the proposition of offering greater expertise and a wider range of products while providing ease in delivering bulky items to customer's homes was seen as an attractive proposition. In addition, it provided a suitable alternative to the convenience of 'superstore' shopping and would offer an early response to the competitive threat of Tesco Baby Direct in the midst of similar activity from other retailers such as Mothercare and the Early Learning Centre.

The approach taken to this case study

The approach taken was the same as that described in the previous case. Data was collected from interviews conducted with members of the BW baby category team and the MABD project team, Alison Biddulph the

MABD Product Manager, the internal specialist groups or teams associated with the project, such as Information Systems, Group Telecommunications, Finance, Personnel, and members of the Executive Managers who have the ultimate decision making authority. Usually, although not exclusively, the business unit supplies the project manager or leader for whom the work is being conducted. This generally implies, although this is certainly not always the case, that the incumbent has the skills and capabilities to run such a project. Contract documentation, recruitment and training material, service level agreements and call handling statistics were all utilised.

4.2 The mail order process in focus (Process logic)

Introduction

This first section examines the work business process under review and, using the 'Activity Record' technique, presents the five prime activities and tasks that make up the process, namely: (i) Receive the 'inbound' calls, (ii) Identify the customer & information, (iii) Take the order, (iv) Initiate other processes, and (v) Close the call. It is not the intention to include all the processes that go to make up the complete end-to-end MABD business

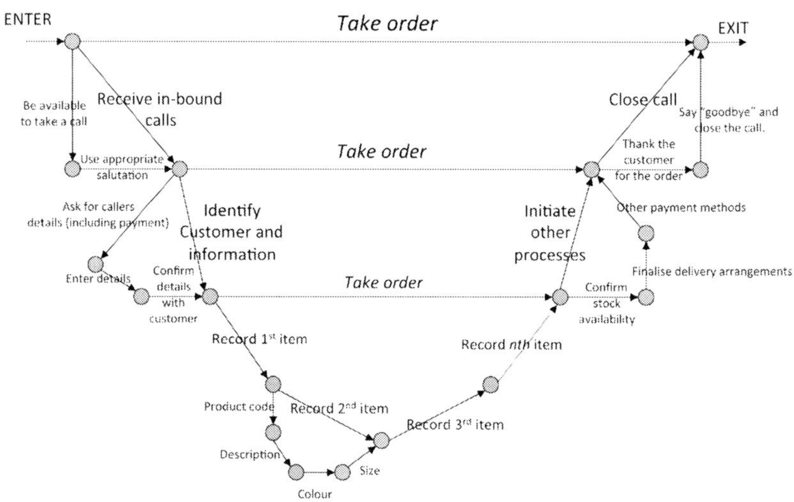

Figure 4.1: An Activity Record of the Mail Order process

however, warehousing and despatch processes are discussed because of the closely coupled association with the process under investigation. The Process starts with an inbound call from a customer, and ends with a finished order and all the associated components (picking lists, despatch notes, invoices and merchandise) being complete for despatch. Figure 4.1 shows an Activity Record of the call centre process as utilised for mail orders.

Each of the activities is described in full as follows:

Activity One: Receive 'inbound' calls

The process starts with an 'inbound' call from customers who call a local rate telephone number which is available between the hours of 7 AM and 10 PM daily, and 8 AM to 8 PM at weekends. The MABD catalogue contains a description of the ordering process and advises that customer reference code, credit/debit card, Loyalty Card and delivery address details are to hand. Although not mandatory, customers are advised to plan their call using the order form inside the back cover of the catalogue, which ensures that the correct product code, product description, colour, size and unit price, (where applicable) are readily available, thus reducing the call duration. Loyalty Card points are available to those customers with a BeingWell Loyalty Card, and simply quoting the card number will ensure that a loyalty scheme points voucher is included with the merchandise. Payment is made normally by credit/debit card quoting the relevant card details, although payment can also be made by cheque and gift voucher, but this would then involve a postal transaction. Since its launch the daily volumes of orders have been approximately 300 - 400, with a peak of in the region of 1000 per day around the Christmas period.

'Mailsales', an independent mail order company located in Plymouth, were chosen to receive the calls and handle the customer orders placed by telephone for the Mother and Baby products. A key component of handling inbound calls is the ability to take the calls quickly and efficiently in an appropriate customer friendly way, but also ensuring that a sale is achieved. BeingWell is '*the*' most trusted brand on the UK high streets, a position it defends vigorously especially when outsourcing any of its services. The Mother & Baby Direct Product Manager confirmed this by demanding: *"Very high levels of service because that's what people expect from the BeingWell brand, consumers have an expectation of that"*.

A unique local rate telephone number was secured for MABD and made available to Mailsales, who at the time used an FDX ACD telephone system to handle and route calls to their operators. They subsequently changed to a Rockwell, and in keeping with many organisations have more recently migrated to a Lucent Technologies system.

A dedicated team were assigned to the MABD account and were given specific product knowledge training as well as an overview of the BeingWell trading philosophy and customer awareness guidance. Operators were required to work shifts to cover the extended trading hours offered by this mail order operation, and BeingWell engaged a full time employee to scrutinize Mailsales constantly, which included time to screen how they manage customers, listen in on calls, and generally make sure that the whole process operates efficiently.

Activity Two: Identify customer and information

The transaction with a customer requires an exchange of personal and product information, which is captured as part of the order fulfilment procedures and retained for subsequent problem resolution and future orders. To do this Mailsales use a system called 'Mail-it'[12], which is a modular suite of software products that supports mailing house, fulfillment operations, and direct sales organisations. It is operated in over 150 companies, and a further 400 companies use its features and functions indirectly. It links directly to third party systems such as Post Office Address File, BACS[13], Electronic Funds Transfer, and industry standard word processing, spreadsheet and EIS (Executive Information System) packages.

When placing an order customers are asked to quote the 'Customer Reference Number' printed on the catalogue, which uniquely identifies them and enables the Operator to quickly access their customer records. Screens tailored to the MABD requirements appear, and the operator can guide the customer through a series of logically related questions to establish their identity, and to check details such as billing and delivery addresses, methods of payment and Loyalty Card details.

Although MABD is a comparatively routine mail order procedure BeingWell insisted on making a series of amendments to Mail-it, with twenty-eight major system changes being identified, such as:

- The adoption of a seven-digit product code to match the BW product code protocols,
- Routines to allocate Loyalty Card scheme points, and more significantly,
- A major development to handle the sophisticated promotions that match the promotions running in BW stores at any given time, despite advice from industry professionals that this wasn't necessary in a mail order business.

---

12 Mail-it is a product of Johnson Group PLC.

13 BACS – Banks Automated Clearing Services

Although Mailsales have a license to make changes to the Mail-it system (in addition to the normal parameter driven changes), such was the extent of the proposed changes that the software vendors (Johnson Group PLC) were encouraged to get involved with some of the changes. As a consequence of this Mailsales now have to support a 'MABD specific' version of the Mail-it system; resulting in, what should be low cost minor changes, being difficult and costly.

The BeingWell Loyalty Card loyalty scheme has approximately 12 million members, which is a rich source of customer and buying behavioural data. The Loyalty Scheme Operating System (LSOS) holds details of the card-holder, while an allied system CDAS (Customer Data Analytical System) holds details of shopping habits and recent transaction history. The system is the closest application BeingWell has to a dedicated CRM (Customer Relationship Management) facility.

Activity Three: Take order

Taking the order is at the heart of this process, and the operator will require additional information in order to fulfil the customer's order.

Having established the identity and *bona fides* of the caller, the customer will describe the items they want to purchase, and the system will prompt the operator to establish specific details such as colour, styles or size, depending on the nature of the products. Table 4.1 is a process impact matrix of the mail order call centre completed at the time which reveals just how closely coupled the call centre process is with the other information systems used during, and in support of, the process. Listed down the left hand side are the activities involved in the process, and along the top the departments. As can be seen, the call centre has a connection with nearly every activity in the total Mother & Baby Direct operation (as represented by the symbol '■ ').

Customers expect to be told estimated delivery dates, especially if the item is 'out of stock' at the time of placing the order, which will require on-line links to the warehouse inventory systems to establish stock levels and forecast delivery dates. Once ordering is complete and payment details are taken, the system has to perform credit checks, produce pick-lists for the warehouse, calculate any loyalty bonuses, discounts, and in the case of a staff purchase any deductions.

	CUSTOMER SERVICES	CALL CENTE	PRODUCT QUALITY DEVT.	WAREHOUSE	FINANCE	SUPPLY	LOYALTY CARD	BUSINESS UNITS	BUSINESS EXPRESS	STORE	MARKETING
Order Placement		■		■		■	■				■
- Standing Order		■			■	■					
- Deferred Order		■		■	■						
- Baby List		■									
- Gift Vouchers				■		■					■
Customer Payment		■		■	■		■				
- Staff Discount		■			■			■			
- Gift Vouchers		■			■		■				■
Order Fulfilment		■		■	■	■	■		■		
Returns	■	■	■	■	■	■	■		■	■	
Repairs		■	■	■		■			■	■	
- Loan Items		■	■	■	■	■			■		
Customer Queries	■	■	■					■		■	
Inventory Maintenance		■		■		■		■		■	
Pricing		■			■			■		■	■
Promotions/Deals		■		■	■		■	■		■	■
Supply to Warehouse			■	■		■					
- Direct Supply					■	■					
Warehouse Stock		■		■							
Management					■						
Stock Disposal				■	■	■		■			
Stock Recall	■	■	■	■		■		■	■	■	■
Loyalty Interface											
- Points allocation		■				■	■				
- Points collection		■					■			■	
- Data collection		■		■			■				
- Data analysis		■					■				
Customer Credit		■			■		■				
Stock Accounting		■		■	■						
Management Reporting	?	?	?	?	?	?	?	?	?	?	?

Key: ■ Has an impact on the call centre process. ? Not yet defined

Table 4.1: A Process Impact Matrix of the Mail Order Call Centre

Activity Four: Initiate other processes

The MABD warehouse is at Acton Road, Birmingham, therefore the orders, more specifically the pick-list and delivery details, have to be passed from Mailsales in Plymouth to the warehouse in Birmingham to put together the order. Details of the delivery status, any missing items or special instructions for the customer are added here and made available to the Mail-it system in Plymouth. An independent courier (Express Packages), is advised of the delivery requirement along with a shipping order.

Deals and offers traditionally offered in BeingWell stores were also offered via the MABD catalogue, despite the complications this created such as the '3 for 2' deal on nappies where three items are despatched but costs and profits apportioned across two only. This also made the accounting for Loyalty Card points difficult. A series of management information reports were generated to keep control of stock movements for later analysis. Once the order is complete and payment received then the transaction is completed.

Activity Five: Close the call

On conclusion of the telephone call the operator will thank the customer for the order and close the call. The associated documentation is produced automatically at the warehouse, the order is picked, packed and despatched via Express Packages. The process ends.

4.3 The approach taken to the business problem (Decision logic)

Introduction

This second section provides a detailed account of how the Mail Order process was approached and managed from the original concept through to implementation and beyond. As the 'baby category' team was already in existence it formed the core of the project team going forward. Strategic Choice Approach techniques (SCA) are used to understand the decision making approach used by the actors in this case.

Step one: Shaping of problems

This first step examines the judgements about possible connections between one field of choice and another. The Decision Graph, as shown in Figure 4.2,

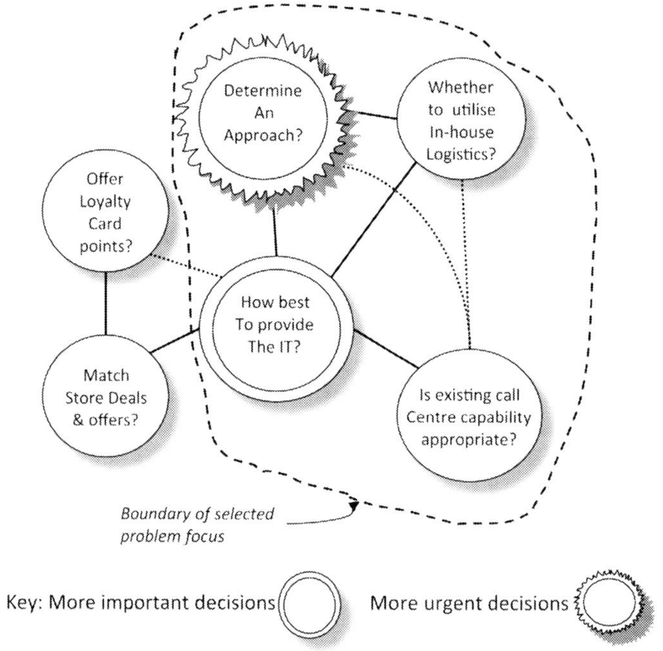

Figure 4.2: A decision graph of the key case decisions

Those decisions shown within the boundary of the problem focus are given prominence over those outside the boundary, however it is realised that all the decisions shown are closely related. Clearly, in this case the initial decision to determine the overall approach was urgently required, as it would influence many of the associated decisions. The four key decisions within the boundary of the problem focus are (i) Determine an approach, (ii) Whether to utilise in-house logistics, (iii) is the existing call centre capability appropriate, and (iv) how best to provide the information technology. To take each decision in order:

Determine an approach?

The project team initially considered two quite different approaches to the problem, these were:

- Acquire or work with a partner who could supply the end-to-end solution (call centre, warehouse and delivery), which was understood to be the preference of the BW Executive at that time, or
- A piecemeal or modular approach looking at each component

individually, with the emphasis on low cost, high speed to market, which at that time was considered a disposable and inherently lower risk approach.

In order to make speedy progress the project manager organised the project into three parallel streams of activity: Call centre, Logistics, and Information Systems, each having a lead person allocated to them, and each reporting into the overall project manager. The Project Manager assigned to 'Call Centres' had the benefit of previous involvement in the strategic positioning work for BW 'direct' products, particularly issues relating to extended inventory of both Health & Travel services as well as Mother & Baby categories. She described the attitude of the participants in this project as:

> *"In many ways the project was approached with the mind-set of a trial despite the fact that some contracts demanded a minimum commitment of two years".*

Traditionally BeingWell are not 'first movers', normally waiting to see what others are doing, but the Tesco initiative did help to focus attention on the launch, and a decision was taken by the Baby Business Category to try and launch in fourteen weeks.

Whether to utilise in-house logistics?

As a retailer BeingWell considered it already had 'warehousing' capability, and a preference was expressed early on in the project to provide the warehousing processes in-house, although there had been discussions with suppliers such as 'GUS' and 'Gratten' who could both supply an end-to-end capability. However this was going to be more expensive than the cost of the current in-house operation, which was attributed mainly to the insistence of BeingWell to conduct the operation 'their way', for example, to configure the information systems to accommodate and mirror every conceivable in-store promotion possible. Therefore the choices were a simple 'yes' or 'no'.

Is the existing call centre capability appropriate?

At that time T.COM were operating the Loyalty Card call centre and there were growing concerns over the relationship and the potential for a clash of interests. An in-house Customer Service call centre based in Head Office had just completed its first year of operation and was handling 1200 calls per day (average). However, the Call Centre selection Project Manager commented:

> *"We knew we didn't have the capability [for call centres] in-house, and it was a struggle to get the company to realise that we didn't have the capability in-house. Having a call centre is not the same as having a call centre that can take and process mail orders. A different set of criteria is required. This is a very different business - the appropriate 'mindset' has to be in place".*

The call centre would need to take payment by credit card, and although payment by card had been done for years in BW stores, the current call centre did not have that capability, and this was made to appear as being a significant issue. This development work coincided with a restriction on any increase to headcount of those who operate the BW Customer Service Call Centre. As one Project Manager commented:

> *"We have a tendency to invest outside the company, due to head-count capping, rather than grow internally, which is almost without considering the financial dynamics of the case"*

The likely options are expressed in terms of: (i) 'yes' the internal call-centre is capable, (ii) 'no' it isn't, or (iii) it could be capable with development.

How best to provide the Information Technology?

The provision of timely and accurate information is essential to provide an effective and efficient mail order operation, and as described earlier, the call centre process is right at the heart of that operation. The call centre will be required to access customer, product, stock, Loyalty Card, payment, and delivery information, much of it in 'real-time', in conjunction with the necessary telephony technology to make this appear 'seamless' to the customer. This is likely to be a combination of existing systems and new functionality not previously used. The choice of how the technology is provided is considered to be the most important, i.e. whether to utilise packaged software and therefore be 'constrained' by the methods of operation that the software supports, or alternatively, utilise existing processes and routines as a framework to develop complimentary bespoke software, to work in conjunction with software packages.

The two key decisions outside the boundary of the problem focus are:

Offer Loyalty Card points?

It was reasonably clear from the beginning of the project that it would be preferable to award customers with Loyalty Card points in much the same way as if shopping in-store. However, as the Loyalty Card scheme had been designed around a face-to-face transaction with the customer, which relied on the customer tendering the card onto which points were physically credited, the provision of points in a non face-to-face transaction was more challenging. Although inelegant this could be easily resolved by providing the customer with a voucher with the appropriate number of points, which could be credited to their Loyalty Card at the next face-to-face transaction in store. This apparent resolution, while not without some difficulty, appeared to be accepted as a pragmatic option thus removing it from the 'critical' decision status.

Match store deals and offers?

Despite engaging third-party organisations for amongst other things their know-how of the mail order processes, BW Marketing insisted on ignoring their advice by including promotional 'deals' in the mail order offer that match those operated in BW stores. This was a decision supported by the internal legal Advisors at that time as they thought it a legal requirement to consistently offer products at the same price regardless of channel to market. Compared with BeingWell the preferred mail order partner (Mailsales) were an inconsequential company and BeingWell took their advice in moderation. BeingWell has a very 'arrogant' approach to these arrangements and has a strong culture of *"we know best"*. As a Product Manager described:

"We chose third parties for their expertise, but didn't listen to them. We said we were open to suggestions, but weren't really, we were 'hamstrung' by the red tape, very little liberty to take decisions. The call centre people were telling us not to do deals. Mail order doesn't lend itself to deals. You are going to get yourselves into all kinds of problems. The customers you get through mail order are not necessarily as price aware, but they are convenience shoppers. The price (say getting three goods for the price of two) is not always going to persuade them to buy from your catalogue".

Step two: Designing the possible courses of action

This second step focuses on designing possible courses of action, and Table 4.2 summarises the key decisions to be taken along with their possible outcomes under consideration.

DECISION AREA	OPTIONS	OPTION LABEL
Determine an approach?	- Modular - Acquisition (e.g. Littlewoods)	- Mod - Acq
Whether to utilise in-house logistics?	- Yes - No	- Yes - No
How best to provide the Information Technology?	- Predominantly Bespoke - Predominantly Package	- Besp - Pack
Is the existing call centre capability appropriate?	- Yes - With development - No	- Yes - Dev't - No

Table 4.2: Options within the boundary of the decision area

A key feature of the decision making process is the interconnectedness of the decisions and the subsequent consequences of those decisions, and that the likely outcome will rely on a compromise between possible options. SCA utilises the Analysis of Interconnected Decision Areas approach (AIDA) to help in understanding the relatedness of these decisions and is useful here to understand how and what decisions have been made. Figure 4.3 shows the results from comparisons of each option within a decision area with every other option within the decision area. This pairing ensures that incompatible or doubtful combinations are highlighted and potentially excluded from future analysis.

		APPROACH?	
		Mod	Acq
Call Centre?	Yes	•	?
	Dev't	•	?
	No	X	?

		CALL CENTRE?		
		Yes	Dev't	No
Logistics?	Yes	•	•	X
	No	?	?	X

		IT?	
		Besp	Pack
Logistics?	Yes	•	X
	No	X	?

		IT?	
		Besp	Pack
Call Centre?	Yes	•	?
	Dev't	•	•
	No	?	•

		APPROACH?	
		Mod	Acq
Logistics?	Yes	•	X
	No	•	•

		APPROACH?	
		Mod	Acq
IT?	Besp	•	X
	Pack	?	•

Key: • = Compatible combination X = Incompatible combination ? = Doubtful compatibility

Figure 4.3: Analysis of interconnected decision areas (AIDA)

The Option Graph in Figure 4.4 diagrammatically represents the outcome from AIDA and it can be seen that despite the possibility of up to twenty-four decision schemes, this is reduced to only six decision schemes, however the number of option bars has increased to seven, and there are nine doubtful combinations (but some of these could be reversed with further work or analysis). Figure 4.4 demonstrates that by choosing 'yes' to the option to utilise in-house logistics capability it immediately causes incompatibilities (option bars) with using packaged application software, as the current BW logistic operation is largely bespoke. Similarly, the acquisition of a third-party organisation that also has logistics capability would be incompatible with wanting to utilise the in-house capability.

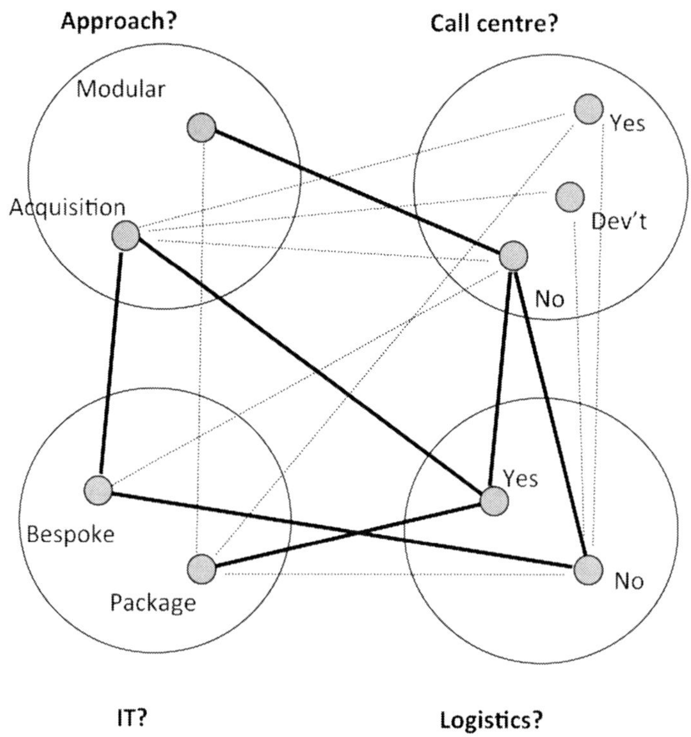

Figure 4.4: Option Graph – Mail Order

Having determined which options are compatible it is then possible to establish which combination of those options can be realistically crafted into feasible decision schemes. A feasible decision scheme is one where it doesn't violate any of the incompatibilities established during earlier analysis, but their inclusion in the final solution is still not automatic.

Figure 4.5 shows that when the compatible options are re-presented to determine what feasible decision schemes are possible only six feasible decision schemes emerge from the analysis, four of those having doubtful compatibilities that would need to be resolved in order to establish if they are truly feasible.

Step three: Comparing the possible courses of action

Having determined a list of feasible decision schemes the next step is to compare each of the schemes in light of what their consequences might be. Table 4.3 lists those comparison areas that emerged to be of importance to

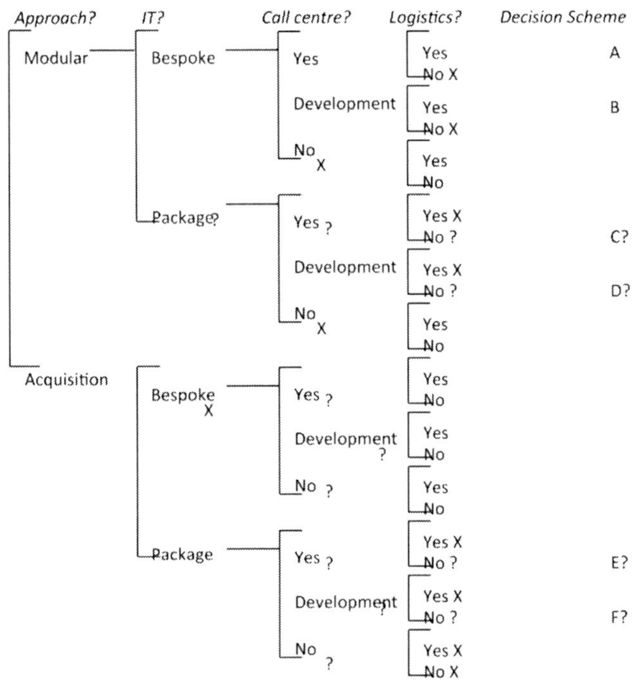

Figure 4.5: Feasible decision schemes for the Mail Order case

the actors in this case, and a comparative measure has been assigned to each comparison type. A working shortlist can be developed from the feasible decision schemes identified earlier, by comparing them against those comparison measures considered by the project team to be the top three comparison areas in this case, namely: *'speed to market'*, *'VBM case positive'*, and *'brand protection'*.

Figure 4.6 shows the assessment of how each feasible decision scheme compared with the desired minimum ratings of at least 'medium' for both speed to market and VBM positive, and at least 'good' for brand protection.

The outcome of the comparison ratings suggests that decision schemes 'C?' and 'D?' should form the working shortlist, as these were the only decision schemes that met the minimum requirements for the comparison measure. However, both these schemes had doubtful compatibility (signified by the question mark), and were very similar in composition; therefore decision scheme 'A' was substituted for decision scheme 'D' to provide a more realistic comparator and was a closer fit to the actual decision scheme chosen by BW. The comparisons of each of the four key decision areas (Approach, IT, Call Centre, and Logistics) and the choices to be made are as follows:

COMPARISON AREA:	COMPARATIVE MEASURE:
Speed to market: Seen as an important response to competition, and a positive impact with City analysts.	Fast ↔ Medium ↔ Slow
Value Based Management (VBM) case positive: Investment decisions are based on 'managing for value' principles and therefore require a positive business case.	High ↔ Medium ↔ Low
Expansion potential: The ability to flex operations in line with demand.	Yes ↔ No
Brand protection: With one of the most trusted brands on the high street BeingWell are extremely cautious about damaging the brand.	Good ↔ Poor
Risk:	High ↔ Medium ↔ Low

Table 4.3: List of comparison areas

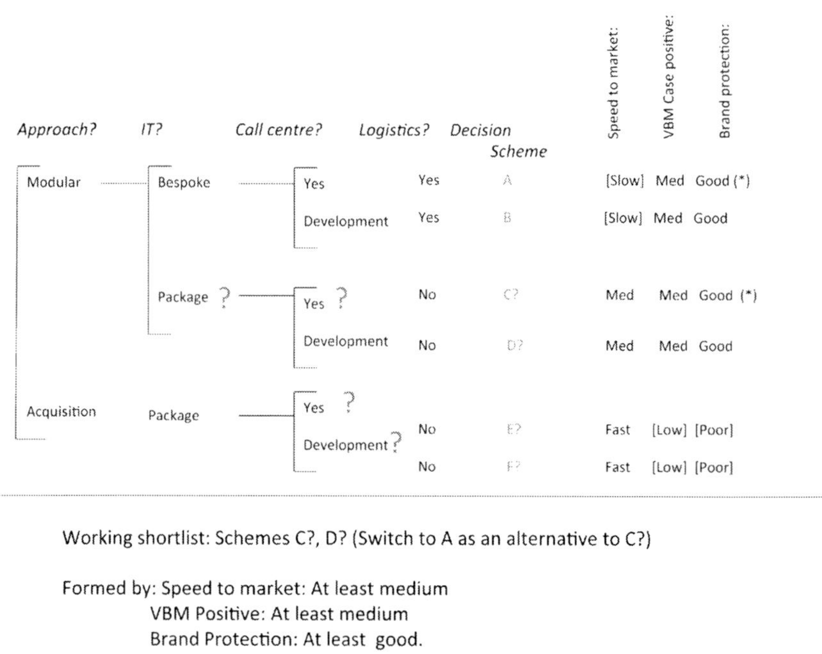

Figure 4.6: Forming a working shortlist – Mail Order

Approach (Modular versus Acquisition)

Discussions took place early on with some of the big names in catalogue and home shopping business for example, Greater Universal Stores (GUS), Gratten, and Littlewoods. BeingWell desire to maintain control habitually precluded joining forces with such established players in other industries, despite the obvious brand leverage BeingWell enjoys.

IT (Bespoke versus package)

Even though at first considered quite separate, the three themes of call centre, warehousing and IT, are closely coupled, as it is the technology that binds them together. Although Mailsales was the preferred call centre partner it was felt that they didn't have the systems capability to make the changes required. Mailsales were asked if they would fund assistance from Johnson Group PLC (the vendor of the Mail-it software) to assist with the changes, and they subsequently agreed. Therefore systems development changes to the Mail-it software would be a tripartite arrangement. Firstly, as Mailsales have licensing rights to modify and tailor bespoke elements of the system, they could undertake 'bolt-on' elements with their small development team that was supplemented with two contractors. Johnson Group PLC, the vendors of Mail-it can undertake the core systems changes, and BW internal IS development staff undertake the in-house systems changes. At one point the changes to Mail-it numbered 46, excluding deals and changes since. As one Business Analyst commented at the time *"It was psychologically more palatable to change the system rather than the people"*.

The option of operating the MABD warehouse by imitating the procedures of a BW store, in order to utilise the stock functionality of the store EPoS systems to quickly satisfy the requirements of a stock-file (held on the store controller), although initially considered to be convenient will in fact be problematic. For example, it will not be possible to disentangle the finance systems elements from the store stock replenishment software, it was also necessary to report stock levels accurately in order to establish accurate financial information. This was aggravated further by the use of seven digit item codes, which had to be translated into 5 digit codes and then back to seven. The Mail-it system can also provide complete order processing and fulfilment functionality, however this has been 'truncated' to allow the Acton Road warehouse to be used. This then feeds into a proprietary system which in turn handles the shipping documentation for the carrier (Express Packages). This approach has generated a considerable number of integration and file transfers between systems. A recent desire to switch to an alternative carrier has revealed the 'hard coded' nature of this system that now requires system changes to facilitate this. Stock-file accuracy for a mail order operation is critical, therefore in keeping with the store approach, stock items are scanned-in to stock at the warehouse. Sales are scanned-out thus ensuring accurate stock figures. This results in a large amount of double handling within the warehouse.

This was also a significant factor in the choice of call centre, as they had to be able to remotely print an order to the Acton Road warehouse. As an IT Business Analyst pointed out:

> *"This sounds very simple, but we later realised that we would be building our own warehouse system. It was a naive view that an order can be printed from the system, at the warehouse, which would allow the picking and packing of the ordered items".*

It was taken as a 'given' that BW had warehousing and logistics capability and the pressure to deliver a solution quickly made it easy to go along with that view. However, referring to the years of experience in Logistics, the Business Analyst went on to say:

> *"What we actually have is years of experience in forty-four ton trunkers and moving pallets between one shed and another. We don't have experience in moving a single item to 'Mrs. Smith' in Acacia Avenue"*

As one Analyst commented *"All of the replenishment taken care of by treating it as a store"*. However, the Systems Development Project Manager observed that:

> *"Trying to make a mail order operation look in the accounts like a BW store turned out to be not a very sensible thing to be doing, we had to go through all kinds of hoops and get extra software written and do things to all kinds of Finance systems".*

It wasn't so much the decision to emulate the store processes that was the problem, but more the consequences of that decision. For example, activities such as bank reconciliation were unnecessarily complicated as the mail order business was logically (even if not physically) treated as a separate company. Ultimately the costs of the changes to BeingWell Finance systems alone were comparable to the total costs of all the other systems changes. A change to the Financial Accountant allocated to this project during its life was also disruptive, each one having a different view on the accounting treatments necessary for this venture.

Call centre (*'Yes in-house' versus 'in-house with Development' versus 'No to in-house'*)

Despite having an adequate in-house call centre in operation at that time, the decision to tender externally was taken. As the Call Centre Project Manager described it:

> *"To change things internally would have taken longer, so an option could have been to put a mail order processing system into the Customer Service call centre. We all felt that would take longer to do, and that it was easier to remove the politics and just go outside"*

An invitation to tender (ITT) process to select the call centre vendors was used, *"which was frankly hard work"*, and over complicated the process. It was based very much around the 'system' rather than the 'service'. Five companies were initially short listed and invited to tender. Four of those organisations took part in the initial selection process, the fifth declining to respond to the ITT due to a recent internal restructure. Of the four, BeingWell already had a relationship with two of them for call centre services (T.COM for Loyalty Card, and Mailingcomp for 'Active & Independent')[14]. Two of the four were call centre specialists and the others IT companies. These companies were included at the request of BW Information Systems department. Responses to the tender documentation were scored against pre-determined criteria and the respondents invited to make presentations to the project team. Visits to each of the respondent's premises, and demonstrations of systems and references from other clients were all sought. The tender process took an elapsed time of approximately six weeks with a final short list of two companies. The capability, client base and systems capability of all the companies were quite diverse. Those rejected at the earlier stages demonstrated that they didn't understand 'mail order' processing, and they also fell down on customer service. In trying to leverage additional income from their call centre infrastructure at hugely inflated costs they confirmed their lack of understanding of price sensitivity in the mail order business. Lots of 'test scenarios' were undertaken, mainly due to the IS influence, meant that testing was literally *"treated as an exam"*, with us not telling partners what we expected to test, which didn't make for good partnership working. As one Business Analyst pointed out *"We are a big company and can be extremely 'crushing' in terms of confidence etc."*. So much so that some refused to tender because of the amount of customisation work involved.

14 Active & Independent is a mail order based catalogue for the elderly or infirm who require specialised equipment such a walking frames, wheel chairs, and specially adapted household appliances.

Mailsales were chosen because of their customer service credentials and active blue chip client base, coupled with an accommodating and 'chatty' customer friendly style. Maintaining high standards was central to the BeingWell philosophy and strategy, so much so that they insisted on having some involvement in the selection of staff, which has consequently led to unsuitable staff being removed from the MABD account. A key perceived reason for this call centre being 'outsourced' was the ability to handle a financial transaction during order taking, as they weren't being conducted in-house at that time.

Logistics (*'Yes' in-house versus 'no' in house*)

Despite Mailsales having additional floor space and therefore expansion capability a five-year lease was taken out on a new BeingWell warehouse at Acton Road in Birmingham. Two thousand lines, the majority from the main central warehouse, and Birmingham Common Stock Room, would be stored at Acton Road to satisfy MABD. During this project a major BeingWell warehouse was badly damaged by fire, which diverted much needed warehousing systems expertise from the project, and temporarily commandeered the Acton Road warehouse as an emergency facility, which had been intended for use by Mother & Baby Direct.

BW has a number of warehouses at its Head Office site, along with numerous locations around the city centre. Warehousing capability (operationally) was considered a core competence of a retailer, and BeingWell was no different in that respect, but the information systems were deemed not suitable. The corporate standard warehousing software package 'Austin'[15], which is heavily customised, was briefly considered but in reality would be a sledgehammer to crack a nut. A new system was required to support Acton Road. However, this perceived capability manifest itself in an over-engineered specification of requirements, which was profoundly influenced by how the existing warehouse processes operate. With 'perfection' the goal, throwing away what had been developed was a real risk.

Comparisons under uncertainty

In Table 4.4, the two short-listed decision schemes (labelled 'A' and 'C?') are compared against each other in terms of all five comparison areas listed earlier.

15 Austin: Warehouse automation computer software.

	A	C?	
Approach? IT? Call centre? Logistics?	Modular Bespoke Yes Yes	Modular Package Yes No	
Comparison Area:			**Comparative comment:**
Speed to market (Fast-Medium-Slow)	Slow	Medium	Likely to be more difficulties in combining the components in 'C' than in 'A'. However, 'C' might be quicker to market. High uncertainty.
VBM Case positive (High-Low)	Medium	Medium	Both very similar, however both are high in uncertainty.
Expansion potential (Yes-No)	Yes	Yes, Slightly Better	Difficult to assess however, external organisations might have greater capacity to grow than internal functions.
Brand protection (Good-Poor)	More Secure	Less Secure	Assumes better control if the majority of components are kept within the company.
Risk (High-Medium-Low)	High	High '+'	Both schemes have 'high' risk elements. On balance, more control with scheme 'A'.

Table 4.4: Comparison under uncertainty

This comparison table is a more complete comparison that takes into account all of the comparison measures (and not just a sub-set) which includes a more general mix of comparison types.

Step four: Choosing commitments for action through time

The final step in this process is the formation of proposed commitments to action through time. Table 4.5 is a cumulative list of uncertainty areas identified by the actors in this case and captured during the analysis, which have been categorised into one of the three UE, UV or UR uncertainty types, and an indicator to the salience of this uncertainty to the final decision. The most salient uncertainties identified by the actors were the ability to mix package and bespoke software (?PACKFIT), the time difference between deployment of those (i.e. bespoke and package) (?BESDEV), and the unknown levels of customer demand for the products via this channel to market (?SALESPROF).

UNCERTAINTY AREA	LABEL:	TYPE	SALIENCE:
? The doubtful ability to support a mixed range of in-house and/or external modules with packaged software.	?PACKFIT	UE	• •
From 'Speed to market' comparison: ?The ability to trade off quality in favour of speed.	?SPEEDQUAL	UV	•
From 'Expansion potential' comparison: ?Will expansion potential be truly favourable, and more practical with third parties.	?EXPANPOTL	UE	•
From 'Speed to market' comparison: ?The 'real' time differences between package adoption and bespoke development.	?BESDEV	UE	• •
? The likely levels of customer demand, average order size, and the impact of cannibalisation of sales.	?SALESPROF	UE	• •

Table 4.5: Comparing uncertainty areas

For example, at the point when the project team needed to request finances and secure Executive approval from the Investment Decision Committee there remained some key financial uncertainties. This was recorded in the *'Investment Decision meeting documentation'*.

7th July

Financial Review

Key uncertainties in the areas of customer demand, average order size, and the impact of cannibalisation of sales preclude the accurate forecasting of value creation. On current estimates and a 10.5% cost of capital, the project generates a 10 year NPV of £16.0m, a discounted payback after just three years yields a net annual cash flow benefit of c£5m from 00/01 onwards. Economic profit streams increase from £(1.4m) in 97/98 to +£3.7m in 00/01. Cannibalisation has been built up from Product Group level and averages 15%.

Source: 'Investment Decision meeting documentation'.

The use of an 'uncertainty graph' helps to put these uncertainties into perspective by grouping like types together and comparing their likely relevance to the final decision. Figure 4.7 shows the uncertainty graph for the Mail Order case and the concentration of uncertainties of the UE type. This diagram would help in determining which uncertainties will be most influential on the final outcome and which can be deferred for the moment. None of the uncertainties have been classified 'high' in salience, and are therefore unlikely to be too inhibiting.

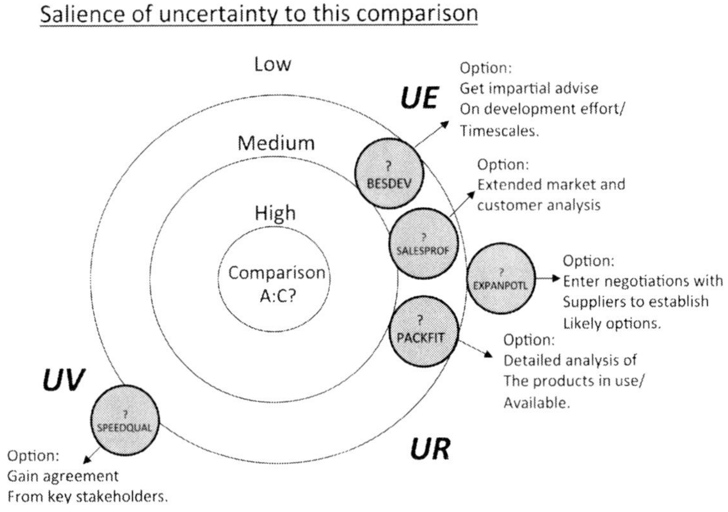

Figure 4.7: Uncertainty graph – Salience of uncertainty to this comparison

Commitment package

A decision has to be made as to how much exploration should take place and what decisions can be made immediately. By choosing a call centre partner in reality the choice of call centre software had also been made. Similarly, choosing to de-couple the fulfilment activities from the ordering activities by operating the warehousing in-house forced yet another technology choice. Therefore, the selection criteria for the systems to support the call centre become principally:

(i) The ability to integrate with the warehouse system,
(ii) The ability to calculate and print Loyalty Card vouchers[16], and
(iii) Stock replenishment (Mailsales have a 'virtual' stock).

Figure 4.8 below relates the actions to the timing of the decisions in this case.

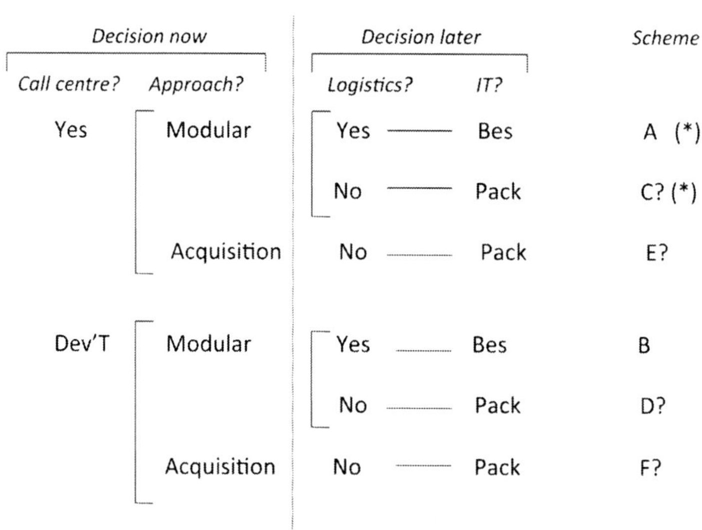

Figure 4.8: A comparison of the feasible action schemes

Strategic Choice Approach uses the concept of the 'commitment package' as the method for determining the choice between those actions that have to be taken immediately, those actions that require further exploration to reduce the salience of areas of uncertainty, and finally the other arrange-

16 When it is not possible to add Loyalty Card points to the customer's card directly, vouchers are sent to customers that can either be added to the card during a transaction in a store or redeemed against the next purchase.

ments that need to be made to enable actions to be deferred. Table 4.6 sets out the commitment package framework for this case and is a summary of the commitments and actual decisions taken in this case now, and those that were deferred to later.

	DECISIONS NOW		**FUTURE DECISION**	
	Actions	Explorations	Deferred Choices	Contingency Planning
Approach:	Withdraw from negotiations with possible acquisition companies.			.
Call centre:	Engage in a contract with Mail-sales.	Prepare the internal call-centre for the increased capacity		Limit contractual arrangements to increase flexibility
		Continue to evaluate the in-house offering versus third party suppliers		Use a third party to regulate the flow of usage as sales rise etc.
IT:	Investigate bespoke software development versus package software	Examine maintenance and systems changes as they attract a premium thus increasing the operations costs.	Choose between IT types	Choice of logistics might have IT implications. Consider them as early as possible

Table 4.6: Commitment package framework – Mail Order

Having taken into account the decisions, options, and incompatibilities that emerged in this case, the actual decision scheme chosen by BW (i.e. a '*modular*' approach, '*bespoke*' systems, '*no*' to utilising the existing in-house call centre, and a *'yes'* to using in-house logistics), did not emerge as one of the feasible decision schemes.

4.4 The alignment of the actors in the network (Alignment logic)

Introduction

The third approach uses techniques from Actor Network Theory to understand the alignment of the actors to the proposed approaches. The 'process inscription/specialisation framework' is used to analyse two critical dimensions that capture the characteristics of work business processes, and the components that make up those processes, these are: *the degree of specialisation, and the degree of inscription.* The two dimensions can be plotted on a graph, and Figure 4.9 below shows the output for the Mail Order case.

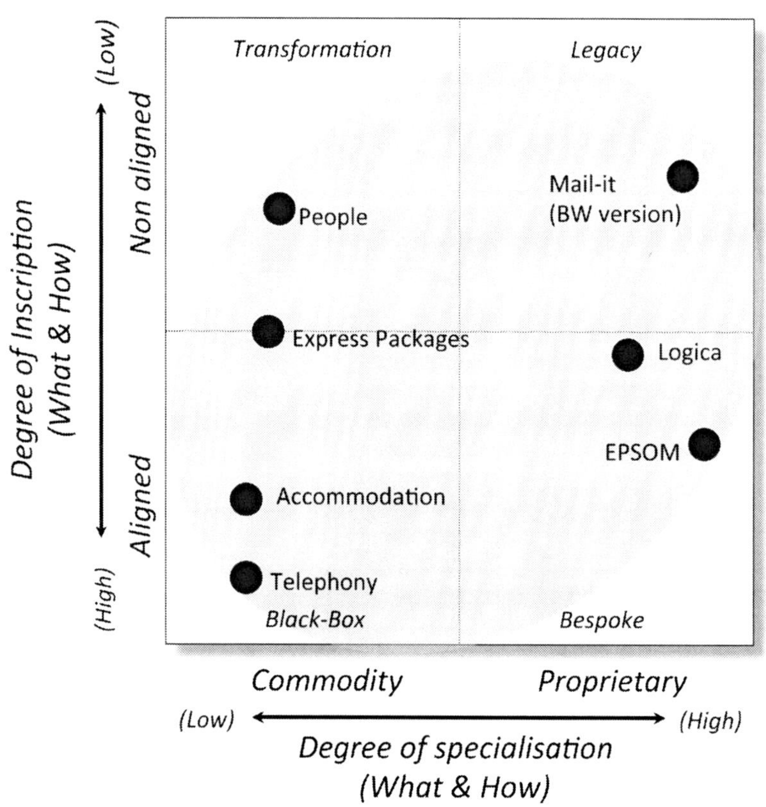

Figure 4.9: Mail Order process inscription/specialisation framework

The spread of results around the framework demonstrates that there is little consensus about the alignment of the interest of the actors in the network, or of the composition of the process components. The Mail Order case represents a dysfunctional process.

People – call centre agents

The non-alignment of 'people' reflects the broad spread of opinion and lack of agreement of the actors involved as to whether the skills required by the call centre agents are 'specialist' because of the nature of a sales environment, or that they are a 'commodity' and could easily be satisfied by appropriate training and development.

Express Packages

The services of a courier 'Express Packages' were used to fulfil the orders placed upon MABD. Although the courier business is relatively self-contained and was comparatively easy to incorporate in the overall process, its position on the border of 'black-box' and 'transformation' reflects the influence it can exert on the way the final process is operated, i.e. Express Packages will have their own operating requirements, constraints, achievements and business objectives they will try to inscribe into this process.

Telephony & accommodation

Once again both 'telephony' and 'accommodation' occupy the black-box space, which reflects the 'commodity' nature of these components, and that the actors consistently see them as commodities in relation to this process.

Mail-it, Logica, and EPSOM - Information Technology

The prime call centre software used in this case (Mail-it), has been so heavily tailored to BeingWell requirements that it is no longer possible to upgrade to later versions of the software. The interests of the actors, which are numerous includes the vendors (Johnsons), the agents (Mailsales) and the customer (BeingWell), and are quite different with regard to this software which means that decision-making is difficult, system enhancements problematic, and change control almost non-existent. The remaining two software components (Logica and EPSOM) are both wholly owned bespoke products either developed in-house by BeingWell own staff, or by a third party to BeingWell own specification and are now both supported in-house, so while proprietary they do reflect the requirements of the process and are therefore aligned.

4.5 A longitudinal view: Mother & Baby Direct - Mail Order

Introduction

From its launch the Mother and Baby Direct team went on to produce a further five catalogues, the last being produced over two years later, which was stretched out to the end of the year in the run up to the Christmas trading period. Despite being well received by its customers, (they were offered extended inventory that you couldn't get in a BeingWell store, Loyalty Card points, deliveries to their home and price matching) the business was continually under review as it enjoyed below average margins on many of the lines, loss leaders on high volume lines such as nappies, and the cost of acquiring customers (marketing and mailing lists) remained expensive.

Developing the call centre process (MODULAR) (BESPOKE) (NO) (YES)

The general (MODULAR) approach towards this mail order venture can be characterised by the phrase *"this is just another way to sell products"*. This attitude prevailed, even down to the way catalogues were produced, and a lack of appreciation of the interconnectedness of the components of the process. Despite the proliferation of consultants engaged in projects within the company at that time, BeingWell kept to a minimum the external assistance on this project as they weren't prepared to pay for mail order consultants to understand the business of selling products. This led to poor decisions surrounding issues with Trading Standards e.g. that catalogue prices for items could differ from those sold in BeingWell stores (they subsequently convinced Trading Standards that this is not an issue), and the volatility of lines could be different (and changed frequently) during the six-month cycle of a catalogue. BeingWell is also a prestige brand and most suppliers are extremely keen to include BeingWell on their lists of clients, which can lead to suppliers over promising and under delivering, as was the case with Mailsales on this occasion.

The decision not to utilise the in-house call centre (NO), was justified by Mother & Baby Direct customers. Regular positive feedback confirmed that they were happy with the outsourced call centre. Service levels agreements were in operation for answering calls whereby 80% of calls should be answered within 15 seconds, with no more than 3% of calls lost (i.e. hanging-up before being answered). However, it required rigorous governance to ensure the operators had comprehensive product knowledge, and that the service was provided in keeping with the BeingWell ethos. A member of staff from the local Exeter BeingWell store was permanently located within Mailsales to be the *"eyes and ears on the ground"*. Helen Fudge (Call Centre Project Manager) commented:

> *"One thing we have absolutely learned about outsourcing a call centre is, if money is an object, and service is an object, then you need so much more control than you would probably need if you are just doing a short-term campaign".*

There was a need to closely manage the third-party call centre. A tariff had been agreed for each of the services provided such as receiving an 'inbound' call; making an 'outbound' call; handling correspondence or fax transmissions; BW is charged accordingly. There were examples where this has been abused with additional outbound calls being engineered in situations when ad-hoc enquiries were made of the warehouse (outbound call), and then a return call to the customer (a further outbound call). Correspondence could also be generated requiring additional handling thus incurring additional charges. In this way the placing of a single order might have generated a number of additional chargeable activities, which is clearly beneficial to Mailsales, but not to BW.

Meanwhile, Mailsales had been acquired by Seville Call Management (Europe), who had subsequently been acquired by Logic-Systems, a privately held company, majority owned by Opel Corporation of Vancouver, Canada. Although some of the original Mailsales management team were still involved with the company, the initial move to Seville was threatening the relationship, and increased charges for the dedicated team that operated the MABD account were being actively pursued. However, this was short lived and the new management team from Logic-Systems brought a completely fresh approach to the way of doing business that was in the end to prove beneficial to both parties.

Mailsales used the 'Mail-it' system, which was extensively modified to accommodate the requirements of MABD (BESPOKE). Such was the scale of the changes demanded by BeingWell that it has become impossible to migrate to the later fully supported versions of the Mail-it system, which in itself became a limiting factor.

Internal organisation changes within the Marketing function saw the Mother & Baby Direct team move from being a stand-alone function within the Healthcare Business Unit to join forces with the Customer Development team. Meanwhile an e-commerce module was being developed for the BeingWell.co.uk website once again in time to capitalise on the Christmas trade. The website offered 1500 lines yet without the significant production costs of a catalogue, but having the flexibility to quickly make changes as the market demanded. Mother & Baby Direct was kept 'ticking-over' due to the latent demand while building 'www.BeingWell.co.uk'. The warehouse at Acton Road (YES), and Call Centre (Mailsales) previously used by Mother & Baby Direct were still needed to fulfil orders for the Internet operation. Orders via 'www.BeingWell.co.uk' were emailed to Mailsales who took the payment using the 'Mail-it' system, processed it via typing-in the order rather than receiving it as a telephone input, then sent the output to the warehouse for processing in much the same way as before. MABD officially closed for business twenty-eight months after it started trading.

> 4 July
>
> **BEINGWELL MOTHER AND BABY DIRECT CATALOGUE CLOSES**
>
> The BeingWell Mother & Baby Direct Catalogue is closing on 31st August. The service has closed as we can no longer deliver the level of service required through the catalogue and see the internet as the best route to develop the BeingWell Direct services.
>
> The BeingWell Direct service will continue through the online shop at www.BeingWell.co.uk where additional health and beauty products may also be bought. Further announcements regarding the development of the BeingWell Internet site will follow shortly.
>
> BeingWell Internet Ventures

The core BeingWell dedicated team was reduced in numbers towards the end. They had come to consider themselves as employees of BeingWell, staff discounts being the only BeingWell employment perk they didn't receive. The team liked dealing with BeingWell customers as they generally received less abuse and foul language from their customers than they did from other accounts. As call numbers reduced, the general customer service calls were redirected to the Customer Service call centre in head office, and any product related calls (then numbering only two or three per week) were directed to product managers.

The emergence of new e-commerce channels

The last quarter of the same year saw the announcement of the BeingWell.com initiative with Thames Media, and the focus of any new activity moved away from the BeingWell.co.uk site to the BeingWell.com site. The following announcement was released on 12th October:

> 12 October 2000
>
> **BEINGWELL AND THAMES MEDIA TO LAUNCH HEALTH AND BEAUTY INTERNET BROADBAND BUSINESS**
>
> The BeingWell Company PLC ("BeingWell") and Thames Media ("Thames Media") today announce the formation of a new, independent Internet and broadband company designed to be Britain's leading e-business for health, beauty and well-being.
>
> Health and beauty are two of the world's largest growth markets. In the UK alone, and excluding the National Health Service, sales of health and beauty products and services amount to £11 billion a year.
>
> The new company will combine the complementary strengths of BeingWell and Thames Media to provide an exceptional range of health and beauty products and services, together with information and advice from leading experts. It will also provide an interactive forum for individuals to exchange personal experience and consult the experts online and on air by phone.
>
> By creating the new media leader in consumer health and beauty in the UK, with 10,000 products available from day one, the company intends to become the natural platform for all those with an interest in well-being, including professional associations, government bodies, commercial organisations and interest groups.
>
> 2000 The BeingWell Company PLC. All rights reserved.

The combined TV and website had approximately 10,000 lines and was designed to be easy for customers to understand and operate, although it was still recognised that customers like to be able to contact you directly. By this time Seville had been taken over by Logic-Systems, who successfully built on the existing partnership with BeingWell to offer a totally new service from a call centre newly established in Dublin, Ireland. Working in conjunction with several partners (Manhattan Associates for the warehousing and logistics, SAP for systems, Logic-Systems for call centre and email), BeingWell.com was launched in March 2001. An overriding objective was to keep the new infrastructure as 'vanilla' as possible. As Jonathan Cave the Managing Director, BeingWell Internet Ventures said:

> *"If we have to change a little bit to accommodate some quirks of SAP then question whether that is easier, or is it spending £200,000 to develop, configure or modify a system that then means we have to spend half as much again every time we have another patch or another upgrade that gets offered to us almost for free, but we end up paying hundreds of thousands of pounds to configure it because of the mess we have made of standard systems".*

4.6 Summary

This is the third case and describes the approach taken by the Mother & Baby Direct team to establish a call centre process for mail order. This was an important first step for BeingWell as it planned to enter the 'alternative shopping' arena both to gain understanding of the customers requirements, and to provide a response to the competitive threat from other 'direct' mother and baby catalogues. As described in the earlier chapters the techniques of SCA, Activity Records, and the Inscription/Specialisation framework were used to understand the process, decision, and alignment logics in this case.

The preferred choice that emerged from the project team was to adopt the MODULAR – BESPOKE – NO - YES approach, which didn't feature as a feasible decision scheme when retrospectively applying the SCA technique. The post hoc analysis conducted here identified decision scheme 'A' (MODULAR – BESPOKE – YES – YES), as that which most closely fit the requirements as expressed by the actors in the network, which utilised the in-house call centre alongside the predominantly other 'in-house' components. The significant difference between the two is the decision to outsource the call centre, which appears to disregard the closely coupled nature of the components in this process. This close coupling is in complete contrast to the loosely coupled nature of the components observed in the Loyalty Card case in the previous chapter. This is reflected in the increase in the number of option bars and subsequent increase in sensitivity of each decision on every other decision. The preferred choice appears dysfunctional which is supported by the lack of alignment of the actors involved. For example, the lack of agreement that 'specialist' skills are required, and the numerous interests that exist in the provision of software.

The next section explores the final case study that examines the call centre process as required by BeingWell Health & Travel Insurance Services.

CHAPTER FIVE
Case Study Four - Health & Travel Insurance Services

5.1. Introduction

BeingWell Insurance Services (BWIS) provides a range of health and travel insurance products to customers of BeingWell including: Dental, Family Health, Accident, and Accident Insurance especially for children. Travel products include: Gap year, Annual, Single Trip, and Winter Travel packages. Products are available through BeingWell high street stores, where upon completion of an application form instant cover is arranged upon paying the premium, (unique for this type of service), or by telephone through a call centre, or alternatively by post. All the products are underwritten by Majestic Insurance Group (MIG). BWIS was launched in April 1998 and is a wholly owned subsidiary of The BeingWell Company PLC.

The call centre supporting the BeingWell Travel Cover products is operated by Majestic Insurance Group (MIG) at their 'Corporate Partnership Division' in Cardiff, from where they also operate similar schemes for companies such as Sainsburys, Lloyds and HSBC Bank. The call centre also receives some calls direct from BW store staff that require assistance with product knowledge and product queries as they serve customers in store.

After only 24 months in operation it has achieved market leadership in the direct travel market, with over 400,000 policies sold to three quarters of a million customers, with an income in excess of £15 million. The key objectives and general principles of the venture are shown below:

> 12th November.
>
> **Objectives of the venture[17]:**
>
> To jointly contribute skills and assets for mutual (win-win) gain.
>
> To ensure that both parties reach their acceptable minimum profit levels and then distribute additional profits on an agreed basis.
>
> To review profit shares on a periodic basis (every three years) but to strive for cost and profit transparency at all times.
>
> Source: BW/MIG partnership statement of principles.

17 Source: BW/MIG partnership statement of principles.

6th November.

Travel insurance general principles[18]:

Cover will at all times be geared to provide the policyholder with genuine and beneficial cover, which at no time will contain so much small print to make a claim impossible.

To provide benefits that encompass the needs of the traveller in difficulty abroad, not as a vehicle purely by which financial recompense is received in the UK.

To give security and peace of mind of the BeingWell name and brand in a practical and meaningful way.

Source: BeingWell Travel working document.

The approach taken to this case study

The approach taken was the same as that described in the previous case. Three sections now follow which in turn examine: (i) the detail of the process under review, (ii) the approach to decision-making, (iii) and the alignment of the actors in the network. Interviews were conducted with BWIS Operations Managers Greg Eisenhauer and Chris Cockayne, and BWIS Managing Director – Robert Hickin, as well as other project team members. Unrestricted access was granted to project archives such as partnership agreements, business results, and claims history, as well as other related material and documentation.

5.2 The Insurance Service process in focus (Process logic)

Introduction

This first section examines the work business process under review and, using the 'Activity Record' technique, presents the five prime activities and tasks that make up the process, namely: (i) Receive the 'inbound' calls, (ii) Identify the customer & information, (iii) Take the order, (iv) Initiate other processes, and (v) Close the call. It is not the intention to include all the processes that go to make up the complete end-to-end Insurance business. The call centre process starts with an inbound call from a customer, and ends with a finished policy including all the associated components (additional

18 Source: BeingWell Travel working document.

questionnaires, travel documents) completed for despatch. Figure 5.1 shows an Activity Record of the call centre process as utilised for Health & Travel cover.

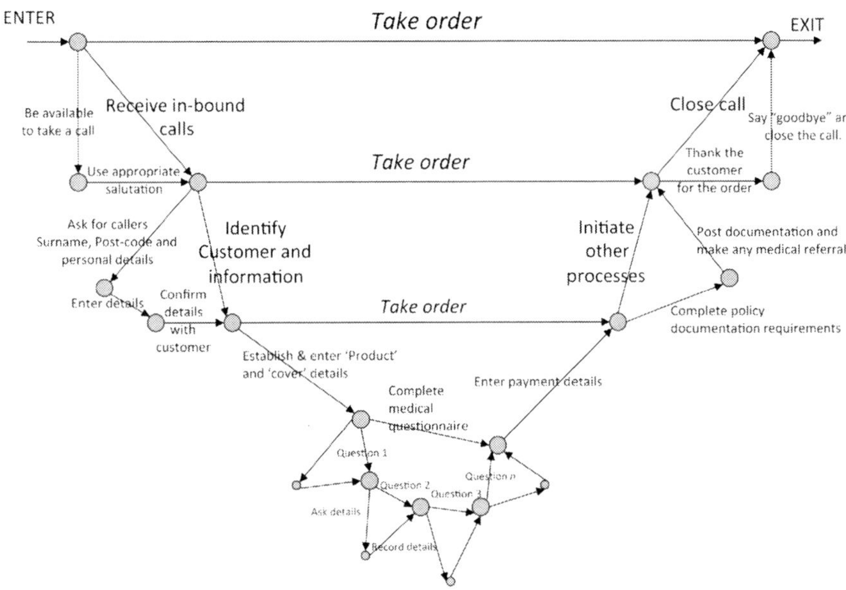

Figure 5.1: An Activity Record of the Insurance process

Each of the activities is described in full as follows:

Activity One: Receive 'inbound' calls

A workforce of approximately twenty-five, which are dedicated to the BeingWell account, work in three shifts to cover the 8 am to 8 pm operation five days a week, with an 8 am to 6 pm operation on Saturdays. The centre is not operated on Sundays. Staff are dedicated to BeingWell Health and Travel Cover but can, and do on occasions, provide overflow back up for the other clients serviced from the centre.

Grouped into three teams, each team works a rotation of the three shift patterns: 8 am to 4 pm, 9 am to 5 pm, and midday to 8 pm. Each shift has a break for lunch of one hour, and in addition a mid-morning and mid-afternoon break of ten minutes per occasion. Each team member has a regular workstation in the call centre which they are encouraged to personalise (family photographs as screensavers etc.), and each shift are seated together in teams which ensures that they are with their shift colleagues rather than being dispersed around the room. With a predominantly young workforce (the majority being under twenty-five years old), the atmosphere is lively and energetic; the room is decked with national flags from around the world to signify the link with 'travel', and the constant background 'noise' generated by the telephone conversations in progress at any time adds to the lively atmosphere.

Activity Two: Identify customer and information

The Agents use a system called 'NEWTON', which is an Image and workflow system developed in-house by MIG to service their Home Insurance business. This has subsequently been heavily modified and redeveloped to support the BeingWell Travel products. Upon answering a call the Agent enters the customers surname and postcode, which then takes the agent into the first of a series of logically related screens to enter the customers personal details. Unless a customer has previously purchased insurance products from BWIS before, the customer will be 'unknown' to the call centre. However the information is retained for subsequent problem resolution and future orders.

Activity Three: Take order

The subsequent screens are: 'product and cover' details, 'medical questionnaire', and finally 'payment details'. The Agents enter the details on the screen by asking the customers a series of questions. The style isn't too prescriptive and although not totally flexible the system will allow the agent to skip to a relevant question should the customer offer that information out of the preferred sequence. The medical questions are the only 'scripted' questions the agents follow. The system is quite basic and doesn't extend to on-line help or features to handle frequently asked questions, and Agents rely upon paper 'crib sheets' and the ability to ask for advice from a nearby colleague. The open plan environment facilitates such an interaction.

Activity four: Initiate other processes

Where more detailed medical information is required, referral to the medical team relies on the completion of the customer and product details form, which is passed to the referral team, all this while the customer is waiting 'on-hold'. Upon completing the call the data is passed via the mainframe systems to Birkenhead where policy documentation is printed and posted directly to the customer.

Activity five: Close the call

On conclusion of the telephone call the Agent will thank the customer for the order and close the call. The associated documentation (Policy and cover papers) are produced automatically and dispatched to the customer. The process ends.

5.3 The approach taken to the business problem (Decision logic)

Introduction

This second section provides a detailed account of how the Insurance process was organised and managed from the original concept through to implementation and beyond. The approach is documented following the steps involved in the Strategic Choice Approach technique (SCA), and has therefore been split into the four logical sections used by SCA of shaping, designing, comparing, and finally choosing.

Step one: Shaping of problems

This first step examines the judgements about possible connections between one field of choice and another. The Decision Graph, as shown in Figure 5.2 depicts those decisions seen by the actors in this case to be key to the outcome of the project. The decisions shown within the boundary of the problem focus are given prominence over those outside the boundary, however it is realised that all the decisions shown are closely related. Clearly, in this case the initial decision to determine the overall approach was urgently required, as it would influence many of the associated decisions.

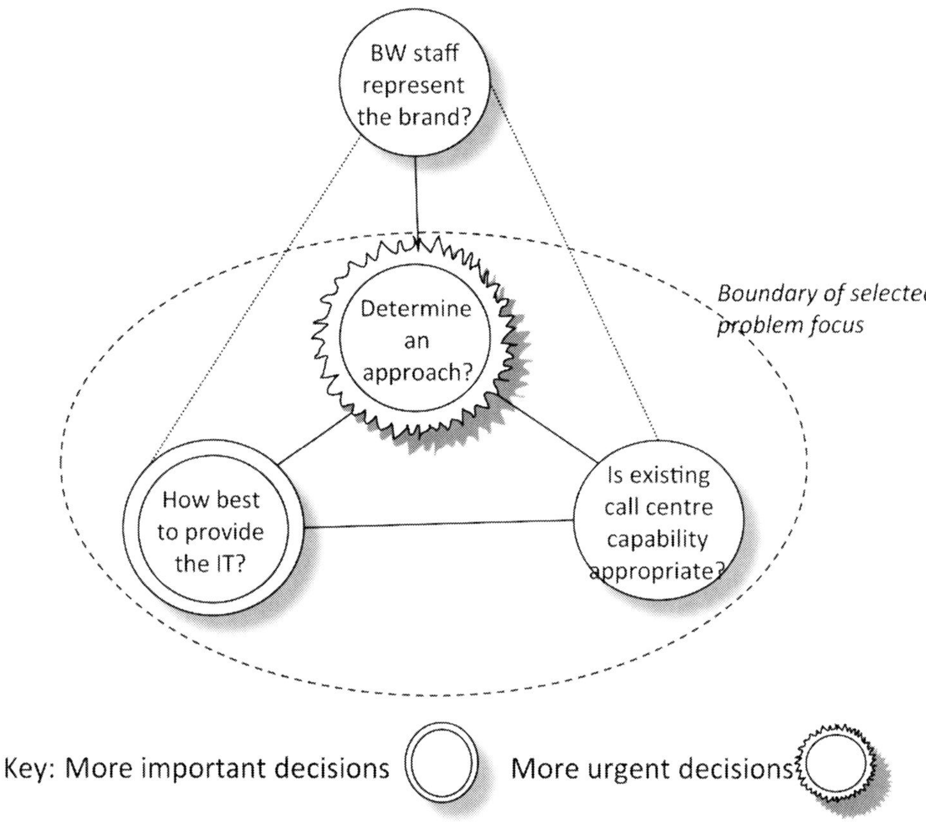

Figure 5.2: A decision graph of the key case decisions

The three key decisions within the boundary of the problem focus are: (i) Determine an approach?, (ii) How best to provide the IT?, and (iii) Is the existing call centre capability appropriate? To take each decision in order:

Determine an approach?

Two quite different approaches were considered to this problem, these were:

1 To conduct the administration of the schemes in-house, or
2 To engage a partner to administer the schemes.

Whichever approach is adopted it was clear that it must abide by the BW service philosophy, as this is central to the proposition and is documented within the 'Service Level Agreement' (SLA)[19], as follows:

Service Level Agreement

"This agreement is subject to the underlying principle that in its administration of this business MIG will reflect BWIS customer service culture and values in respect of: quality of communications both written and verbal; quality and speed of response; complaint handling and escalation, and recruitment and training of staff. Irrespective of the MIG location where administration is carried out, MIG staff will reflect BWIS culture and values as though BWIS themselves employed them.
In determining the levels and standards of service emphasis is being placed on qualitative delivery and measurement. The greatest focus is placed on the perceived value and feelings of BWIS customers in all of their contact and dealings with MIG".

Source: BWIS/MIG Service Level Agreement.

A pragmatic decision had already been taken not to initially 'de-couple' the call centre activity with that of the processing activity, which was a direct trade-off between the 'speed to market' and choice of operation. The city analysts had branded BeingWell as *"unfashionable"*, *"predictable"*, and *"lacking in pace"* when bringing new products and services to market when compared with the grocers. As one team member commented:

"At that time there was much criticism of BeingWell and its apparent lack of ability to bring new products and services to market quickly. Our preferred approach is to be 'retail engineers' and analyse everything precisely, rather than to act quickly and decisively".

Table 5.1 is an extract from an internal annual results presentation that compares the new products and services introduced by other well-known high street retailers over the preceding five years, and those introduced by BeingWell. Clearly BeingWell are not as pro-active as their competitors.

19 Source: BWIS/MIG Service Level Agreement

MARKS & SPENCER	TESCO	Sainsbury's	BEINGWELL
Financial Services	Petrol	Wine on the internet	Low calorie lunchtime sandwich range
Home Furnishings	Pharmacy	Loyalty Card	
Gift Services	Banking	Banking	
	Photo	0-5 Club	
	Dry Cleaning	Home shopping	
	Gift Services		
	Home Shopping		
	Travel Insurance		

Table 5.1: A comparison of new products and services introduced by well-known UK high street retailers over the preceding five years. Source: The BeingWell Company Internal Annual Results.

How best to provide the IT?

The complete end-to-end process requires a number of systems changes and enhancements be made to existing systems. For example, that the in-\store EPoS system can record the insurance product sale with an appropriate transaction type that will be recognised by the associated finance systems (sales ledgers) for subsequent reconciliation, or the allocation of Loyalty Card loyalty scheme points, including any points awarded as an incentive to purchase. Policy proposal information will need to be captured at a store and transmitted for processing, and the telesales process will need to capture additional information such as the customers Loyalty Card number (7 digits), the staff discount number (17 digits), and any mailing preferences the customer has registered so that either the partner or BeingWell don't send unsolicited mailings to customers. Therefore, this was largely a choice between developing and/or enhancing bespoke applications, or utilising existing packed software products.

Is existing call centre capability appropriate?

The two previous projects to utilise a call centre in their process (Loyalty Card and Mother & Baby at Home) had both chosen third party organisations to operate the call centre. Only the BeingWell Customer Service project had decided to set-up an in-house operation. A Telecommunications Business Analyst said of the telephony requirements for Health and Travel Insurance project:

> *"The requirements from a telephony point of view are very standard. We have the technical and telephony capacity in-house to satisfy 'all' of the outsourced call centres. There is no capital investment exposure and telephony is now cheaper in-house due to economies of scale".*

At this point it was too early to know from the other cases which of the options chosen would be the most appropriate for this case. Therefore, the choices considered relevant by the actors involved in the case were: (i) utilise the existing internal call centre (i.e. Customer Service), (ii) outsource the call centre activity to the insurance partner, or (iii) set-up a new internal call centre.

Only one key decision lay outside the boundary of the problem focus as follows:

BeingWell staff represents the brand?

BeingWell recognises the difference in brand values, as perceived by the customer, between traditional Financial Services organisations and is own 'trusted' brand image, of which it is extremely protective. As the BWIS Operations Director put it: *"We think we are the only ones capable of representing the brand properly"* For this reason all BeingWell sales staff undergo *'Selling the BeingWell experience'* training which provides background to the BeingWell Company, its ideology, and 'what BeingWell expects' in customer service. The aforementioned training is supplemented with sales techniques and telephone skills training which are provided by external organisations. Brand protection is important to BeingWell: *"We like the ability to control the interface with the customer".*

Step two: Designing the possible courses of action

This second step focuses on designing possible courses of action, and Table 5.2 summarises the key decisions to be taken along with their possible outcomes under consideration. A key feature of the decision making process is the interconnectedness of the decisions and the subsequent consequences of those decisions, and that the likely outcome will rely on a compromise between possible options. SCA utilises the Analysis of Interconnected Decision Areas approach (AIDA) to help in understanding the relatedness of these decisions and is useful here to understand how and what decisions have been made.

DECISION AREA	OPTIONS	OPTION LABEL
Determine an operating approach?	- In-house administration - Partner to administer the scheme	- In-house - Partner
How best to provide the Information Technology?	- Predominantly Bespoke - Predominantly Package	- Besp - Pack
Is existing call centre capability appropriate?v	- Utilise existing internal call centre - Outsource to the insurance partner - Set-up new internal call centre	- Existing - Partner - New

Table 5.2: Options within the boundary of the decision area

Figure 5.3 shows the results from comparisons of options from each decision area, with the options from every other decision area. This pairing ensures that incomparable or doubtful combinations are highlighted and potentially excluded from future analysis.

The Option Graph in Figure 5.4 diagrammatically represents the outcome from AIDA. Obviously, with fewer decision areas the potential for feasible combinations is also reduced. However, it can be seen that despite the possibility of up to twelve decision schemes, this was reduced to only five compatible decision schemes, and generated three option bars and three doubtful combinations (but some of these could be reversed with further work or analysis). Figure 5.5 demonstrates how by choosing 'partner' as the preferred operating approach it immediately creates difficulties (option bars) if using package software (as the partner is likely to use their own tailored products), and it would be unlikely to decouple the insurance

IT?	APPROACH? In-house	APPROACH? Partner
Besp	•	•
Pack	X	X

IT?	CALL CENTRE? Existing	CALL CENTRE? Partner	CALL CENTRE? New
Besp	•	•	•
Pack	•	?	•

Call centre?	APPROACH? In-house	APPROACH? Partner
Existing	•	?
Partner	?	•
New	•	X

• = Compatible combination
X = Incompatible combination
? = Doubtful compatibility

Figure 5.3: Analysis of interconnected decision areas (AIDA)

administration undertaken by the partner and the administrative elements of the call centre, hence reducing the likelihood of the 'new' internal call centre option.

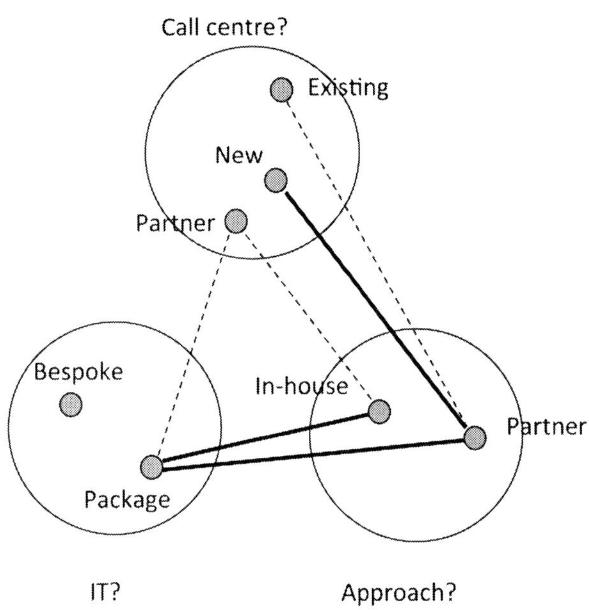

Figure 5.4: Option Graph – Insurance Services

Having determined which options are compatible it is then possible to establish which combination of those options can be realistically crafted into a feasible decision scheme. A feasible decision scheme is one where it doesn't violate any of the incompatibilities established during earlier analysis, but their inclusion in the final solution is still not automatic. Using a diagram similar to a decision tree it is possible to map the possible decision schemes so that they can be logically assessed for future consideration. Figure 5.5 shows that when the compatible options are re-presented to determine what feasible decision schemes are possible only five decision schemes emerge from the analysis, two of those having doubtful compatibilities that would need to be resolved in order to establish if they are truly feasible.

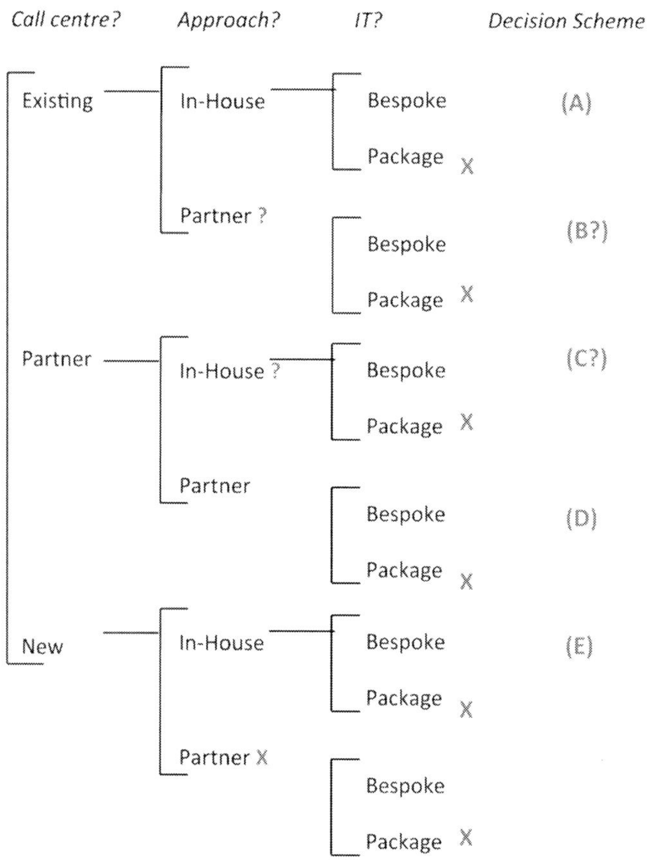

Figure 5.5: Feasible decision schemes for the Insurance Services case

Step three: Comparing the possible courses of action

Having determined a list of feasible decision schemes the next step is to compare each of the schemes in light of what their consequences might be. Table 5.3 lists those comparison areas that emerged to be of importance to the actors in this case, and a comparative measure has been assigned to each comparison type.

COMPARISON AREA:	COMPARATIVE MEASURE:
Speed to market: Seen as an important response to competition, and a positive impact with City analysts.	Fast ↔ Medium ↔ Slow
The ability to reflect BW brand values and service: With one of the most trusted brands on the high street BeingWell are extremely cautious about damaging the brand.	Good ↔ Average ↔ Poor
Compliance with FSA and ABI regulations: These are mandatory requirements and non-negotiable.	Yes ↔ No
Flexibility to undertake all of the administrative operations if desired: Any partner would have to demonstrate flexibility to allow BeingWell to undertake any or all of the administrative, underwriting or risk carrying activities within an agreed timetable and subject to legal and regulatory constraints.	Easy ↔ Difficult ↔ Unlikely

Table 5.3: List of comparison areas

A working shortlist can be developed from the feasible decision schemes identified earlier, and compared against those considered to be the top three comparison areas in this case, namely: *'speed to market'*, *'the ability to reflect BW brand values and service'*, and *'flexibility to undertake all of the administrative operations if desired'*. Figure 5.6 shows the working shortlist along with the assessment of how each comparison area compared with the desired minimum ratings of at least 'medium' for 'speed to market', at least 'average for 'brand values', and must not be 'unlikely' for 'flexibility'.

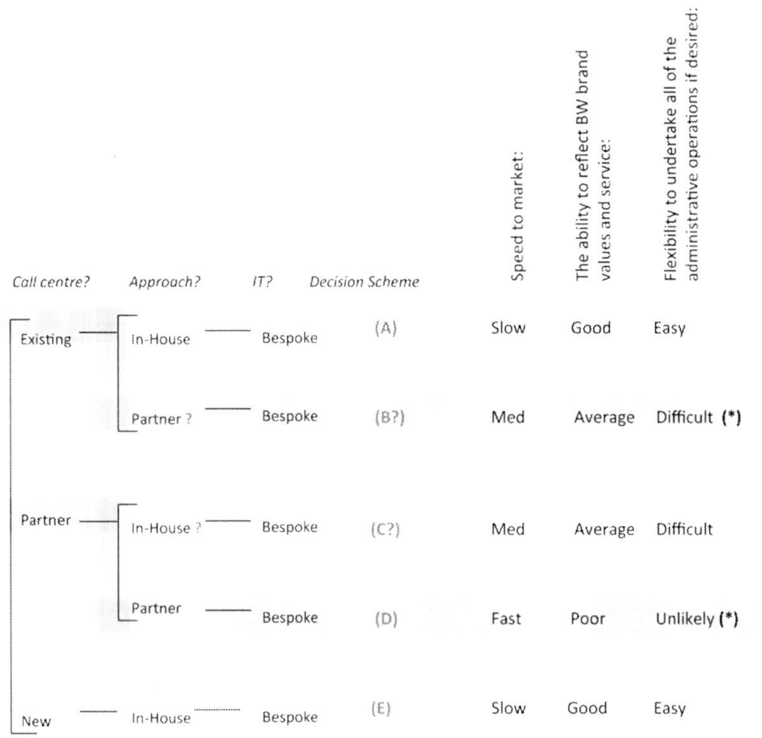

Working shortlist: Schemes B?, D

Formed by: Speed to market: At least 'medium'
Brand values: At least 'average'
Flexibility: Must not be 'unlikely'

Figure 5.6: Forming a working shortlist

The outcome of the comparison ratings alone suggests that decision schemes 'B?' and 'C?' should form the working shortlist, as these two feasible decision schemes were the only ones that met at least the minimum requirements for all the comparison measures. However, both these schemes had doubtful compatibility (signified by the question mark), and neither of these schemes had been chosen by BW. The actual scheme chosen and later implemented by BW was scheme 'D', despite the 'poor' rating of its ability to reflect brand values largely due to relying so heavily on partners, and its 'unlikely' rating for flexibility to undertake the administration, largely due to its dependence on third parties. It was actually chosen for its speed to market. For the purpose of further comparison and analysis, decision scheme 'C?' was substituted for decision scheme 'D' to provide working comparisons that are more aligned to the actual case. The comparisons of each of the three key decision areas (Call Centre, Approach, and IT) and the choices to be made are as follows:

Call centre (*Existing versus partner versus new*)

The most likely partner was based in the Cardiff area, which is home to many blue-chip call centre operations, 'BT' and 'Orange' to name just two. Consequently there is a large pool of mobile and flexible workers, mostly seeking temporary work in the area, which might well have had relevant experience with other companies. Unlike some of the other call centres operated by MIG this one does not require agents with foreign language skills as most of the callers are English speaking, however previous sales experience and, obviously, a good telephone manner is essential. For this reason interviews for vacant positions are often conducted by telephone. Although Agents develop an understanding of the medical conditions of customers they are not expected to make any judgements on this. A medical referral team would be available to take calls where additional medical knowledge is required to have a conversation with the caller. Such a team would comprise experienced Agents and medically trained staff such as nurses.

The decisions not to initially de-couple the call centre and the processing activity, largely favours using a partner to handle both activities. However, it is perfectly possible to administer them separately, and any partnership agreement would need to reflect this.

Approach (*In-house versus partner*)

BW wanted to retain the right to undertake all the administration should it so desire and therefore any partnership agreement had to reflect this. Compliance to the relevant FSA (Financial Services Act) codes of practice, and regulatory authorities such as ABI (Association of British Insurers), are satisfied by MIG, as the provider of the financial services, with BWIS acting as agents only in this relationship. BeingWell Insurance Services products are VAT exempt, therefore to avoid any unnecessary tax complications BWIS would have to be located in a separate office building and not in the new Head Office complex. An extract of the key relevant elements of a partnership statement of principles is shown below:

Extract of the key elements of: Partnership statement of principles

MIG has agreed to assist BW set up a 'virtual' or 'real' insurance company and for BW to take (on an agreed basis) a shareholding in that insurer up to 100%.

MIG will provide BW with maximum flexibility in its aspiration to undertake any or all of the administrative, underwriting or risk carrying activities within an agreed timetable and subject to legal and regulatory constraints.

MIG will administer the business at an agreed cost.

Source: 'Partnership statement of principles'.

There was a pressure to do the right thing, versus the increasing pressure from the Chief Executive to just 'do it quickly'. The BWIS Operation Manager said:

> *"The desire for speed of launch precluded a trial, which might have given us an earlier indication of the size of the business, and provided some evidence and improved confidence".*

IT (*bespoke versus package*)

The sale of Health & Travel Insurance through a high street pharmacy chain is not that common; expecting to purchase an 'off-the-shelf' software package to handle this was unrealistic. Many of the routines and procedures would need to be closely integrated with existing systems (payment at tills in stores), so interfaces with existing legacy systems was an important consideration. All five of the feasible decision schemes rely on utilising 'predominantly bespoke' IT in their solution. Typically any partner would already be using a tailored application (often bespoke) to administer similar business.

Comparisons under uncertainty

In Table 5.4 two of the five short-listed schemes (labelled B? and D) are compared with each other in terms of all four of the comparison areas listed earlier.

B?		D	
Existing Partner Bespoke	Call centre? Approach? IT?		Partner Partner Bespoke

Comparison Area:		**Comparative comment:**	
Speed to market: (Fast ↔ Medium ↔ Slow)	Medium	Fast	The fastest speed to market is where the partners' infrastructure that is already in place is utilised, as in scheme 'D'.
The ability to reflect BW brand values and service: (Good ↔ Average ↔ Poor)	Average	Poor	Scheme B? is considered to have slightly more control over brand values by being able to control the call centre operations. However, both schemes are unlikely to be 'good'.
Compliance with FSA and ABI requirements: (Yes ↔ No)	Yes	Yes	Compliance with the Financial Services Act (FSA) and Association of British Insurers (ABI) code of practice is mandatory and non-negotiable.
Flexibility to undertake all of the administrative operations if desired: (Easy ↔ Difficult ↔ Unlikely)	Difficult	Unlikely	Neither option would easily facilitate BWIS undertaking all the administration. In each option either the call-centre or the administration would need to pass to BWIS.

Table 5.4: Comparison under uncertainty

This provides further opportunity to make additional forms of comparison to the crude assessments that were made in earlier short-listing. The 'textual' rather than 'numeric' descriptions convey uncertainty, which is explored in the following section.

Step four: Choosing commitments for action through time

The final step is the formation of proposed commitments to action through time, and the judgements about the management of uncertainty. Table 5.5 is a collection of uncertainty areas that have been identified throughout the analysis, which have been categorised into one of the three UE, UV or UR uncertainty types. The most salient uncertainties identified by the actors in this case were (i) retaining the call centre activity while outsourcing the operation to a partner (?CALLPART), (ii) using the existing call centre while a partner undertakes the administration only (?FLEXADMIN), and (iii) whether bespoke applications will actually be a better 'fit' with existing legacy systems than packages (?LEGACY).

UNCERTAINTY AREA	LABEL:	TYPE	SALIENCE:
?Possible infeasibility of utilising the existing internal call centre while adopting the approach of working with a partner.	?CALLPART	UE	• • •
From 'Flexibility to undertake all of the administrative operations if desired: comparison: ? The ability of the partner to undertake the administrative work while operating an in-house call-centre.	?FLEXADMIN	UR	• • •
From 'Speed to market' comparison: ? The ability for bespoke solutions to be a better fit with legacy systems than packages.	?LEGACY	UE	• • •
? The unknown volume and frequency of call-centre traffic.	?TRAFFIC	UE	• •
From 'The ability to reflect BW brand values and service' comparison: ? The ability for a third party to adequately represent the brand values of BW.	?BRANDVAL	UV	• •

Table 5.5: Comparing uncertainty areas

Figure 5.7 shows the uncertainty graph for the Insurance case and the cluster of uncertainties of the UE type. This diagram would help in determining which uncertainties will be most influential on the final outcome and which can be deferred for the moment. Three uncertainties have been classified 'high' in salience (utilising an internal call centre while working with a partner, the ability for the partner to undertake the administration while operating an in-house call centre, and the ability for bespoke solutions to be a better fit with legacy systems than packages) and are therefore likely to have a significant influence on the final outcome. Indications of the options likely to resolve those uncertainties are also indicated.

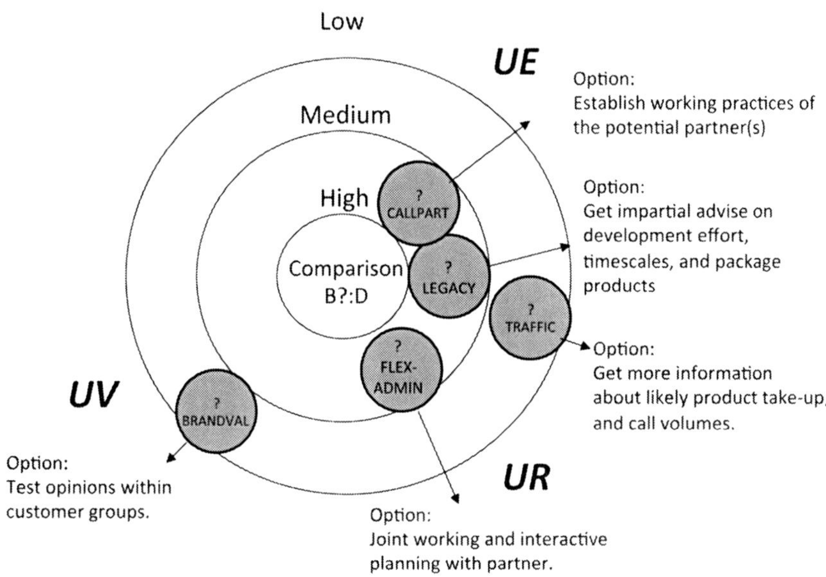

Figure 5.7: Uncertainty graph – salience of uncertainty to this comparison

Commitment package

A decision has to be made as to how much exploration should take place and what decisions can be made now. In practice the decisions are made throughout the project, and by rearranging the feasible action schemes so that the more 'urgent' decision areas can be brought forward to earlier branches of the decision tree, or those decisions where there is little or no choice, then flexibility can be engineered into later decisions. Figure 5.8 shows a reworking of the decisions to reflect those that must be taken sooner, and those that can be deferred.

Decision now		*Decision later*	*Scheme*
Call centre?	*IT?*	*Approach?*	
Existing	Bespoke	In-house	A
		Partner?	B? (*)
Partner	Bespoke	In-house	C?
		Partner?	D (*)
New	Bespoke	In-house	E

(*) Short listed decision schemes

Figure 5.8: A comparison of the feasible action schemes

The decision regarding approach was considered the most urgent at the outset based on the assumption that all other decisions (call centre and IT) would naturally follow on. However, in the interest of expediency it emerged that as long as flexibility was maintained (that is that no decision taken now would preclude the long-term flexibility of the approach), then the call centre decision should take priority. As the IT decision would remain the same (i.e. Bespoke) regardless of whichever scheme was chosen, then that decision had by implication already been made.

Strategic Choice Approach uses the concept of the commitment package as the method for determining the choice between those actions that have to be taken immediately, those actions that require further exploration to reduce the salience of areas of uncertainty, and finally the other arrangements that need to be made to enable actions to be deferred. Table 5.6 sets out a summary of the actual decisions taken in this case now, and those deferred to later.

	DECISIONS NOW			FUTURE DECISION	
	Actions	Explorations		Deferred Choices	Contingency Planning
Call Centre:	Utilise partners call centre capability.				
Approach:	Utilise partners administration capability.	Establish working practices of the potential partners.		Move administration activity in-house	Joint working and interactive planning with partner.
IT:	Adapt partner software to support new business venture.	Obtain impartial advice on development effort, timescales.			

Table 5.6: Commitment package framework - Insurance Services

The decision scheme actually chosen by BW (i.e. a *'partner'* call centre, *'partner'* approach, and *'bespoke'* IT), was labelled as scheme 'D'.

5.4 The alignment of the actors in the network (Alignment logic)

Introduction

The third approach uses techniques from Actor Network Theory to understand the alignment of the actors to the proposed approaches. If we plot the process components for the Insurance case study on to a process inscription/specialisation framework, which represents the view as defined by BeingWell (Figure 5.9), the following can be observed.

The final case (Insurance) shows a grouping of the process components around the centre of the framework, however there is no consistency to that grouping, with both 'people' and 'NEWTON' being in the non-aligned space. This would suggest that there is some ambiguity about the final solution. To take each component:

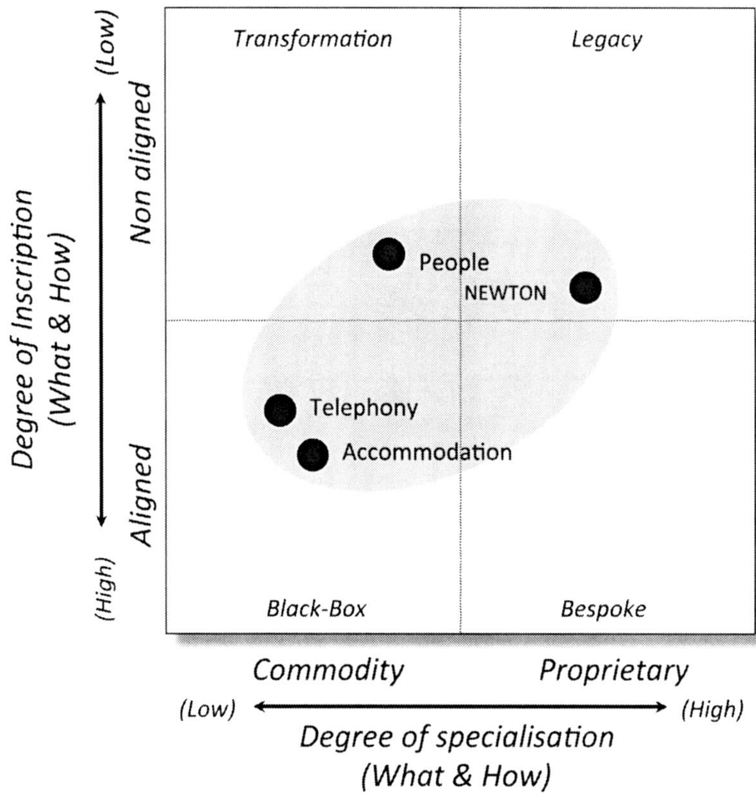

Figure 5.9: Insurance process inscription/specialisation framework

People – call centre agents

The positioning of 'people' in the transformation space reflects the non-alignment of the interests of BeingWell, and the employees of the Insurance Agents (Majestic Insurance Group), who rigidly apply staffing levels that are consistent with the union agreements they have in place with their employees. Governance of call handling is considered excessive by BW and staff turnover is high. Although there is some USDAW representation BeingWell is predominantly a non-unionised workforce, and an independent staff council represents the majority of employees and there is a 'clash' of culture and styles between the two organisations. However, MIG unions insist on what BeingWell consider to be a 'top-heavy' management structure, and are prescriptive about ratios of Call Centre Agents to Supervisors.

Each new Agent undergoes approximately three weeks of training in order for him or her to operate effectively. During week one they undergo a 'Freshman's course which is aimed at providing information on the basics of the Insurance industry, background the MIG, the Association of British Insurers (ABI) code of practice, and health and safety. Week two is an introduction to the BWIS products they will be handling plus the opportunity to 'listen-in' on calls taken by experienced Agents so that they can be exposed to the appropriate techniques. In week three they will handle calls with the assistance of an experienced Agent being on-hand to help should they have a problem.

NEWTON – Information technology

The NEWTON software is bespoke and is an adaptation of a Majestic Insurance Group proprietary system and therefore occupies the 'legacy' space. BWIS are wholly dependent on MIG to support this product and are heavily constrained by their capability (or lack of it), desire, and capacity to do the enhancements and changes required. Prioritisation of systems work is not easy when MIG have more 'value creating' activity to focus on.

Telephony and accommodation

Once again 'telephony' and 'accommodation' appear in the black-box space and have been consistent in doing so throughout all four cases. Agents sit at 'turrets' that receive the calls, and ceiling mounted electronic display units are positioned at strategic points around the call centre so that they are visible to all the Agents. The displays are constantly updated to show the incoming call traffic by client, the source of the call, either 'internal' i.e. transferred from another call centre or a normal customer call, the number of calls waiting, how long calls have been waiting, and the number of Agents available to take the calls.

5.5 A longitudinal view: Insurance – Health & Travel Insurance

Introduction

BWIS entered a three-year agreement with MIG to provide health & travel insurance underwriting, as well as the call centre and administrative support required for their new venture. BWIS valued MIG's experience, expertise and understanding of the insurance administration and underwriting markets, and the travel business grew quickly outstripping the most optimistic predictions, and a positive relationship developed between the two companies. Three years on, at the renewal of the contract, BWIS entered into a new arrangement with AIG (Europe), a change largely transparent to their customers, and business continues to flourish. BWIS now enjoy market leadership in its travel sector and are steadily developing its health insurance market.

Developing the call centre process (PARTNER) (PARTNER) (BESPOKE)

BWIS's decision to outsource the call centre (PARTNER), and the administration (PARTNER), to MIG was influenced heavily by speed to market considerations. Upon entering MIG's Corporate Partnership Division call centre at Cardiff, it's not easy to forget that this is a tele-sales environment. The top three performing Agents names are emblazoned on a flip chart entitled 'Crazy Conversions', which is a fortnightly incentive scheme encouraging Agents to exceed the target of 55% of calls converted into sales, of which 18% should be sales of the annual travel product. The rewards, a selection of digital cameras or portable CD players, are displayed to encourage performance. The walls carry slogans such as *"If you don't ask the question you can't sell the product"*. These initiatives are sponsored by MIG although BW have sponsored some team initiatives resulting in a 'murder mystery' weekend at a local hotel. Some incentives are team based (shifts), which encourages a healthy inter-team rivalry. The amount the Agent can directly influence a sale is limited principally to the telephone manner they adopt, and ensuring that they ask the right questions. For example, *"are you travelling again?"* is a direct lead into converting the customer to an annual travel product. Motivational games are used to break the routine monotony and quick 'buzz' sessions convened to fire-up the Agents.

The use of an extensively modified in-house systems NEWTON (BESPOKE) had been a pragmatic decision based on speed of deployment, however there was an increasing frustration from BWIS that they were disadvantaged by being locked in to a legacy system, with limited ability to change and develop functionality to suit the business need.

Following a first year interim review BWIS expressed a desire to review two key areas over time: (i) the systems disadvantage, i.e. that it should not be locked-in to legacy systems, and (ii) BWIS has a non-unionised workforce, however MIG unions insist on, in the opinion of BWIS, a 'top-heavy' supervisory and management structure. The then Operations Manager expressed a view that *"If we were doing this again today we would build our own call centre"*.

Qualitative and quantitative data is collected on call handling, call monitoring via questionnaires with customers, through stores, claims, and through telesales. The service levels in place are reviewed every three months and include specific targets for things such as response times 85/15 (85% of the calls answered in under 15 seconds), which has now been revised to 90/10, (90% of the calls in under 10 seconds). An agreement also exists where BeingWell could install a Call Centre Manager if necessary.

Analysis of the costs

BWIS operate an 'open book' accounting approach with MIG so each party understands the cost dynamics of the operation. Despite having a healthy relationship between the two companies the regular reviews highlighted a significant issue that was to change dramatically the arrangements. When analysed closely it became clear that, at a cost of around £12 per insurance sale, MIG were losing money on the processing of each policy. Traditionally the systems and procedures in place were based around motor and household business, typically returning premiums of at least £300 per policy, which was more than adequate to cover the £12 administration charge. However, with travel premiums typically around £40 the £12 fee couldn't be sustained. This prompted a joint examination of the relationship and provided the opportunity to look for call centre alternatives. Although there were no issues with claims or loss ratios this also prompted a re-examination of the major insurance underwriters at that time. What also emerged was the existence of third-party administrators (TPA's), who position themselves as intermediaries by providing administrative support, typically call centre based and the associated mechanisms to support that, between a travel insurance underwriter and the company providing the brand, in this case BeingWell Insurance Services. The emergence of the TPA's (at that time only two major TPA's in the UK were separate from an insurance company), heightened the desire to de-couple the call centre activity from the underwriting, the direct opposite of the original decision taken some three years earlier to consider them as being closely-coupled. This de-coupling was now considered beneficial, and acceptable, as it increases flexibility to change underwriters independently of the call centre providers.

The outcome from this review was to move to European Travel Group (ETG) for travel insurance underwriting, and Insurance Support Services (ISS) for TPA services.

The result was a significantly reduced administration fee of each policy sale to a third of that charged by MIG. It prompted MIG to consider the services of a TPA for its own travel insurance processing, and to consider a strategic decision not to enter arrangements of the type it had with BeingWell in the travel insurance market. Of course engaging a TPA would have been impossible three years earlier as they didn't exist. Typically starting as travel insurance providers these niche players have developed through their role as travel insurance providers to the trade. Leveraging technology, telephony and insurance know-how, they used capabilities to become cost effective intermediaries.

The restructuring didn't stop here for BWIS, as this new approach also facilitated the use of a portfolio of underwriters to support a range of product types such as Dental insurance, Health and Cash Plan, each using different TPA's. The BWIS Operations Manager said:

> *"The business model of using third parties but branding it as BeingWell is a really efficient way to operate as a division, it enables moving in to new products with the same business model".*

The BWIS team when reviewing the recent changes, as follows, expressed that they are now more relaxed about changing underwriters as they now have the experience of having been through it. It helped that AIG and IGIS had worked together previously, resulting in AIG allowing IGIS to settle claims directly (thus improving the customer service to BeingWell customers) in the event of a claim. There was however some initial apprehension when IGIS were taken over by Churchill Insurance. IGIS provided a Windows based system (developed in-house) as well as an Internet site for on-line business, which now accounts for 4% of all policy sales.

5.6 Summary

This case study describes the approach taken by the BWIS team to establish an Insurance call centre process. The nature of this partnership venture is not only to satisfy the needs of both partners, but also to provide the peace of mind and security to customers that the BeingWell brand values brings to the Insurance market. As in the previous chapters the process, decision, and alignment logics are examined using the techniques described in detail in the earlier case studies. The actual choice of the BWIS team was decision scheme 'D' i.e. PARTNER – PARTNER – BESPOKE approach. This decision reflects the desire of the Chief Executive for speed of implementation, which was to take priority over other considerations. As with all the previous cases telephony and accommodation components were considered commodities, so were the people once the mystique of the Insurance industry was understood. The limited choice of software and the need for speed of deployment led to the adoption of the partners' software, which in itself limited further future options. The non-alignment of BWIS and the partner organisation on matters relating to governance of the call centre process reflects the different culture and approach of the two organisations.

CHAPTER SIX
Case Study Analysis (inside-out)

6.1 Introduction

The purpose of this chapter is to analyse in detail the findings from each of the four case studies both individually and collectively using cross-case analysis. To do this the chapter is split into four sections: Firstly, the *process logic* is examined to understand what the processes are actually about, their individual characteristics, and how similar (i.e. common) is each to the other processes under review. The second section examines the *decision logic* i.e. what decisions were considered and how they were made. It uses the tools and techniques of the SCA approach to do that, namely decision areas, options, decision schemes, comparison areas, and uncertainty. The third section examines the *alignment logic*, i.e. alignment and non-alignment of the actors in the network with the aid of three concepts from actor network theory: *inscription*, *translation*, and *irreversibility*. It uses the inscription/specialisation analysis framework to help understand these concepts as seen in the four case studies. Finally, the concluding section discusses the 'patterns of activity' identified and the integration of the three logics using a conceptual model of commodity business process adoption.

6.2 Process logic

Introduction

The purpose of this first section is to understand the process logic, which concentrates primarily on the characteristics of the call centre process. In addition to determining whether the processes are similar (i.e. common) to the other processes under review, it also examines some of the related non-process characteristics that influence the eventual make up of a process. In the original research design it was envisaged that 'structure', as one of the business process characteristics, would form a subunit of analysis to enhance the insight into the cases. In practice, the analysis has been conducted at a level below that at which structural issues emerge, therefore no structural analysis has been included. Activity Records of the four cases are used to help with the comparisons.

The language used to describe business processes

Keen & Knapp[i] maintain that there is no established body of common language about business processes as a whole; however despite this the language used to describe processes is important. For example, the 'call centre' process as researched in this thesis has quite reasonably been described as:

- A *'complaint handling'* process - in the Customer Service case,
- An *'account servicing'* process - in the Loyalty Card case, and
- An *'order taking'* process - in the Mail Order and Insurance cases.

All three examples above are principally the same, and the components of the process are similar. However, those concerned with the 'workflow' or 'industrial engineering' school would find a description that describes the inputs and outputs of the process more informative (i.e. complaint handling or taking an order), whereas the 'work coordination' school would prefer a more generic descriptor (call centre). Pentland[ii] describes the development of a grammatical model of organisational processes that consists of a lexicon of basic elements and rules or constraints for combining them[iii]. He uses an example from Salancik and Leblebici[iv]; a simple grammatical model for a restaurant might be 'order, cook, serve, eat, pay', or 'cook, order, pay, serve, and eat' if a fast food restaurant. A simple description would fit this analysis also, as the call centre process could (and was in earlier chapters) be described as 'receive the inbound calls, identify customer & information, handle the complaint/enquiry/order, initiate other processes, close the call'. Halē[v] would describe the generic or *horizontal* process as the 'call centre' process, whereas the departmental or functional process *(vertical)* would be described as the order taking, complaint handling, or Loyalty Card administration. However this process view of organisations is not fully realised, and has been described as *'cognitive dissonance'*[vi] (integrated processes yet fragmented organisations pulling in different directions). It is clear that the terminology is confusing and a lack of clarity surrounding process descriptions does add to the confusion when trying to establish the nature of a process, its content, and purpose. In this research the approach taken has been wherever possible to describe the generic (or horizontal) process, i.e. 'call centre'.

The similarity of the processes under review

What is immediately noticeable with the processes as depicted in Figure 6.1 is the similarity of the tasks and activities that make up that process. At the highest level of detail then each process comprises five activities: (i) Receive inbound calls, (ii) Identify customer and information, (iii) the process specific activity be it handle a complaint, service the account, or take an order, (iv) Initiate other processes, and (v) close the call. At a lower level of detail the sub-activities are again similar, i.e. questions are asked of the caller and their responses recorded, or linked processes such as documentation (invoices or shipping details) are initiated. It is only at the lowest level of detail that the dialogue or questions might appear to be different; the links to systems that are specific to that process, for example the links to the Loyalty Scheme Operating System (LSOS), or Underwriting System (NEWTON), and the linked processes could be quite diverse, for example to a logistics system or gift vouchers catalogue. The question therefore is, do the specific activities and tasks justify different approaches for the whole, which is common? Davenport[vii] asks this question of systems and processes when considering the role of ERP's in an organisation. He makes the distinction between small single business organisations where there is really no decision to be made, suggesting that systems and processes covered by the system should be the same wherever they appear within that business.

However, in larger more complex or multi-business organisations the problem is more acute. This is particularly true for global organisations where products, customers, regulations and taxation can vary widely in different parts of the business and different countries. In the four case studies researched there isn't a global dimension but four quite different business areas are covered. We have already seen that, depending on your frame of reference, the process under review could be considered to be 'order taking', 'complaint handling', or even 'account servicing'. With such diversity of views on a single business process it is not hard to see why the final solution can turn out to be so different in each case. If the tasks and activities that are actually conducted within the call centre were the only consideration, then in this particular process it might be possible to do it in a common way. However, in addition to the activity within the process there are other *characteristics* of a process, ranging from how the 'BeingWell culture' may differ from case to case, through to the nature of any 'investment specificity' of the process, or the impact of history (administrative heritage), timing, individuals, their knowledge and competence in that particular part of the business. In order to understand this further there follows a series of issues that bear on the question of whether the processes can be treated as similar or not. The issues are grouped into four categories: (i) information and knowledge, (ii) cultural differences, (iii) administrative inheritance (where we are now), and (iv) assets, governance and commoditisation.

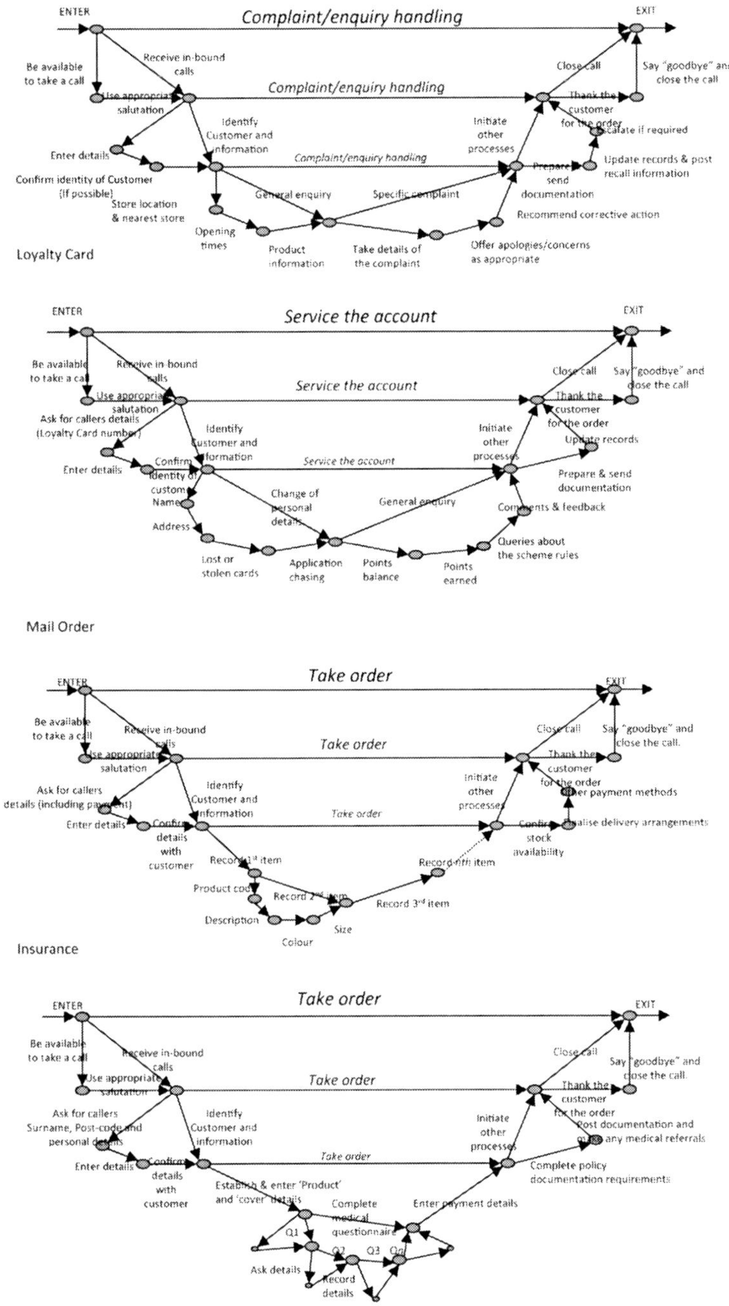

Figure 6.1: Activity record composite

Information and knowledge

How closely coupled is the process with other processes?

Clearly the more closely coupled a process is to any other process then the more likely that information and data is exchanged between the two. Dependencies between processes can be critical, for example in the mail order case the interdependency of the call centre, supply chain, and a third party delivery courier was key, in contrast to the Loyalty Card case where although links to other processes exist (card fulfilment) the association is loosely-coupled and easily managed. Teng et al[viii] argue that these degrees of mediation (inputs and outputs) can be reduced, and collaboration (information exchange) can be increased, by the appropriate use of information technology. In the case of call centres as described earlier, the customer is demanding more closely coupled processes, as the call centre manager in the Customer Service case commented:

"Initially just getting the job done was good enough and links with other processes were ignored, today customers expect more. Customers expect to do several transactions while, in their perception, on the phone to Being-Well".

Kock et al[ix] determined that there is a correlation between data, information and knowledge exchanges within business processes. From their research they conclude that there exists an information exchange threshold above which knowledge is likely to be transferred as well. A process that has a low information exchange threshold (i.e. a high proportion of knowledge is exchanged) might indicate training needs, or an opportunity for method improvements or re-engineering. A low information threshold is unlikely to be consistent with a 'commodity' process, or those that require minimalist involvement. However, a high information threshold would be supportive of a commodity i.e. lots of data but little knowledge is passed. In all four cases, although varying in each case, the thresholds of information is high (i.e. a low proportion of knowledge is exchanged between functions engaged in the processes).

Attainment of the call centre capability

It might sometimes be obvious when an organisation has attained a capability in a particular process, but how does an organisation recognise when it has attained that capability, is there a formal announcement or a public celebration? Depending on the particular capability, a firm might have to go through a long and difficult learning process in order to acquire that capability. Where this exists (and there is no way to avoid it), it is said to be path dependent (Barney 1999)[x]. The combined Loyalty Card / Customer Services call centre is, by any analysis (i.e. people involved, know-how, technology deployed, structure, or calls handled), a fully operational and functional call centre. However, during the interviews the Customer Services Manager commented: *"Now that we own the technology we can now handle calls as efficiently as a 'proper' call centre"*. This Freudian slip does perhaps reveal how the organisation actually perceives this facility, as somehow not being 'proper' when compared with that of third parties. Is this a reflection of the general alignment of actors towards the Customer Service call centre? Do they think that just because it is internal it can't be effective and efficient? Even the most passionate supporter of the centre (the Customer Services Manager) was 'conditioned' to think that it was, in some way, sub optimal:

"The Loyalty Card call centre is perceived as being small, which it is in commercial call centre terms, but the value and impact of it is important".

When it is not clear what actions an organisation should take to create a capability it can be described as *'Causal ambiguity'*. Barney (1999)[xi] suggests that this causal ambiguity is likely to exist where the capabilities are *"taken for granted, unspoken, and tacit attributes of a firm"*. In making an asset specific investment by purchasing the Lucent telephony equipment, Group Telecommunications had *'taken for granted'* that the call centre capability had been achieved, or was at least achievable, yet they had no real clarity about this when entering into the transaction.

Know-how

Know-how spans both the process and decision logic but will be discussed here. Consider the different types of know-how in these cases: (i) the know-how of the process under investigation (in this case call centres), (ii) know-how of the industry / channel type e.g. mail order, insurance, loyalty schemes, and (iii) know-how of adopting processes (relevant particularly to decision logic).

Know-how of the process (call centres) in each case is similar. The telephony know-how was easily available in-house, and advice was sought from Group Telecommunications at different points in the process depending on the project. Customer Service being the first initiative involved Group Telecommunications (GT) from the outset. Loyalty Card was heavily influenced by the third party organisations involved in the trials (T.COM) that already have knowledge of call centres, and might not have known of the existing internal call centre capability. GT were not approached with regard to the telephony arrangements until the decision to outsource had already been taken. For Mother & Baby Direct, the approach was very much *"we want to do it this way, is there a problem?"* This was partly because they had learnt a little about call centres, and partly because they didn't believe that they needed advice. Know-how of the industry/channel is specific to each case. Typically the knowledge (know-how) transfer was good in technical areas between GT and Information Systems as they had some continuity across the projects such as telephony and systems integration. Some people were involved in all the different initiatives. However, knowledge transfer was poor in the business areas such as Marketing.

"Before a customer can buy a new product first they must learn about it"[xii]. Know-how of adopting processes is similar to the know-how required by a customer buying a new product; they need to learn about it. Building on earlier work[xiii], Doyle describes the *'adoption process'* as comprising five stages: Awareness, Interest, Evaluation, Trial, and Adoption.

- *Awareness*: Awareness has to be created for the product,
- *Interest*: Adopters need to be encouraged to find out more about the product or service,
- *Evaluation*: Decisions are made as the whether the product or service will meet the particular needs. Opinion formers are important at this stage,
- *Trial*: Trials are conducted and a decision to adopt (or not) is made, and finally
- *Adoption*: Regular use is made of the product.

In the Insurance case, elements of this adoption cycle can be observed as the BWIS staff became more *aware* of the capabilities of third party organisations, had the opportunity to *evaluate* and *trial* this approach during the initial contract with MIG, and they were ready to embrace (i.e. *adopt*) that method when prompted by a contract renewal.

Cultural difference between 'retail' and 'financial services'

The BeingWell brand values and the customers' 'trust' in that brand is engrained in everything the organisation does, which extends beyond how it sells its products and services. Although difficult to describe or capture, there is most definitely a 'BeingWell way of doing things' which is liberally applied in its processes and procedures. This 'BeingWell way' is accompanied by an arrogance of 'knowing best', which is brought into sharp contrast when its processes or procedures come into contact with those of other organisations, *"If you want a job done properly, then do it yourself"*[xiv]. A quite noticeable cultural difference was observable between the financial services call centre agents and BW store staff. The call centre staff that only ever deal with customers 'remotely' find it difficult to understand why BW store staff appear hesitant to sell financial services products. They would often contact the call centre to check product details or ask for advice. However, the call centre only has four products to deal with, whereas the diversity in the store is much greater. Typical questions asked by the stores are:

"Is Tenerife included in Europe or is it World-wide"? "Do I have to put the product through the till (Epos) twice if two people are travelling"? "The customer has a medical condition, can they still purchase the cover at store or do they have to telephone you"?

Administrative inheritance (where we are now)

Davenport[xv] describes how companies instead of *'starting from scratch'* will *'start from what is possible or easily accomplished'* in one of the leading enterprise systems. He describes a shift in how companies engineer (or reengineer) processes by thinking in parallel about the supporting information systems needs rather than by designing an elegant solution that is then supported by the appropriate technology. However there is evidence to suggest that this extends beyond purely enterprise systems. For example, in the Mail Order case the BW stores EPoS system, because of its ability to check stock in and out of a stock file, calculate payment, and then link to the central accounts system, was bastardised and used as a warehouse system. Mail-it, the mail order system used by Mailsales, was heavily modified to suit the needs of the call centre. NEWTON, MIG's bespoke insurance underwriting system, was modified and used as the basis on which the health & travel insurance products were sold. In contrast to enterprise systems that largely incorporate 'best practice' designs, this approach was driven by the desire for convenience, pace, and perceived low cost. This approach of redesigning packages as presented and making them firm specific by blending them with the existing organisational practices is referred to in the literature as '*Appropriation*' (Clark & Staunton 1989)[xvi]. Appropriation undermines the notion of 'plain vanilla' implementation and any best practice prescription from the vendor, and therefore 'appropriation' has to be distinguished from 'implementation'. Hislop et al[xvii] describe how a company might implement a new technology but not actually use it in terms of it becoming routine or fully embedded; it is the unpacking and re-blending of new ideas to develop firm specific solutions.

Assets, governance and commoditisation

Asset specific investments

Asset specific investments are likely to be more effective in their optimal application, but less widely applicable than general investments. The contribution to value of an asset specific investment is high but outside options are weak, and the organisation is then effectively locked-in to a relationship with that asset. In contrast, a general investment though not as effective in enhancing value, strengthens outside options and hence may be chosen to avoid lock-in. The decision of the BeingWell Group Telecommunications function to purchase telephony equipment as a group-wide asset can still be considered as a general investment, as a whole industry of independent firms utilises a common asset technology, thus avoiding lock-in to any one firm[xviii]. However, the dominance of Lucent Technologies in the telephony market could give rise to fears of it being an 'owner-specific' investment, especially if the technology purchased is unique to that firm. The investment in this technology does imply that there is an expectation that it will be utilised within the Group and that there will be benefit from providing this capability.

Telephony is a commodity

It is an important finding of the research that the telephony, a key component of the call centre process, is actually a commodity, and in all four cases it was also seen, and accepted as, a commodity.

Although not the case at the commencement of the research, all four cases will end up operating on telephony equipment from the same supplier. Despite the deregulation in the telecommunications industry, and the breaking-up of monopoly supplier's contracts with increased competition from the many new players, the telecommunications industry is heavily regulated and standardised. This facilitates an approach where any number of supplier's equipment can be connected to a growing number of networks. Such is the ubiquitous nature of telecommunications; in both the Customer Service and Loyalty cases it was possible to 'rent' the telephony requirements from a local cable supplier as a 'managed service'. This also provided flexibility to grow the requirements as the business grew by renting more capability. Later, as the need became more understood, the service was brought in-house when GT purchased the Lucent equipment. Telephone numbers are easily transferred (albeit attracting a fee) as in the Loyalty case where previously T.COM had the number that was later transferred to BeingWell, thereby removing the need to change the published number to customers. Alignment of interests (and therefore low interest in telephony) was made possible, as everything you wanted to do was achievable and relatively simple thereby raising few problems.

Location and accommodation

Modern telephony allows the call centre to be positioned anywhere. There are numerous examples, such as BT Directory Enquiries and IBM Global Services help desk, where call centres are located in different parts of the country (or even the world) and service customers elsewhere around the globe. In the cases researched, while proximity to the customer might not be a critical factor, the distance from other elements of the supply chain could well be (such as the warehouse and supply facilities). Technology has reduced the impact of physical distance as files and data can be passed electronically, thus removing the need for physical proximity. There is added value for Customer Service staff from being 'physically close' to the marketers. Governance can be made more difficult if call centre staff are *'out of sight and out of mind'*. Standard office environments are suitable for call centres although out of hours access and staff facilities (such as restaurant facilities) might need to be available around the clock.

Governance

Four different business models appear across each of the four cases: The first being the in-sourced service provision of customer services; the second is an in-sourced Loyalty Card service having previously been outsourced; the third is the outsourced provision of a sales function (mail order); and finally a 'joint venture' sales operation (insurance). Clearly in a joint venture the freedom to act, and flexibility is limited. The governance issues are more restricting and joint consultation and decision-making is likely. The individual interests of the companies could be competing because of the separation of ownership and control, which gives rise to an agency relationship (the subject of agency theory). For example, when operating an outsourced call centre what will be the behaviour, approach and empathy of the agent with the customer? Will they have the ability to escalate any issues to someone with sufficient authority to handle a potential life threatening complaint?

The subconscious association between commodities and outsourcing

There appears to be a subconscious association that some people make between a business process that might usefully be classified as a commodity, and that of outsourcing, the emphasis being placed on *'how'* the process is undertaken rather than *'what'* is done. This association while understandable is perhaps a little misleading. Using the definition of commodity processes as described earlier, it could reasonably lead you to think that if the process isn't specific to your business, and is readily available to you and does not return 'excessive' value to your business, then why not let someone else perform it for you? This might be a 'reasonable' conclusion, but not necessarily an effective or sensible solution when considering costs, potential sources of innovation, or a portfolio of processes. Does anyone ask the question 'could the commodity process be made firm specific, unique, and therefore be a source of excessive value or competitive advantage'? In isolation it might not be, but when considered alongside a portfolio of processes, be they commodity or not, then this could change. An example from the core BeingWell business (Dispensing Services) shows that for a nationwide chain of Pharmacies such as BeingWell, it was possible to turn the commodity process of 'dispensing drugs' into a leveraged process, i.e. *a processes that, while not specific to a particular company, is more valuable to it than to others,* because its national coverage and economies of scale will allow it to offer added value services to its customers such as 'E-Pharm'[20] (patient prescription records held centrally). E-Pharm enables any BeingWell pharmacist to have access to patient records and be aware of any drug interactions from previous prescriptions, thus providing a safer and more convenient service at any store the customer chooses to visit.

To take this even further, BeingWell could turn this now leveraged process into a proprietary one, i.e. *the company-specific processes around which an organisation builds a business*. To use a 'Loyalty Card' example Walgreens[21], the American Drug Store Chain, through their subsidiary Walgreens Health Initiative (WHI), have done just that, by positioning themselves as the providers of a pharmacy ID card, linked to their health plans, that electronically checks claim-processing eligibility, prescription price, and reviews the prescription for possible conflicts. This service operates not only in its own 2,500 stores but is now extended to a retail pharmacy network of over 43,000 pharmacies including other participating leading "big-name" chain pharmacies such as Wal-Mart, Kmart, Eckerd and Albertson's.

By thinking of some processes as *commodities*, companies outsource products and services to third parties. Callon[xix] suggested that by doing so they risk not being able to disentangle themselves from former users, producers and prior context. Once a transaction has been concluded, it is necessary to sever the 'purchaser / vendor' relationship that existed during the transaction. If the purchaser remains entangled then they can never escape from the web of relations. BeingWell appear to follow the broad maxim that commodity can't be valuable or important so outsourcing (non-core) processes must be the right approach.

Process logic summary

Returning to the question posed earlier, do the 'specific' activities and tasks justify different approaches for the whole, which is common? Despite the diversity that occurs at the very lowest level of the process, and the fact that

20 E-Pharm is a record of all the prescribed medicines dispensed for the cardholder at any BeingWell Pharmacy. It has a unique registration number ensuring a confidential service is offered and is free of charge to all customers.

21 Founded in 1901, Walgreens is a national retail pharmacy chain with over 3000 stores, and Walgreens Health Initiatives is the managed care division of Walgreen Co. Walgreens Health Initiatives designs prescription drug benefit programs that meet organizations' goals for cost containment, while providing members with comprehensive and convenient pharmaceutical care.

processes are described differently in different situations, there seems to be a 'core' that is common, with a 'surround' that is fairly specific. Throughout the examples cited in this section there is evidence to support that the core of the call centre process is common, while the same evidence reinforces the specific nature of some of the surrounding factors. It has been established that the tasks and activities undertaken at the heart of the process are the same in all cases. It has also been established that two key components of the call centre process (telephony and accommodation) are in themselves commodities. They were identified as such in all four cases. They were also seen to be commodities by the actors in the network. Investment in telephony is not considered asset specific and is generally applicable, as telephony can be used in any call centre process. Know-how of the process is fairly common and readily available. Call centres aren't generally location specific, and standard office facilities are suitable for most requirements.

There are however some notable differences that support the 'surround' being 'specific'. It has been established that a process can differ in its information exchange (i.e. if knowledge is also passed), and in its closeness of coupling with other processes. Information exchange and close coupling introduce dependency. Industry or channel know-how will be specific depending on the nature of the call centre. The culture (norms, values and beliefs) of the organisation will be specific to that business, as will utilising existing software products as a fast or inexpensive entry strategy. Utilising existing software products compounds the uniqueness of that particular situation. A lack of (i) any obvious mechanisms for recognising when a relevant capability has been achieved in an organisation, and (ii) know-how of the commodity adoption process, may lead to confusion and lost opportunities.

6.3 Decision Logic

Introduction

In the previous section the emphasis was on the nature and composition of the business process. This section examines what decisions were considered and how they were made. It uses the tools and techniques of the SCA namely decision areas, options, decision schemes, comparison areas, and uncertainty. In each of the four case studies some initial decisions were implicit from the approach adopted to solve the problem. In the Customer Service case it had been decided to address the problem of poor complaint and enquiry handling, probably by incorporating a call centre, but they didn't know how they were going to go about it. The initial trials of the Loyalty Card had indicated that it would be well received and sought after by customers however, issues such as whether to use 'smart-card' technology were central to the deployment strategy. In the Mail Order case the decision to enter the mail order business for mother and baby items had already been taken, but the proposed method of operation was not clear at that time. Finally, in the Insurance case it was clear that the products were the first in a range of health and travel related insurance products to be sold through BW stores, but once again the method of deployment was vague. This analysis examines those decisions that were in focus at the time of determining how to satisfy the requirements of the call centre process, which in each case was integral to the success of the operation. Table 6.1 is a summary of the results from the various analytical techniques used. The descriptions that follow step-through the table contents and explore the underlying reasons for the outcomes.

CASE	APPROACH	DECISION AREAS		OPTIONS		DECISION SCHEMES			
	'Structured' or 'Anarchic'	Inside problem boundary	Outside problem boundary	Option bars	Doubtful options	Possible decision schemes	Incompatible decision schemes	Doubtful decision schemes	Feasible decision schemes
CS	Structured	4	5	10	3	24	20	0	4
LC	Structured	4	4	3	4	36	15	13	18
MO	Structured	4	2	7	9	24	18	4	2
INS	Structured	3	1	3	1	12	7	2	3

Table 6.1: Summary results of the decision logic analysis techniques

Approach - structured versus anarchic decision making

In all four cases the decision making approach can be characterised using Pinfields' (1986)[xx] taxonomy as being *'structured'*, that is it followed an ordered progression from recognition to resolution[xxi]. This is in contrast to being *'anarchic'*, that is the decision is as a result of a fortuitous combination of problems, solutions and participants (or happenstance)[xxii]. Despite the obvious lack of overall decision making techniques or framework used in the case studies, the approach to these initiatives typically recognised that there was a strategic consequence for the organisation, that goals and objectives were relatively clear and understood, participation in the process was expected, and a recognition of the need for orderly progression through the decision phases.

		CUSTOMER SERVICE	LOYALTY CARD	MAIL ORDER	INSURANCE
Inside problem focus boundary	Process specific decisions	Obtain or acquire call centre capability?	Obtain or acquire call centre capability?	Is existing call centre capability appropriate?	Is existing call centre capability appropriate?
		BeingWell own staff to handle enquiries or complaints?			
		Determine an approach?	Determine an approach?	Determine an approach?	Determine an approach?
	Related decisions	How best to provide the IT?	How best to provide the IT?	How best to provide the IT?	How best to provide the IT?
			Whether to use Smart-card technology?		
				Whether to use in-house Logistics?	
Outside problem focus boundary	Process specific decisions	Separation of written and oral work?			
		Effective complaint handling?			
		Provision of the telephony?	Obtain or acquire call centre telephony?		
			Whether to move the call centre in-house?		
			Use BeingWell staff to handle the calls?		BeingWell staff represents the brand?
	Related decisions	Match the in-store experience?		Match store deals and offers?	
		Maximise customer relationships?			
			Extend scheme to other BeingWell companies?	Offer Loyalty Card points?	

Table 6.2: Summary of the decision areas inside and outside the boundary of the problem focus, split by process specific and related problems[22].

22 Naming conventions: Although in each case the terminology used by the actors might have been slightly different, for the purpose of analysis I have been as consistent with descriptions as possible so that it is clear that the same decision is actually being considered. Where this application of common terminology would be misleading or could imply a different decision under consideration then it has remained unchanged.

Decision areas

As seen in earlier chapters the decision areas, as represented by the decision graphs, map the terrain of the decisions in focus and comprise a rich mix of policy, operational, financial and other decision types within a single approach. This diagrammatic representation of the decision areas and their connectedness with each other further enhances the analysis by describing 'links' between decision areas, notably where their joint consideration might materially alter any decision outcome. Therefore the boundary surrounding the selected problem focus encapsulates those decisions that were considered key at that time by the case study actors and Table 6.2 is a summary of the decision areas considered both within and outside the problem focus in each case. It also shows the decisions split between (i) those decisions which relate directly to the call centre process (i.e. *'process specific'*), and (ii) those associated decisions that are closely-coupled with the process specific ones but could apply equally to other processes as well (*'related decisions'*).

What is immediately clear from Table 6.2 is that despite the apparent similarity of the processes in question: (i) there is a wide variety of decisions inside the problem focus boundary; (ii) the impact, importance, and variety of the *related decisions* that are within the boundary of the problem focus, which include those decisions labelled by the actors involved as most 'important' and 'urgent', and (iii) how a single decision, such as whether to use BeingWell own staff, could be treated so differently across all the cases or even not considered at all. The next section examines these questions in more detail.

Process specific decisions within the boundary of the problem focus

The primary 'process specific' decision, and one considered by all four initiatives, is 'how to provide the call centre capability?' Table 6.3 further summarises the 'process specific' decision areas and includes the options considered in each case.

		CUSTOMER SERVICE	LOYALTY CARD	MAIL ORDER	INSURANCE
Inside problem focus boundary	Process specific decisions	**Obtain or acquire call centre capability?** * Develop in-house * Outsource to third party	**Obtain or acquire call centre capability?** * Utilise internal call centre * Outsource * Set-up new internal call centre	**Is existing call centre capability appropriate?** * Yes * With development * No	**Is existing call centre capability appropriate?** * Utilise existing internal call centre * Outsource to the insurance partner * Set-up new internal call centre
		BeingWell own staff to handle enquiries or complaints? * Yes * No			

Table 6.3: Summary of the process specific decisions

The following sections take each question within each case in order.

Customer Service - Obtain or acquire call centre capability?

The requirement for a call centre was first encountered during the Customer Service case, and as no other in-house call centre existed at that time the possible options for that case were perceived as being restricted to either developing an internal call centre from scratch, or outsourcing it to a third party. The strong preference by all the actors to use BeingWell own staff to represent and protect the brand (discussed in the next section), was a key driver to the decision making process and the task altered to become 'achieve this' rather than a choice of alternatives. The ready availability of experienced Customer Service staff already employed as Customer Service Advisors, albeit with limited telephone skills, was a main influence. The trend by retail industry competitors was to make available the opportunity for customers to get closer to the company and the company to its customers, and to handle complaints/enquiries in a more immediate way (i.e. by telephone). This more immediate interaction provides the occasion to try to turn a negative situation into a positive one, therefore an in-house option was certainly generally favoured by the industry.

Customer Service - BeingWell own staff to handle enquiries or complaints?

Considerable emphasis had been placed on the importance of accountability and a strong feeling existed among many of the stakeholders in the Customer Service case that this had to be a BeingWell operated call centre if they were truly going to provide the level of service required, have the commitment and wherewithal to resolve complaints, and to fulfil the 'psychological contract' between employer and employee as first described by Schein[xxiii], i.e. the assumptions, expectations and mutual obligations with the organisation to ensure that this happens[xxiv]. This subsequently favoured the use of in-house staff, which ultimately led to the setting up of the in-house call centre. The Customer Service Manager commented:

"Customers trust BeingWell so much that they are offended if they find out they are talking to someone not from BeingWell. Customers expect us to be fair, and that we treat them in a quality way, like they are in a store".

Significantly, the managers in the Customer Service case were the only ones to express such a strong view of the importance to BeingWell of using their own staff in this situation. The managers in the Loyalty Card case, who openly regarded the task as relatively simple, and those in the Mail Order case, who considered that 'Mail Order specialists' were key to the success of the business and subsequently outsourced that part of the operation, did not share this feeling. However, there was considerable anxiety about Financial Services staff handling calls from BeingWell customers on their behalf in the Insurance case. A clear objective of the insurance proposition from BeingWell was that the experience should be in keeping with the quality, safety and security customers have come to expect from the BeingWell brand; as protection of that brand is seen as all important, and it was questioned whether this really could be performed by Financial Services staff who were notorious for poor service. Despite this view the related decision area 'BeingWell staff to represent the brand?' was included as a decision area in the Insurance case but outside the problem focus.

Loyalty Card - Obtain or acquire the call centre capability?

Although the cases are unrelated, their chronology is important when considering these decisions. In the second case (Loyalty Card), which lagged behind the Customer Service case by five months, the existence of the Customer Service call centre provided an additional option. However, in complete contrast to the first case the prevailing view in the relevant part of the business at that time was that the call centre provided little opportunity for competitive advantage and was relatively 'low priority' when compared with the other operational issues under consideration, specifically smart-card production, and mass marketing of the card launch. This view was expressed quite clearly by the Loyalty Card Programme Manager:

> *"We didn't have a call centre established in BeingWell at that time, and the BW (Customer Service) call centre was in its infancy. We had no idea about the volumes of calls we were going to get, therefore staffing up internally was going to be tricky. Our expectations were that the Loyalty Card was going to be 'big', but it had the potential to be 'enormous'. Sourcing it externally would make the lead times to establishment quicker than trying to do it ourselves. The call centre was subcontracted to T.COM during the two trials so we didn't learn much about call centres because of the way we had done it".*

This call centre process was initially considered a commodity in this case, as the services had been (and could continue to be) purchased from a third party and the related routines were reasonably simple. The decision not to utilise the existing in-house call centre probably made setting up an alternative dedicated call centre an unviable proposition. Although an uncorroborated observation, it was suggested by the Loyalty Card Programme Manager that at launch there was an expectation that in the future the call centre would be moved to the BW site. Uncertainty surrounded the likelihood of setting-up a new internal call centre when one already existed for another service.

Mail Order/Insurance - Is existing call centre capability appropriate?

Both the Mail Order and Insurance cases had the benefit of following, and therefore learning from, the progress made by the Customer Service call centre, which by the time of their launch had been in operation for twelve months. This could have been a rich source of information and possibly an additional option when determining how to proceed. However, there is little evidence to suggest that this opportunity was actively pursued, or that a Customer Service call centre would be an acceptable alternative for a mail order or financial services call centre. There was uncertainty surrounding the potential of any call centre to expand to the predicted demand of the mail order operation, or the as yet unknown volumes of the insurance operation.

Related decisions within the boundary of the problem focus

The *related decisions* within the boundary of the problem focus are not process specific decisions but nonetheless are closely coupled with the process in question. Two particular decisions (overall approach, and how best to provide the IT requirements) arise in all cases. Two other decisions are considered i.e. whether to use smart-card technology, and whether to use in-house logistics. Table 6.4 shows a summary of the related decisions along with options under consideration.

Determine an approach?

Decisions regarding the method of approach appear to be the most important or critical ones surrounding this particular process. They include a diverse range of decisions on organisation structure (such as centralisation), procurement (in-house versus outsourcing), acquisition of companies or service providers, and partnership (as in the Insurance case). In all four cases the outcome of this decision significantly shaped the outcome of other related decisions. For example, the decision to approach the problem in a modular fashion in the Mail Order case set the scene for a complicated mix of packaged, legacy, and bespoke software development. Alternatively, entering a partnership with another company, as in the Insurance case, introduced significant compatibility issues such as working practices, location of offices, and staff recruitment.

		CUSTOMER	LOYALTY CARD	MAIL ORDER	INSURANCE
		Determine an approach? * Do nothing * Centralisation of teams * Centralisation management of teams	**Determine an approach?** * Controlled trial or pilot * Get a third party to administer the scheme * In-house administration	**Determine an approach?** * Modular * Acquisition	**Determine an approach?** * In-house administration * Partner to administer the scheme
Inside problem focus boundary	Related decisions	**How best to provide the IT?** *Predominantly Bespoke *Predominantly Package	**How best to provide the IT?** *Predominantly Bespoke *Predominantly Package	**How best to provide the IT?** *Predominantly Bespoke *Predominantly	**How best to provide the IT?** *Predominantly Bespoke *Predominantly
			Whether to use Smart-card technology? * Yes * No		
				Whether to use in-house Logistics? * Yes * No	

Table 6.4: Summary of the related decisions inside the problem focus boundary

How best to provide the IT?

The call centre process is 'information intensive'[xxv], and the closely coupled nature of the call centre process to related processes introduces the potential for a high information exchange, and as IT is the principle exchange mechanism this is a significant factor. Typically any debate was around software and not hardware. Although there were some compatibility issues surrounding the use of different operating systems or centralised versus distributed models, hardware was not an issue and the general 'open' nature of hardware made most likely combinations possible. At that time there was no formal IT strategy in place across these operating divisions and there was a general backlash by business users to bespoke systems, which they perceived had limited functionality, were slow and difficult to change. A general preference prevailed (albeit unofficial) for packaged software. However, interfaces with existing legacy systems would not be easy, and there was the increasing challenge of 'customisation' of packages to the way BeingWell wants to operate.

The call centre process relies on the timely provision and capture of information, typically in 'real time' while talking to a customer. It is also likely that the software is the link to related processes, and in some instances this association will be a closely coupled one. All four cases faced a similar decision regarding the use of either packaged software (i.e. a pre-written software application package specifically for a defined purpose such as customer contact, warehousing or mail order), or alternatively bespoke software, which could be provided either internally by in-house development staff or subcontracted to a third party. It was also the case that decisions that might initially appear to be unrelated to any technology decisions actually had significant technology consequences. For example, the decision taken to use a mail order bureau for Mother & Baby Direct determined by association that the software product eventually used was the same as that used by the bureau, which in turn required the bespoke development of an order fulfilment system.

Whether to utilise smart-card technology?

In the Loyalty Card case a key consideration in the operation of the card was to avoid the 'home store' concept as adopted by most retailers (i.e. a pre-designated or *'home'* store at which customers predominantly shop and where their personal card details are retained on-line) in order to circumvent the problems associated with centralised data storage and retrieval. This approach works well when the card is used regularly in the home-store only (as often the case with supermarkets), and is more memory efficient for the in-store technology that holds the data, but is less convenient or customer-friendly when used in other stores. Unlike supermarkets, BeingWell customers prefer the freedom to shop at any store and will regularly shop a portfolio of stores. A card that uses a memory chip rather than a magnetic stripe will enable the use of the card at any store, and can also accommodate the data required for some of the likely future initiatives such as additional information in the form of a talisman including drug interactions, allergies, patient medical records, in addition to the standard Loyalty Card details such as the loyalty points accrued and personal details. However, this does have far reaching consequences. Firstly, it requires the installation of memory-chip card reader technology at all 1500 BeingWell stores; secondly, as all current Loyalty Card administration software assumes a magnetic stripe card and the 'home-store' configuration, bespoke software needs to be developed to administer the scheme.

Whether to utilise in-house logistics?

A fundamental feature of the Mother & Baby Direct operation is the provision of warehousing, order picking and fulfilment. The existing logistics infrastructure to support 1500 BeingWell stores is an extensive operation, employing c6000 staff in central and regional warehouses, as well as seventeen regional distribution centres, plus a limited workforce of drivers, the majority being provided through three preferred contract haulage companies. With such a pedigree it is easy to understand why, when faced with the decision to either make new arrangements for this associated process or to utilise what was already in operation, the in-house option is the most pragmatic. However, the closely coupled nature of the call centre process to the other processes (fulfilment, logistics, and delivery), make it a highly integrated operation that requires close coordination of all the components.

Process specific and related decisions outside the boundary of the problem focus

The range of decisions that appeared outside the boundary of the problem focus varied between cases. The decisions ranged from the separation of written and oral work in the Customer Service call centre, through to extending the Loyalty Card scheme to other BeingWell Group companies. It also included some decisions that might have been expected to be positioned within the problem focus boundary, such as the provision of telephony (Customer Service case). However, it transpired that this was quite legitimate as the telephony in this case was considered a commodity and although central to the proposition in the case was easily obtained. The actors in the case were happy to accept its 'black-box' status.

Decision options and decision schemes

This section considers the impact of doubtful and incompatible option bars on the ability to generate feasible decision schemes. Figure 6.2 is a composite of the four option graphs used in this case that represent the option bars (solid lines), and doubtful options (dashed lines). We can see from the case studies that the number of option bars (including doubtful options) is inversely proportional to the number of feasible decision schemes generated, i.e. the greater the number of option bars the fewer feasible decision schemes can be generated. The range of possible options derived from the decision areas takes no account of the interconnectedness of these options, other than each option within a decision area should ideally be mutually exclusive. By comparing linked pairs of options from the different decision areas a 'compatibility matrix' is produced. This approach enables the deter-

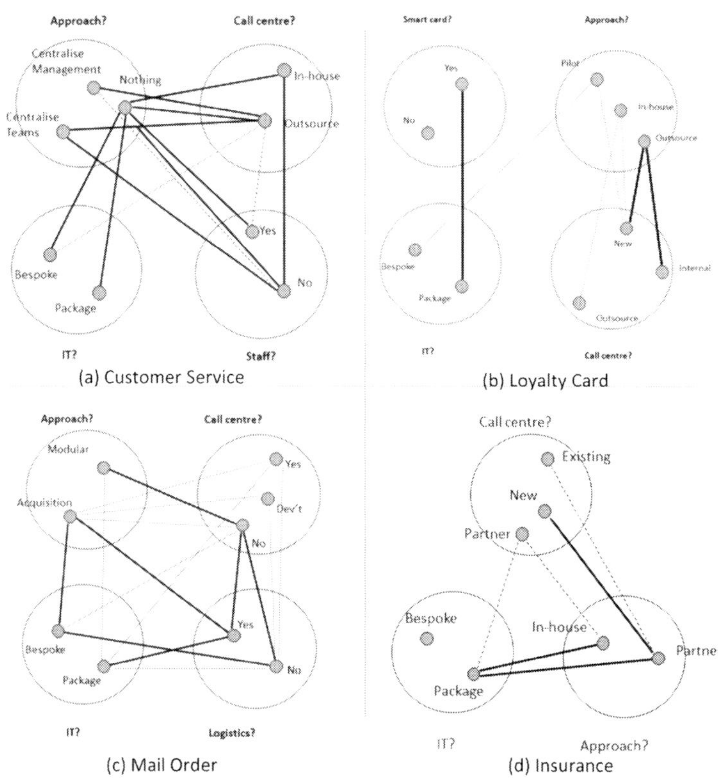

Figure 6.2: A composite of all four option graphs

mination of possible decision schemes, incompatible decision schemes (i.e. those schemes that include option bars), doubtful decision schemes where additional information is required or the likelihood is uncertain, and feasible decision schemes from which a likely solution might be found.

Table 6.5 shows the summary of the output from the compatibility matrices for the four cases.

CASE	DECISION SCHEMES			
	Possible decision schemes	Incompatible decision schemes	Doubtful decision schemes	Feasible decision schemes
CS	24	20	0	4
LC	36	15	13	8
MO	24	18	4	2
INS	12	7	2	3

Table 6.5: Summary of the compatibility matrix results

There were a wide variety in the number of possible, incompatible, and doubtful decision schemes. This had a direct impact on the number of feasible schemes that are accessible to each case. For example, in the Loyalty Card case the highly compatible nature of the decisions under consideration, as can be seen by the number of feasible decision schemes available to it (i.e. eight, four times that of the Mail Order case), with significantly reduced incompatible or doubtful options, could be treated as a commodity and easily outsourced. In contrast, the Mail Order case has only two feasible decision schemes available to it thereby suggesting a limited range of alternatives and reduced flexibility. It can therefore be seen that having high compatibility of options and a greater choice in decision schemes (i.e. flexibility), is important for a process to be considered a commodity.

Comparison areas of decision schemes

The comparison areas were derived from the outputs, objectives, or goals that were considered important by the actors in each case, and act as a measure of appropriateness of the alternative decision schemes. There is a significant spread of comparison areas being used in the four cases, which surprisingly includes few outputs, objectives or goals relating purely to the call centre. Table 6.6 displays the comparison areas in logical groupings along with the description of the comparison used and the associated measure. Notwithstanding a concentration of 'customer service' comparative criteria, which might be expected in the Customer Service case, there is no real pattern to the comparisons. Once again the uniqueness of each situation has been reflected in the variety and range of comparators emerging.

Managing uncertainty

SCA recognises three types of uncertainty when faced with decision making; these are (i) uncertainties about the working environment (labelled UE), usually resolved by obtaining more information, (ii) uncertainties about related decisions (labelled UR), usually resolved by improving coordination, and (iii) uncertainties about guiding values (labelled UV), usually resolved by providing clearer objectives. Tables 6.7, 6.8 and 6.9 contain the uncertainties expressed by the actors in each case, grouped into the three categories and ranked in order of salience (most salient first).

Uncertainties about the working environment appear to be the most frequent but this is quite normal for this type of analysis[xxvi]. Only those with a high salience (···) are likely to make any great impact in the case, and there is an even distribution of uncertainties listed against all four cases. The related decisions gave rise to uncertainties of availability of suitable office accommodation, the lack of Customer Service call centre experience, and the ability to cope with the rapid take-up as indicated by the trials. The true cost of outsourcing was unknown, and doubt was being expressed as to whether an in-house call centre could be used even if a partner was acquired, or the ability of a partner to undertake the administrative work while operating an in-house call centre. Uncertainties arising during the decision-making stages included doubt that packaged software would be more difficult to integrate than bespoke software, the assumption that in-house development resource would be available to build a bespoke application, the ability of an outsourced call centre to use 'company specific' bespoke software, the doubtful ability to support a mixed range of in-house and /or external modules with packaged software, the real time differences between packaged software adoption and bespoke development, and finally the ability for bespoke solutions to be a better fit with legacy systems than packages.

Bounded rationality and Satisficing

In three of the four cases (CS, LC and INS) the actual decision outcome in the case and the outcome from the SCA were closely aligned (i.e. the outcome was contained within the decision scheme options). As the analysis

COMPARISON AREAS OF DECISION SCHEMES			
COMPARISON AREA	CASE	DESCRIPTION	MEASURE
COST/PRICE/ VALUE	LC	Cost effective administration:	Effective ↔ Break even ↔ Ineffective
	CS	Cost:	High ↔ Medium ↔ Low
	MO	Value Based Management (VBM) case positive:	High ↔ Medium ↔ Low
CUSTOMER RELATIONSHIP/ SERVICE RELATIONSHIP	CS	Prompt and effective resolution of complaints:	Greater than 90% Less than 90%
	CS	Consistency of delivery in performance and communication:	High ↔ Medium ↔ Low
	CS	Opportunity for information feedback contributing to increased sales and profit:	Yes ↔ No
	CS	Maximise customer relationship opportunities:	High ↔ Medium ↔ Low
RISK/ COMPLIANCE	MO	Risk:	High ↔ Medium ↔ Low
	INS	Compliance with FSA and ABI requirements:	Yes ↔ No
GROWTH/ SCALABILITY/ EXPANSION	LC	The ability to enhance new initiatives:	Yes ↔ No
	LC	Scalability to include other BeingWell Group companies:	High ↔ Medium ↔Low
	LC	The ability to support new retail products and services	Good ↔ Average ↔Poor
	MO	Expansion potential:	Yes ↔ No
FLEXIBILITY	LC	Flexibility to cope with high demand:	High ↔ Medium ↔ Low
	INS	Flexibility to undertake all of the administrative operations if desired:	Easy ↔ Difficult ↔ Unlikely
BRAND/ REPUTATION/ VALUES	CS	Protection and enhancement of BW's reputation:	Good ↔ Poor
	INS	The ability to reflect BW brand values and service:	Good ↔ Average ↔ Poor
	MO	Brand protection:	Good ↔ Poor
SPEED	INS	Speed to market:	Fast ↔ Medium ↔ Slow
	MO	Speed to market:	Fast ↔ Medium ↔ Slow

Table 6.6: Comparison areas of decision schemes

CASE:	UNCERTAINTY AREA - UE	LABEL:	TYPE:	SALIENCE:
CS	From 'Managing customer relationships' comparison: ? That packaged software will be more difficult to integrate than bespoke software.	?PACKINT	UE	•••
CS	? The ability of an outsourced call centre to use 'company specific' bespoke software.	?BESPOUT	UE	•••
CS	? No real 'Customer Service' call-centre experience.	?EXPERT	UE	•••
CS	? Will a call centre improve customer service	?SERVPLUS	UE	•••
LC	? The true cost of outsourcing.	?OUTCOST	UE	•••
INS	From 'Speed to market' comparison: ? The ability for bespoke solutions to be a better fit with legacy systems than packages.	?LEGACY	UE	•••
INS	? Possible infeasibility of utilising the existing call centre while adopting the approach of working with a partner.	?CALLPART	UE	•••
CS	? The uncertainty of the project being worth the investment in in-house telephony	?TELINVEST	UE	••
LC	? The ability to cope with the rapid take-up as indicated by the trials.	?TAKE-UP	UE	••
MO	? The doubtful ability to support a mixed range of in-house and/or external modules with packaged software.	?PACKFIT	UE	••
MO	From 'Speed to market' comparison: ?The 'real' time differences between package adoption and bespoke development.	?BESDEV	UE	••
MO	? The likely levels of customer demand, average order size, and the impact of cannibalisation of sales.	?SALESPRO F	UE	••
INS	? The unknown volume and frequency of call-centre traffic.	?TRAFFIC	UE	••

Table 6.7: Uncertainty areas (UE)

CASE:	UNCERTAINTY AREA - UR	LABEL:	TYPE:	SALIENCE:
INS	From 'Flexibility to undertake all of the administrative operations if desired: comparison: ? The ability of the partner to undertake the administrative work while operating an in-house call-centre.	?FLEXADMIN	UR	•••
CS	From 'Cost' comparison: ? The assumption that in-house development resource will be available to bespoke an application.	?DEVSKILLS	UR	••
LC	? The likelihood of setting-up a new internal call centre when one already exists for another service.	?NEWCALL	UR	••
LC	? The likelihood of outsourcing the call centre when an 'in-house' administration option has been chosen.	?IN-OUT	UR	••
CS	? Availability of suitable office accommodation.	?ACCOM	UR	•
MO	From 'Speed to market' comparison: ? The ability to trade off quality in favour of speed.	?SPEEDQUAL	UR	•

Table 6.8: Uncertainty areas (UR)

CASE:	UNCERTAINTY AREA - UR	LABEL:	TYPE:	SALIENCE:
CS	? Soft benefits are difficult to quantify.	?SOFTBEN	UV	••
LC	From 'Scalability to include other BeingWell Group companies' comparison:? The real likelihood that other Group companies will require the Loyalty Card.	?GROUP CARD	UV	••
INS	From 'The ability to reflect BW brand values and service' comparison: ? The ability for a third party to adequately represent the brand values of BW.	?BRANDVAL	UV	••
MO	From 'Expansion potential' comparison: ? Will expansion potential be truly favourable, and more practical with third parties.	?EXPANPOT L	UV	•

Table 6.9: Uncertainty areas (UV)

is based on the views of the actors involved this confirms the validly of this approach as it should represent those views as it was meant to do. However, in one case (MO) the actual outcome was not represented as a possible decision scheme, which suggests that if the analysis was accurate (as it appears to be in the other cases), then the actual outcome is inconsistent with the objectives as described within the case. Bounded rationality[xxvii] is a central theme in the behavioural approach to economics, which is used to designate rational choice that takes into account the cognitive limitations of the decision maker. What this in fact does is to recognise the actual capacities (limitations) of the human mind in a decision-making situation, recognising that the optimum decision is not computable within feasible limits of effort. While there is no evidence to suggest that bounded rationality is the cause for this rogue outcome, it is useful to consider that there are practical limitations exaggerated by speed of decision-making, limited time, or just a shortage of know-how that could lead to a decision of this type.

Slow and strategic versus fast and technical

Davenport[xxviii], when describing the implementation alternatives for Enterprise Resource and Planning systems (ERP's), utilises a simple grid (Figure 6.3) to focus on the two key dimensions of 'speed of implementation', versus 'the amount of business change and value' to which the company aspires. Described as the 'fast-technical' implementation, this focuses on speed of implementation with as little business change as possible. This can mean quick relief to an existing system or new product/business initiative launch. The two options labelled 'strategic' attempt to maximise business change and value through a 'quick win' or 'long-term competitiveness', while the 'slow-technical' approach characterises a poor implementation. A common theme emerging from the four case studies in this thesis is the desire for a fast implementation, and there are numerous examples of how this desire for 'speed' has forced a tactical rather than strategic solution. While these might result in short-term benefits, they do not make for a robust long-term business solution. For example, the decision to utilise the BW store stock system in the Mother & Baby Direct warehouse in order to provide stock control functionality quickly was a 'fast-technical' implementation but at best could only provide quick relief without long-term stability.

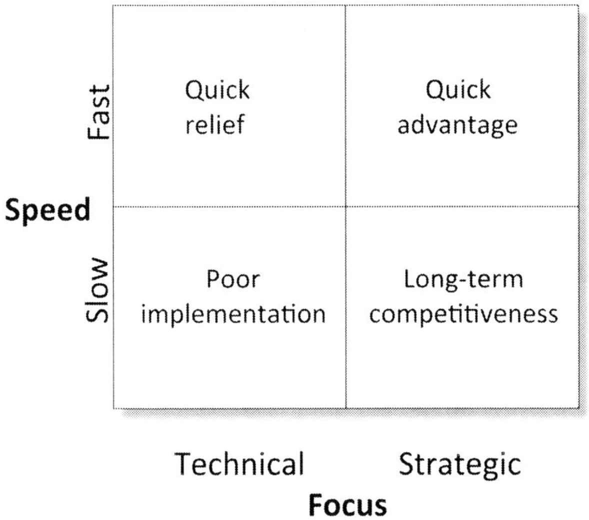

Figure 6.3: Alternative implementation approaches (Davenport 2000)

Decision logic summary

Building on the process logic summary in the first section, once again the uniqueness of each situation has been reflected in the variety and range of decisions that were taken in each case. The decision-making in all four cases was approached in a 'structured' way, i.e. recognising that they had strategic consequences, goals and objectives, an expectation of participation, and a recognition for orderly progression. The decision areas fell into two types labelled *'process specific'* decision areas, and *'related'* decision areas. There were a wide variety of decisions made within the problem focus boundary, which reflects the differing order in which they are taken, at different times, having different requirements, comprising different tasks, made by different actors, with different skills and abilities. For example, one component of the call centre process (people) was observed being treated in three different ways (the insistence of them being BeingWell own staff; the use of mail order specialists; and the low skill / low cost option). The variety and influence of the 'related decisions' also has a considerable impact on the final outcome. These decisions will often have no direct connection with the process in question, but they will influence the final outcome. For example, the chain of dependent decisions that arose from the decision to use a smart card in the Loyalty Card case, which in turn triggered software and hardware decisions. Uncertainty about the working environment is prominent in the related decisions, and the speed of implementation can force short-term and unsustainable decisions. Option bars and doubtful options are inversely proportional to the number of feasible decisions schemes generated, and there were a wide variety and range of comparison areas in use.

One important observation is that where there are more feasible decision schemes processes are treated as commodities. This leads to the question – how do processes (in their business aspects) come to be treated as commodities?

6.4 Alignment Logic

Introduction

This section examines the alignment (and non-alignment) of the actors in the network with the aid of three concepts from actor network theory: *inscription* – embodied patterns of use or behaviour, *translation* - how actors manipulate or force other actors into positions that suit themselves, and *irreversibility* – the strength of the inscription. The analysis in this section uses the inscription/specialisation analysis framework to help understand these concepts as seen in the four case studies. The areas of alignment and non-alignment for the components of each process are considered initially, followed by evidence of inscription and translation. This then leads to an analysis of the movement between different states over time and the subsequent irreversibility of the inscriptions and translations.

Alignment of the actors in the network

Figure 6.4 shows the inscription/specialisation analysis framework with the process components from each case plotted together in groupings of (a) software, (b) people, (c) telephony, (d) accommodation, and (e) miscellaneous. Once again it is apparent that despite the similarity of the processes in question there are significant differences in alignment of the actors, for example: (i) the telephony and accommodation components occupy the 'black-box' space in all cases and are therefore fully aligned; (ii) there is a significant difference between the alignment of the 'people' components in the Customer Service and Loyalty Card cases (black-box), and the alignment in the Mail Order and Insurance cases (Transformation); (iii) the relative isolation that the software application package for Customer Service enjoys in the 'black-box' space, when compared with all the other software deployed in the cases, and (iv) in the Mail Order case the use of Express Packages as a courier on the border of the aligned and non-aligned space reflects the third party translation that is present, however there is total alignment that it is a commodity, reflected in its positioning to the left of the framework.

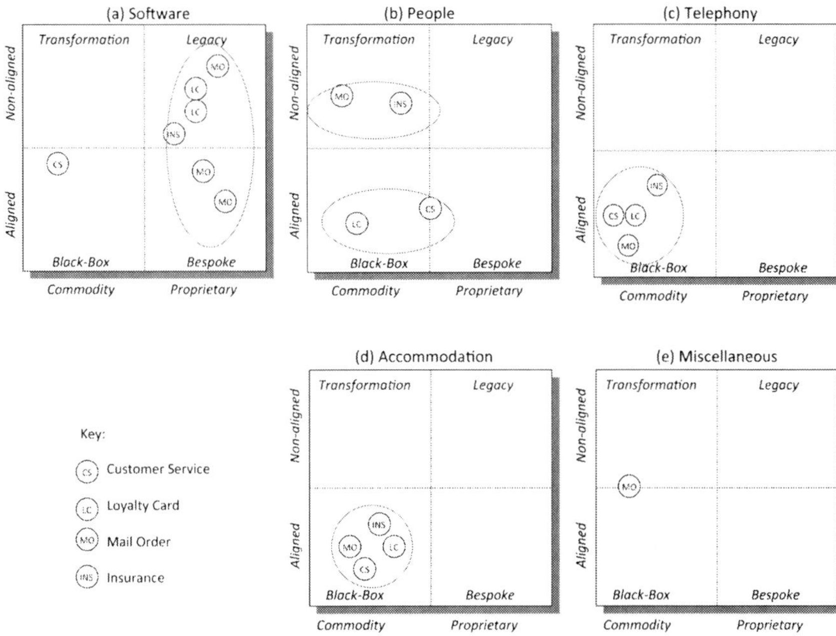

Figure 6.4: Case study process components grouped by type

The sections that follow examine the telephony and accommodation, the people, and the software in more detail.

Telephony and accommodation

Telephony and accommodation consistently appeared in the black-box space, but there is a need to be clear that this is not suggesting that telephony and or accommodation would always occupy this space. In a quite different process the accommodation required might be central to the proposition, for example the location and proximity of a retail outlet to its customers as part of a sales process, and therefore be more susceptible to changes in requirements. Standard office accommodation was adequate in each of the cases studied. The telephony requirements in these cases were also very similar, and although provided through different means i.e. rented from a cable company, or a system purchased from a vendor and operated in-house, the functionality was consistent. It was generally accepted by the actors that whatever was required from a telephony perspective was likely to be possible, and it was accepted (at least in this industry sector) that the equipment and services would have the capability to do what was required of it. The telecommunications industry is strictly regulated and compliance with standards and protocols is vital to preserve connectivity and the integrity of the telephone networks. Consequently there are a variety of vendors offering managed services, lease and rental arrangements, as well as companies such as BT and Lucent selling the telephony capability (equipment and services) for the provision of DIY services, but all comply to the same standards and protocols. However, the choice of deployment can have an impact on the degree of inscription. For example, the influence a telephony provider can have on the business process will be restricted as far as the functionality it provides, but it can have significant commercial and contractual influence through the rents charged for the use of the equipment or service.

In the Mail Order case the telephony component was so closely coupled to the provision of the call centre capability from a third party, that it almost disappeared from the view of those involved. While this does give the vendor (in this case Mailsales) the opportunity for a high degree of inscription, it had reached a point where the actors in the network were so comfortable with such a low visibility of the telephony that it became almost undetectable despite its criticality. The more automatic something appears, even the simplest device, which might attract little or no attention, will not persist without the intervention of people[xxix]. For example the Kodak instant camera, which we all take for granted, requires an army of technicians, engineers and scientists to make it work and to continue to develop and enhance it. If this has become a 'black-box', then the *"blacker the black box is"*, the more likely it is that it will rely on 'people' to ensure that it has momentum.

People engaged in the call centre process

The people involved in the call centre process have commodity skills: knowing how to handle calls by following pre-defined scripts and prompts is no longer a proprietary skill, any competent person can do it. Described as unskilled or semiskilled labour *"easy to replace and low value add"*, and while any organisation might need plenty of these people its success does not depend on them as individuals[xxx]. One candidate is likely to be as good as another, typically training time is short, and one good advert would attract many suitable candidates.

In the Customer Service and Loyalty Card cases there was clear alignment of the interests of the actors in the network with regard to the people involved albeit for quite different reasons. In the Loyalty Card case the task of the call centre operators was considered quite simple, the routines were easy to handle and required no specialist know-how or training, and all the actors agreed with this view. However, in the Customer Service case there was a perceived 'value' to BeingWell that the Customer Service Advisors should be their own employees, even though the skills of the people engaged in the call centre were fundamentally viewed as commodity skills. Being the shared view of all the actors involved legitimised this view. Despite the circumstances being very different the important issue is that there is active support for both these respective views and therefore they are both fully aligned.

In the two cases where the call centre was outsourced (Mail Order and Insurance) there was little alignment of the interests of the actors in the network with regard to the people engaged in the call centre process, and there is evidence of opportunities being taken to translate other actors in the network. For example, this non-alignment manifests itself in both cases as *'intermediate governance'*[xxxi], i.e. the complex contracts, procedures and arrangements BeingWell put in place so as to guard against opportunism. This included insisting on being involved with the delivery of training to their agents' employees, on being involved with the recruitment, and on having an on-site presence to check how the business was being managed.

Software used in the call centre process

An immediate contrast can be seen between the software package used in the Customer Service case (Enquiry Q) which is within the black-box space, and that of the remainder of the software products that are largely bespoke developments with varying degrees of alignment of the actors in the network. In the customer service case, a standard product Enquiry Q was purchased and, using the parameter driven software and 'user exits' that allow for local customisation, was modified to suit the then limited requirements. It was a conscious and deliberate action by the project team to contain the implementation of procedures that could be supported by this software product in an attempt to keep ongoing support costs and complexity to a minimum. However, on a number of occasions it was acknowledged that the limited functionality was placing a restriction on the business requirements (for example the integration of Enquiry 'Q' with the Loyalty Card Operating System). Abrahamson's work [xxxii] on fads and fashions emphasises how firms adopt what appear to be effective and efficient solutions, rather than because they actually are. Scarborough[xxxiii] extends this by describing how suppliers build on this perception by 'blackboxing' new solutions suggesting that they will 'fit' in any situation. However, at the time of implementation the actors involved in this case universally accepted this approach. The benefits of using 'vanilla software[23]' are described as 'tactical' flexibility[xxxiv], i.e. the flexibility gained by utilising a standard product was at the expense of long-term strategic flexibility. Robertson and Powell suggest that flexibility, albeit a nebulous attribute may be either tactical or strategic. 'Tactical flexibility' attempts to account for perceived (or known) future occurrences, and strategic flexibility concentrates on the ability to differentiate for competitive advantage.

In contrast, the software that handled the Loyalty Card operation (LSOS) was originally commissioned as a bespoke development from a third party, as at that time BeingWell 'Loyalty Card' was the only 'smart-card' based loyalty scheme in Europe, and had quite specific requirements when considering its longer-term development. Its accompanying software (CDAS) was also a bespoke development by a third party, both products being supported by third parties. Fleck[xxxv] described as *'Innofusion'* the concept where users' system design changes are reflected in the vendor's product and adopted as best practice (an opportunity for inscription from the customer to the supplier). These modifications to systems design introduced by users are taken up by the IS suppliers, and further diffused to the wider community.

In the Insurance case the service being provided was a new business venture and didn't exactly fit with any existing software products on offer. However, the know-how of the insurance requirements at MIG facilitated the approach of taking one of their in-house bespoke software systems and adapting it to suit the BW products. Although recognised as an expedient approach, the inflexibility of the software, lack of functionality, and reliance on MIG to make changes generated a negative perception of the software, and the ever growing list of enhancements and changes was testimony to this, hence its non-aligned status.

In the Mail Order case there are three main software components: the mail order system, the warehouse stock management, and the order placing system. Choosing a specialist mail order partner meant that the preferred software product of that partner (in this case Mail-it) became the default software option. This resulted in many changes to Mail-it, some of them quite detailed, in order to provide the functionality required. This was further complicated by the need to interface with several other non-standard software products that were required within the process such as the Loyalty Card interface and the promotional deals system. The reliance on the vendors to coordinate the changes, the inability to support similar promotional activity as in-store, plus the inability to remain on supported versions because of the number of changes applied, all contributed to the non-aligned view of this product. The other two software products, one the stores stock

23 Vanilla software refers to using the developers' standard product i.e. as in a 'vanilla ice cream (no additional flavours).

system (EPSOM), the other a bespoke order placement system (Logica) while not ideal were accepted as being aligned for what they were intended.

Externalities and overflowing

Callon[xxxvi] describes 'the impossibility of total framing' or what he calls *'overflowing'* when externalities (that is what economists describe as all the connections, relations and effects which are not taken into account when entering a market transaction) have an impact on a process. For example, Express Packages had an agenda in the mail order case to influence the returns procedures in use so that it suited their own method of working. This need not be a negative impact because the outcome of the changes might be mutually beneficial to both parties. However it does highlight the different approaches and drivers of the actors involved. Where 'fusion' of external knowledge/artefacts/methods with internal knowledge/procedures/systems, had changed both in the process phenomenon, has been labelled as *'Articulation'*[xxxvii]. Hislop et al go on to assert that the degree of commodification of the process will influence the articulation process. *"In general, the more commodified a technological system is, the more easily transferable it is. Conversely, the more commodified a system is the more difficult it is for the company adopting it to modify and contextualise it".*

Methods of inscription observed during the cases

Trials, pilots, and speed of implementation

Adopting the trial or pilot approach to implementation is an ideal opportunity to legitimately facilitate translation and inscription activity, and several of the cases suggested that the approach to the business problem was as if it were a trial or pilot. Trials and pilots can easily become 'de facto' standards (i.e. they default to the trial option and never get reviewed and become a legacy), but the incomplete nature of trials and pilots openly allows alternative suggestions and operating options to be legitimately tabled at the expense of a prolonged implementation process.

Hierarchical, intermediate, and market governance.

In the Mail Order case the call centre was under the control of a third party organisation, yet BeingWell insisted on being actively involved in the governance procedures (i.e. the direction and control of affairs, policies, and functions of the call centre). For example, the recruitment and training of staff and the incentive schemes used to motivate staff. Barney[xxxviii] describes three types of governance that have their roots in transaction cost economics; they are market, intermediate, and hierarchical governance. Market governance is perhaps that which is most associated with the provision of commodities. Where companies deal at arm's length and rely on market-determined prices to manage an exchange, but they do run the risk of opportunism when a transaction-specific investment is involved. In contrast, hierarchical governance is applicable when an exchange is brought within the boundary of the firm. For instance when the Loyalty Card call centre was brought in-house the parties to the exchange were no longer independent so control could be exercised in any decision-making. Finally, Intermediate governance, the use of complex contracts, strategic alliances, and joint ventures is applicable when partnering to form a joint venture. An example is the joint venture between BWIS and MIG in the insurance case. Therefore the successful commoditisation of a process will rely on a healthy market governance approach to issues, which is both manageable by the agent and acceptable to the principal.

The influence of key actors in the network

Although actors need not be people, typically the arbiters on decisions concerning the 'design' of a process (and for design read 'what' is done rather than an elaborate engineering activity) are those most closely concerned with the product or service. They will view the process (if they even consider it as a process), from a viewpoint of the 'what' is done and less so the 'how'. Describing a concept called the 'deeper structure', Kutschker[xxxix] suggests that:

> *"The designers produce designs of business processes based on their perception, explanation, and understanding of organisational reality. Values, beliefs, attitudes, and facts are the bits of knowledge of organisational reality".*

In each of the cases examined earlier key actors emerged as being dominant, yet despite this domination and regardless of their position of power, without the alignment of the actors in the network the impact was not sustained in the long run. For example, the insistence by the Mother & Baby Direct Product Manager to use third-party resources in the call centre was eventually overturned, or the pressure applied by the BW Chief Executive to launch the Insurance products quickly and the subsequent change of arrangements at contract renewal. It would take more than the decision by a key actor for a non-commodity process to be considered a commodity, or vice versa just because they want it to be.

Evidence of translation and inscription activity taking place in the non-aligned space

A number of the cases had components that were considered 'commodities' but they also occupied the 'non-alignment' space of the framework, thus signifying the pressure of potential translations from actors in the network. Table 6.10 utilises Hanseth and Monteiro's[xl] 'four key aspects of inscription' to illustrate the current translation activity for those components that were categorised as 'non-aligned'. The table consists of four columns: Column (i), which identifies the explicit anticipations (or scenarios) held by some of the actors during translation; Column (ii), describes how the inscriptions are translated and inscribed into the materials of the inscription (e.g. systems, procedures etc.); Column (iii), lists the actors who inscribe them; and, Column (iv), describes the strength of the inscription (i.e. the effort it takes to oppose or work around them).

The anticipations or scenarios are a mix of both 'what' should be done, for example that LSOS should form the core of a CRM approach; and also 'how' they are conducted, e.g. the outsourcing of the Mail Order call centre in order to secure access to staff perceived as having the appropriate 'specialist' skills. The inscriptions are a mix of formal and overt activity, such as compliance with union regulations or the willing acceptance of advice given by an internal legal Advisor, through to uncooperative behaviour taking every opportunity to discredit that that is the subject of the inscription. Typically the inscribers are formal groups or individuals (a mix of both internal and external to the organisation), but could also be informal groups (competitors), or even intangible artefacts such as the organisations culture. The strength of the inscription is a relative measure rather than an absolute one.

Movement around the inscription/specialisation framework

The case studies as summarised in Figure 6.4 describe the positioning of the process components at their inception. Figure 6.5 shows the movement of some of the process components over a three-year time period.

EVIDENCE OF TRANSLATION AND INSCRIPTION ACTIVITY IN THE NON-ALIGNED SPACE			
(i) Anticipations (Scenarios)	(ii) How they are being translated	(iii) Who inscribes them	(iv) The strength of the inscription
That the Loyalty Scheme Operating System (LSOS), should provide the core of a Customer Relationship Management (CRM) facility	Constant requests for new functionality, coupled with the citing of inadequacies of LSOS, as the reason for not implementing new ideas and business initiatives.	Marketing departments who have these requirements and are not associated with the Loyalty Card scheme.	Despite the obvious advantages, to date this inscription has always ranked less important to those who have the decision-making authority.
That LSOS and CDAS should be operated in-house by the Information Systems Department who have a wealth of experience in running large mainframe applications.	The indifferent service provided by IBM has provided numerous opportunities to challenge the current arrangements, and to demonstrate a lower cost of ownership if operated in-house.	Information Systems Department Management	Very strong. Upon the expiry of the existing contract new arrangements are being made to remove the support from a third party and bring it in-house.
The mail order courier 'Express Packages' wants to incorporate the BeingWell work into their normal operating procedures.	By being prescriptive about the methods they should operate (e.g. the returns procedures if goods previously delivered are faulty or damaged).	The Account Management team at Express Packages.	Some minor changes to the refunds procedures have been instigated by Express Packages.
That the design of the 'Mail-it' system should be modular and kept as generic as possible.	Encouraging long lead times for changes and enhancements, and inflated costs for systems development work.	The systems vendors (Johnsons), and the Agents for the system (Mailsales).	The bespoke changes made to the BeingWell version of Mail-it cannot be upgraded to any later versions supplied by the vendor.
That the skills and experience required for a quality mail order operation were only available from 3rd parties.	An emphasis on the need to use a call centre that had a strong 'sales' orientation and a blue-chip client base (e.g. Harrods).	The call centre Project Manager.	Although a view that was seen as important at the time of the process design, there is a subtle shift to now consider alternatives.
The implementation of manning levels and supervisory structures at MIG were considered by BeingWell to be excessive.	The rigid adherence to agreements made with the incumbent Trades Union.	MIG Management Team and Union representatives	Very strong. These were never amended (despite much activity) during the life of the case.
The inability to take a flexible approach and adapt the NEWTON software to meet the business requirements.	Constant requests for amendments and changes to the bespoke software.	BeingWell Insurance Operations and Marketing Teams.	Considered an irreconcilable issue when reviewing contract renewals.

Table 6.10: Current translation activity in the four case studies

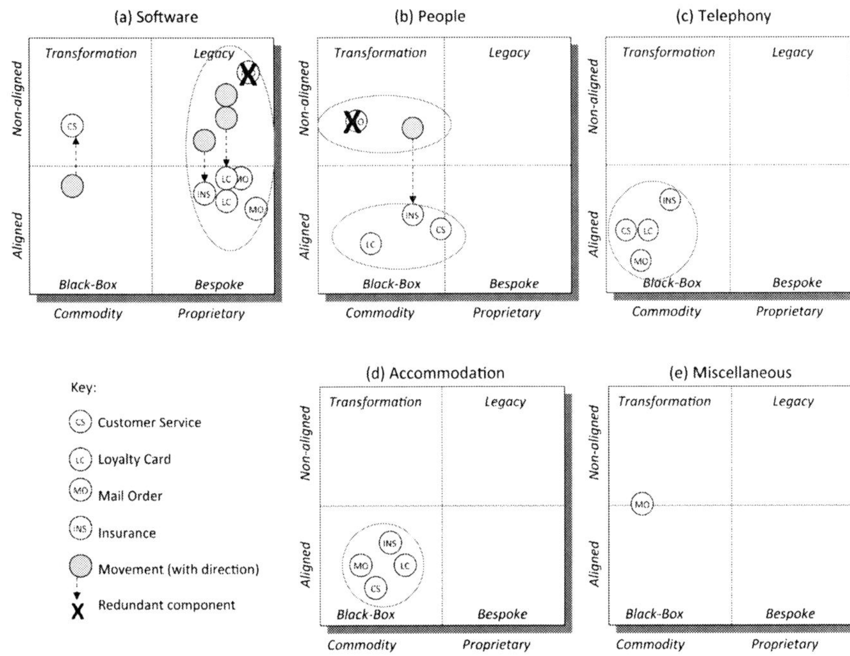

Figure 6.5: Movement due to inscription/translation over time

Initially two of the process components in the Insurance case (people, and software (NEWTON)), were positioned in the 'transformation' and 'legacy' space respectively. A key decision taken early on was to keep the call centre and the associated administration closely coupled, and to use the services of the partner organisation (MIG) to provide these services, a view that MIG clearly supported and inscribed. This meant that BWIS were using third party staff and systems to run their business. There had been a keen desire by BWIS to influence the staff, their training and development, and concerns were expressed about the flexibility and functionality of the NEWTON system. Although this was the view at the inception, when reviewing the arrangements some three years later, with the benefit of the experience of running the operation, the views had changed significantly. The joint realisation by both partners that the unit cost of administering each sale, coupled with the emergence of third party administrators (TPA's) who could undertake the administration separately from the underwriting of the insurance risk, meant that new opportunities were now possible. This de-coupling was legitimised by MIG who now had new information about their own cost structures for this product type that influenced their own strategic direction. This helped in the translation to their new view. Although this process was not considered a commodity at its inception, these developments actively move 'people' and 'software' into the aligned space, as BWIS had learned that third parties *can* effectively operate such a call centre. This positively reflects the growing confidence BWIS has in third parties to undertake the work to the required standard. Similarly, the new software provided by the TPA's is significantly better than the NEWTON system. This looser coupling (or commodification) means that the power of the single third party has been reduced and flexibility to utilise other third-party organisations has been created.

In complete contrast the Customer Service software (Enquiry Q) has been a stable and robust product, but as the call centre develops into new areas of activity this software is increasingly considered an inhibitor to undertaking CRM activity. The inability of the product to interface with existing legacy systems is also seen as an inhibitor. For these reasons the software has moved into the non-aligned space as the pressure mounts to choose an alternative.

The same CRM activity has created pressure to develop LSOS by adding functionality to become the core of a CRM application. As a result concern that a strategically important system such as LSOS is administered by a third-party has grown to such an extent that the decision has been taken to bring it in-house at a suitable point when the contract allows. CDAS has also been fully adopted and is administered in house. Although both are bespoke applications they have now moved into the aligned space.

Telephony and accommodation components remain unchanged. This continues to endorse their commodity status in this process. Express Packages (mail order couriers) remains on the aligned/non-aligned border. Several of the mail order components eventually perished as the mail order business was subsumed into the e-commerce channel.

Alignment logic summary

Using the inscription/specialisation analysis framework the alignment of the actors in the network was assessed for the components of the call centre process. As was the case with both the process logic, and the decision logic, it is apparent that despite the similarity of the processes in question there are significant differences in alignment of the actors in the network. The strength of the alignment of actors (irreversibility) was demonstrated by two decisions in the Customer Service case (to insist on using BeingWell own staff in the call centre, and the determination to work within the boundary of a software package to limit complexity). Both were fully supported by the actors in the network. In complete contrast the decision to outsource LSOS did not have the same degree of support and subsequently that decision was overturned.

The evidence of inscription and translation activity highlights the eclectic mix in the sources of inscription/translation activity. For example, the opportunities for inscription that trials and pilots present, the impact of intermediate governance, the influence of key or powerful actors such as the Chief Executive. The alignment of actors is a dynamic phenomenon as was demonstrated by the movement over time of the people in the Insurance case, the software in the Loyalty Card and Insurance cases, and ultimately the shift from an aligned view of the packaged software in the Customer Service case to a non-aligned view as the business requirements changed over time.

6.5 Integration of the three logics of commoditisation

Introduction

In this final section, the 'patterns of activity' identified in the earlier sections can be represented in a model by the three central logics of commodity business process adoption, which are the process logic, decision logic, and alignment logic. The term 'model' is used as per Suppe (1977)[xli], and later Pettigrew and Whipp (1991)[xlii], *as "a projection in detail of a theoretical position, which depicts a possible system of relationships, events and actions"*. It is not intended as being prescriptive, or a complete checklist, but as a representation of how the mechanisms operate. The model has emerged from examining four internal corporate ventures in one major UK retailer, each endeavouring to establish a call centre process. The result is the identification of a pattern of activity that arises from the observable differences in the way that components of the process, decision, and alignment logic act as either 'facilitators' of commodity adoption, or in contrast 'inhibitors'.

The construction of the model

The model (Figure 6.6) is made up of three vertical sections headed in turn 'process logic characteristics', 'decision logic characteristics', and 'alignment logic characteristics'. Overlaid upon each section are the characteristics that are principally associated with the process, the decision-making, or alignment of actors. The characteristics are not exclusive to one section, some overlap as they apply in both sections. For example, 'low uncertainty' can be characteristic of a reasonably straightforward decision to be made, or similarly of a commodity process. Some of the characteristics could also be linked, for example 'high uncertainty' is linked to 'trials and pilots' thus highlighting the relationship between the propensity to enter trials and pilots where uncertainty is high. It follows that the uncertainty can be reduced from the experience of a trial or pilot. The characteristics shown here are not considered a complete set, as it is envisaged that others might emerge when examining different processes. The process characteristics identified within the case studies are plotted on the model (in a vertical plane) according to their ability to 'inhibit' commodity adoption i.e. above the inhibitor threshold line, or 'facilitate' commodity adoption i.e. below the facilitation threshold line. Those appearing between the two thresholds are neither conclusively inhibitors or facilitators (labelled crossover). Although the model implies a continuous graduation from the most inhibiting characteristic at the top, to the most facilitating at the bottom, the relative positioning is perhaps the most meaningful. For example, the positioning of 'asset specific investment' in the inhibitor space reflects the lack of general applicability and flexibility of such an investment that is much better suited to optimisation. Similarly, 'commodity components' would clearly be synergistic to, and a facilitating characteristic of, commodity processes (such as telephony in a call centre). The four segments of the inscription/specialisation framework graduate the alignment logic from 'legacy' as the most inhibiting to commodity process adoption, through 'bespoke' and 'transformation' to 'black-box' as the most facilitating.

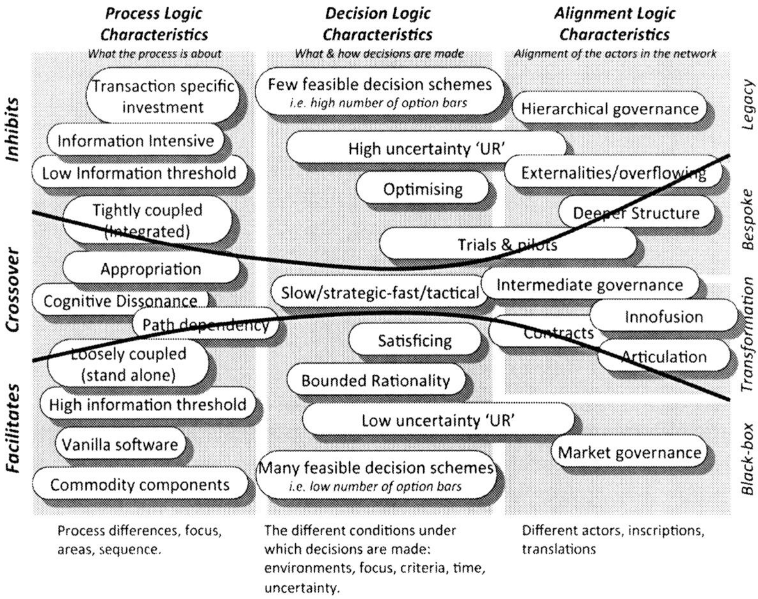

Figure 6.6: Conceptual model of commodity business process adoption: the three central factors (See Appendix 2 – Glossary of terms).

To take each section in order:

The process logic

The first section shows the 'process logic characteristics', i.e. *what the process is actually about* (Figure 6.7).

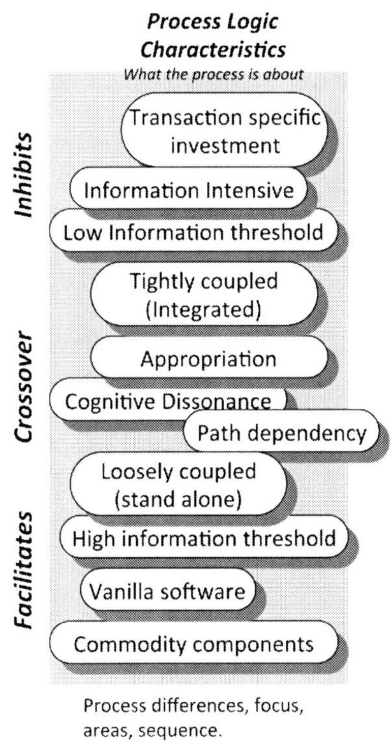

Figure 6.7: Conceptual model – Process Logic characteristics

The characteristics in this section relate directly to the process e.g. that it is information intensive, or has commodity components, or alternatively that it might be the subject of a transaction specific investment. The characteristics of a particular process at any given time might not all reside within one area of the section, and characteristics of a process can change, placing it in different areas of the section over time. For example, the change in strategic importance of the Customer Service call centre as it migrates to become the heart of the bourgeoning CRM activity. Therefore the process characteristics aren't necessarily static, but can be dynamic.

The decision logic

The second perspective is the 'decision logic characteristics', i.e. *'what' decisions are made, and 'how' those decisions are made,* which will also reflect the different conditions under which decisions are being made (Figure 6.8). For example, where there are few feasible decision schemes to choose from, i.e. there are a high number of option bars, then this naturally limits the possible scope making it more difficult to conform to a process which might need to be prescriptive (a feature of its commodity status). However, where there are few option bars this then increases the relative number of feasible decision schemes, and along with them the realistic chance of conformity to a commodity process, i.e. greater choice.

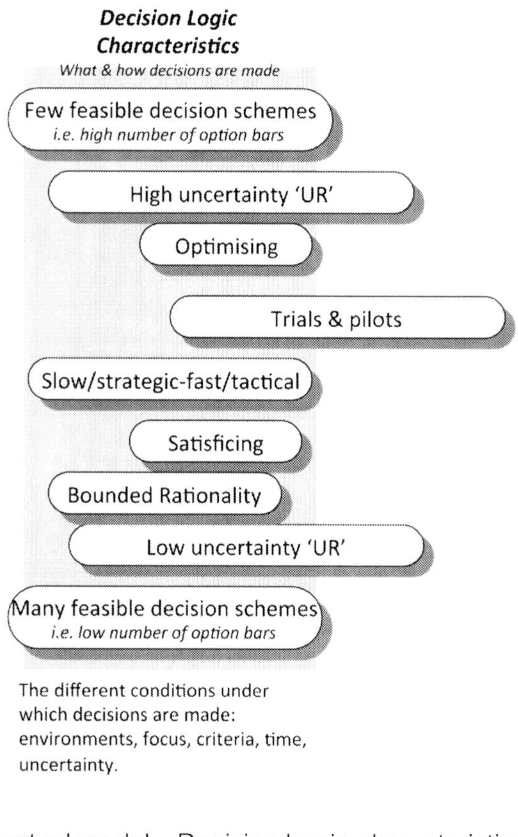

Figure 6.8: Conceptual model – Decision Logic characteristics

Davenport & Prusak (1998)[xliii] describe as "frictions" the many cultural factors that inhibit and prevent knowledge transfer as it tries to move through an organisation, for example, lack of trust, dissimilar culture, vocabulary or frames of reference. Similarly, they also assert that the size of an organisation will be a critical factor. While the probability of the required knowledge being resident within a large and more complex organisation is greater than in a smaller organisation, so is the likelihood that the knowledge is not held locally, or in fact that anyone knows where it exists. What became apparent during this research is that the know-how about call centres didn't transfer very well between cases despite being established at about the same time and the wealth of information and experience the Customer Service call centre had amassed. Once again, depending on individual circumstances the decision characteristics need not be static within one area, as was observed in the Loyalty Card case where despite the initial outsourced implementation being a 'fast / tactical' and satisficing approach, this quickly changed to a slow / strategic optimising approach when 'insourced'.

The alignment logic

The final perspective is that of the 'alignment logic characteristics', i.e. *'the alignment of the actors in the network'*. The alignment logic space is divided into the four characteristics as determined from the inscription / specialisation analysis framework, with 'legacy' being the most extreme inhibitor, through bespoke, transformation, and finally black box, which is the most facilitating characteristic (Figure 6.9).

The alignment of the actors is an important and powerful characteristic, which was emphasised by the almost unanimous alignment of the actors in the Customer Service case to support an in-house call centre against all the odds. This alignment was even strong enough to resist making changes to the software products. We have already seen how alignment moves through inscription / specialisation due to inscription and translation activity, and as a growing group of actors consider CRM to be a strategic way forward then the interest in Customer Service, and the functions it operates, are scrutinized.

Movement over time

Figure 6.10 shows a plot of the conceptual model of commodity business process adoption for each case over three time periods (years 1, 3 and 5). The figure emphasises the variety between cases at different stages of their development, with year one (highlighted) showing a completely different

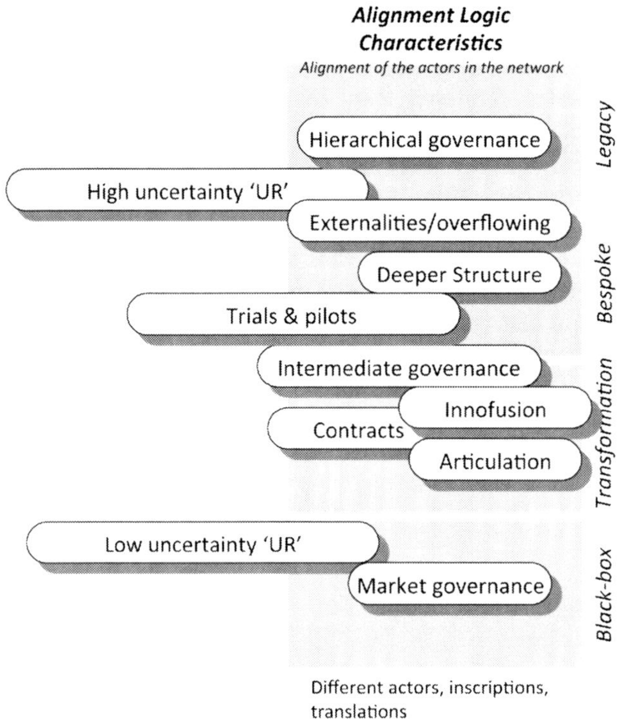

Figure 6.9: Conceptual model – Alignment Logic characteristics

pattern of activity, and starting position for each case, and the subsequent moves through the following years.

The Customer Service case has seen a significant shift in process logic from 'facilitating' to 'inhibiting'. This was largely the result of the shift away from a relative straightforward customer service facility, to a more complex and integrated CRM approach. The decision logic has remained static within 'crossover', and alignment logic within 'bespoke'. The Loyalty Card case now appears to be treated less as a commodity as it has moved out of the 'facilitating' area in both process and alignment logic that will have been influenced by the amalgamation with the Customer Service call centre. The Mail Order case showed no discernible changes before it was closed. However, the Insurance case has shown a significant movement towards commodity with all three logics now considered facilitating. This reflects how it is possible to learn to adopt a commodity process over time. This accurately reflects the Insurance case make up of commodity components, flexibility in options, and acceptance of market governance.

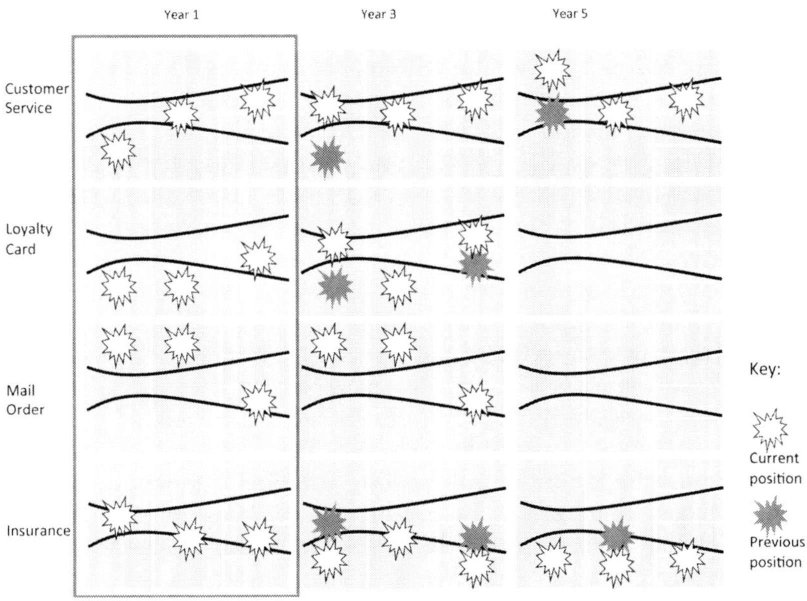

Figure 6.10[24]**:** Plot of the conceptual model of commodity business process adoption

Commodity adoption at different levels of the firm

Although not explicitly discussed within each case, the adoption of commodity business processes in practice takes place at a number of different levels within the businesses concerned. From the four cases we have seen how commodity adoption (of components or full processes) can be at the level of (i) the department, as in the Customer Service case; (ii) the Strategic Business Unit (SBU), as with Mother & Baby Direct; or (iii) at the corporate level, such as Group Telecommunications act of purchasing the telephony equipment on a group-wide basis. This adds a level of complexity to the final outcome as we have seen that decisions are made within the context of the particular business need or situation at a particular point in time. This being the case, then consistency across a multi-business organisation will require specific activity to ensure architectural alignment at the level of the project, programme, department, or corporate levels, can be achieved. The adoption of a complete commodity business process could be a multi-step operation, which might involve a mix of commodity, leveraged and proprietary components while working towards adoption.

24 Year 5: Loyalty Card had merged with Customer Service, Mail Order had ceased to operate, and Insurance had only been trading for four years at that time.

6.5 Summary

This chapter brings together the within-case and cross-case analysis from earlier chapters, and concludes by integrating the three logics of commoditisation (process, decision, and alignment). The chapter opens with the analysis of the process logic, which concludes that despite the 'core' of the process being similar (i.e. the tasks and activities undertaken), the unique context (surround) in which each process is operating, is fairly specific to that situation. The surround can be specific in its information exchange content; its connectedness with related decisions, processes and systems; the culture within which it operates; and the practical limitations of utilising existing infrastructure, software and equipment. Similarly, the mechanisms available to recognise when the relevant capability has been achieved, or the existence, availability, and level of relevant know-how, all go towards creating a *distinctive* situation in each case. The decision logic follows-on and continues the theme of uniqueness, which is significant enough to generate major differences in the decisions being taken in each case. Typically comprising *'process specific'* decisions and *'related'* decisions, there is a wide variety in the scope, order, requirements, timescales, and uncertainty contained within them. Despite the similarity at the core of the business process, the process specific decisions cover a wide range of issues, as do the related decisions which contain those decisions that are fundamental to the process in question and reflect the diversity of contexts in each case. The flexibility to choose between feasible decision schemes is inversely proportional to the number of option bars, and thus the degree of difference between cases builds up. The alignment logic exemplifies the variety in the way that actors view the decisions to be addressed, and how the individual views of the actors involved influence the final outcome. The strength of that alignment (irreversibility) to either adopt or reject commodity business processes (or their components) is dynamic and can change over time. Finally, components of business processes can act as 'facilitators' or 'inhibitors' of commodity process adoption, and the conceptual model of business process adoption reflects the interconnectedness of those components, and that of the three logics. For commodity process to be adopted:

- the process itself has to have features that are similar to other commonly used processes supported by other actors;
- the decision process must not be constrained by too many factors that mitigate against commodity adoption:
- the various actors involved (internal and external) must be aligned behind the belief that the process is a commodity.

In the cases examined here over time, the nature of the process itself ultimately dominated the choice of whether to treat a process as a commodity or not. The distorting factors in the decision process and initial lack of alignment tend to play themselves out. This led in some cases to the adoption of a commodity approach and in others to its rejection. The availability of suitable commodity processes to adopt, also changes over time as illustrated by the appearance of third-party administrators in the insurance case. As the market matures and more options become available, a commodity approach becomes more feasible. However, it is open to a company to decide to reject the notion of a commodity approach and make the design of their in-house processes a source of differentiation.

NOTES ON CHAPTER

i KEEN, P.G.W. and KNAPP, E.M., 1996. *Every managers Guide to Business Processes: a glossary of key terms and concepts for today's business leaders*. Boston: Harvard Business School Press.

ii PENTLAND, B.T., 1994. Process Grammars: A Generative Approach to Process Redesign. In: *New Imperatives for Managing in Revolutionary change, Tokyo, Japan, August 1994.*

iii MALONE, T.W., CROWSTON, K., LEE, J., & PENTLAND, B.T. (1993). Tools for inventing organizations: Toward a handbook of organizational processes. In *Proceedings of Second Workshop on Enabling Technologies: Infrastructure for Collaborative Enterprises* (pp. 72-82). Morgantown, WV: IEEE Computer Society Press.

iv SALANCIK, G.R., and LEBLEBICI, H., 1988. Variety and Form in Organizing Transactions: A Generative Grammar of Organization. In: N. DiTomaso and S.B. Bacharach (Eds.). *Research in the Sociology of Organizations*. Greenwich, CT: JAI Press. 1-32.

v HALE, J., 1995. *From concepts to capabilities – understanding and exploiting change as a competitive advantage*. London: Wiley.

vi STANTON, S., 1999. How process enterprises really work. Harvard Business Review, November/December, 108.

vii DAVENPORT, T.H., 2000. *Mission Critical, Realizing the promise of Enterprise Systems*. Boston, MA: Harvard Business School Press.

viii TENG J.T., GROVER V. and FIELDER K.D., 1994. Business Process Reengineering: Charting a strategic path for the information age. *California Management Review*, 36, (23), 9.

ix KOCK, N.F., Jr., McQUEEN, R.J., and CORNER, J.L., 1997. The Nature of Data, Information and Knowledge Exchanges in Business Processes: Implications for Process Improvement and Organisational Learning. *The Learning Organisation*. 4, 2 pp.70-80.

x BARNEY, J.B., 1999. How a firms capabilities affect boundary decisions. *Sloan Management Review*, 40, (3) 137-145.

xi BARNEY, J.B., 1999. How a firms capabilities affect boundary decisions. *Sloan Management Review*, 40, (3) 137-145.

xii DOYLE, P., 1994. *Marketing Management and Strategy*. England: Prentice Hall.

xiii ROGERS, E. M., 1962. *Diffusion of Innovations*. New York: Free Press.

xiv SAPPINGTON, D.E.M., 1991. Incentive in Principal-Agent Relationships. *Journal of Economic Perspectives*, Vol.5, (2), 45-66.

xv DAVENPORT, T.H., 2000. *Mission Critical, Realizing the promise of Enterprise Systems*. Boston, MA: Harvard Business School Press.

xvi CLARK, P. and STAUNTON, N., 1989. *Innovation in Technology and Organization*. London: Routledge.

xvii HISLOP, D., NEWELL, S., SCARBOROUGH, H., and SWAN, J., 1997. Innovations and Networks, In: *British Academy of Management Annual Conference, September 1997, London*. London: London Business School. P669.

xviii WILLIAMS, I., 1996. *Integration and Investment Specificity*, Discussion paper in Economics and Econometrics No. 9614. University of Southampton.

xix CALLON, M., 1991. Techno-economic networks and irreversibility. In J. LAW ed. *A sociology of monsters. Essays on power, technology and domination*. London: Routledge. p 132-161.

xx PINFIELD, L., 1986. A field evaluation of perspectives on organizational decision-making. *Administrative Science Quarterly*, 31, 365-388.

xxi MINTZBERG, H. and RAISINGHANI, D. AND THEORET, A., 1976. The structure of unstructured decision processes. *Administrative Science Quarterly*. 21: 246-275

xxii COHEN, M.D., MARCH, J.G and OLSEN, J.P., 1972. A garbage can model of organisation choice. *Administrative Science Quarterly*, 17, 1-25.

xxiii SCHEIN, E., 1988. *Organisational Psychology*. New Jersey: Prentice Hall.

xxiv GUEST, D., CONWAY, N., BRINER, R. and DICKMAN, M., 1996. *The state of the Psychological Contract in Employment: Issues in People Management*. London: Institute of Personnel and Development.

xxv PORTER, M.E. and MILLAR V.E., 1985. How information gives you competitive advantage. *Harvard Business Review*, July-August.

xxvi FRIEND, J.K. and HICKLING, A., 1987. *Planning under pressure: the Strategic Choice Approach*. Oxford: Pergamon.

xxvii SIMON, H.A., 1997. *Models of Bounded Rationality, Volume 3, Empirically Grounded Economic Reason*. Cambridge, Massachusetts: MIT Press.

xxviii DAVENPORT, T.H., 2000. *Mission Critical, Realizing the promise of Enterprise Systems*. Boston, MA: Harvard Business School Press.

xxix LATOUR, B., 1987. *Science in Action*. Cambridge, Massachusetts: Harvard University Press.

xxx STEWART T. A., 1997. Intellectual Capital: The new wealth of Organisations. New York: Doubleday.

xxxi BARNEY, J.B., 1999. How a firms capabilities affect boundary decisions. *Sloan Management Review*, 40, (3) 137-145.

xxxii ABRAHAMSON, E., 1996. Management Fashion. Academy of Management Review, 21 (1): 254-285.

xxxiii SCARBOROUGH, H., 1995. Blackboxes, Hostages and Prisoners. *Organization Studies, 16 (6), 991-1019.*

xxxiv ROBERTSON, S. and POWELL, P., 1997. In search of flexibility: The Mercator Case. *ECIS97 Conference Proceedings, June 1997.*

xxxv FLECK, J., 1987. *Innofusion or Diffusation? The Nature of Technological Developments in Robotics.* PICT working paper No.4. Edinburgh University.

xxxvi CALLON, M., 1999. Actor-network theory – the market test. *In:* J. LAW AND J. HASSARD, eds. *Actor Network Theory and After.* Oxford: Blackwell and Sociological Review, 181.

xxxvii HISLOP, D., NEWELL, S., SCARBOROUGH, H., and SWAN, J., 1997. Innovations and Networks, In: *British Academy of Management Annual Conference, September 1997, London.* London: London Business School. P669.

xxxviii BARNEY, J.B., 1999. How a firms capabilities affect boundary decisions. *Sloan Management Review,* 40, (3) 137-145.

xxxix KUTSCHKER, M., 1994. *Re-engineering of Business Processes in Multinational Corporations.* Working paper (No. 95-4). Katholische Universitat Eichstratt, Germany.

xl HANSETH, O, and MONTEIRO, E., 1998. *Understanding Information Infrastructure, Manuscript 27, August 1998.* Available from: http://www.ifi.uio.no/~oleha/Publications/bok.html

xli SUPPE, F., 1977. *The structure of scientific theories.* Urbana: University of Illinois press.

xlii PETTIGREW, A. and WHIPP, R., 1991. *Managing change for competitive success.* London, Blackwell.

xliii DAVENPORT, T.H., and PRUSAK, L., 1998. *Working Knowledge: How organizations manage what they know.* Boston, MA: Harvard Business School Press.

PART TWO:
‘Outside-in’

INTRODUCTION:
PART TWO

In contrast to part one which concentrates on the internal focus that orgaisations can adopt with regard to business processes (inside-out), and the tightly grouped set of case studies used to examine in particular commodity process adoption, part two comprises a series of twenty case studies predominantly business to consumer (B2C) that are based on direct observation through the lens of a customer, consumer, or service user from a wide group of organisations (outside-in), and examines how, in our everyday lives, those business processes good or bad, actually perform when played out for real. All of the case examples were directly observed by the author and were naturally occurring over a period of approximately five years (from 2008 to 2013), and have naturally clustered around three themes, those being: (i) Our relationship with technology and the impact it has on processes; (ii) how processes aren't always designed with the end user or customer in mind, and (iii) the behaviours exhibited by people (actors) within processes, although many of the characteristics observed here appear in cases across all three themes. Each case includes a commentary and some also included dialogue with the process owners (i.e. those organisations/bodies responsible for the process), which gives useful insight into how they operate their processes and how they view what they do.

Organisations are named specifically to add weight, breadth, and significance to the issues observed and particular industries feature prominently and exhibit a competency for operating dysfunctional processes. In general the names of individuals have been altered to protect their identity.

CHAPTER SEVEN
Our Relationship with Technology

7.1 Introduction

What follows in this chapter is a series of case studies depicting how technology impacts upon what we do within processes and our subsequent relationship with it. In contrast to the typical approach to technology writing, I won't be extoling its virtues of speed, integration, connectivity, inter-operability, and all the other attributes regularly associated with it, but more on how we blame, hide behind, demonise, vilify, unquestionably rely on, and despise, all at the same time.

The technology case studies comprise:

T1. Santander's computer says no: How one prominent high street banking institution failed to keep accurate records of accounts on its systems, continued to give false and misleading information to its customers, and then hid behind an inadequate complaints procedure and the Financial Ombudsman Service.

T2. A new form of National Lottery that is on-line ticket purchasing: This case examines the pervasive trend of using on-line ticket websites and vendors for major arts and sporting events, a practice that is becoming little more than an alternative to lottery gaming sites.

T3. User interface: Examples of the problems experienced by users when engaging with technology and in particular the difficulties faced by the old or the technically challenged.

T4. The more information we have the less information we have: How by having more information channels available to us, this increases complexity and in fact we have less reliable information available to us!

T5. Identity crisis: In this age of identity fraud this case highlights examples of the problems with user authentication and the security of passwords which continues to be an issue even with experienced users of technology.

T6. More eBay and email, shopping and Skype : This case explores the challenges of the limited bandwidth available to many parts of the UK and the two tier system of broadband access that excludes many from the services now available via this technology.

T7. Electronic Vehicle Licensing (EVL): This case highlights how despite good intentions a reasonable system can be disrupted by supporting elements that are not adequately monitored or controlled, and will have an impact on millions of users if it is allowed to prevail.

T8. Last chance to avoid the new penalties: This short case highlights how careless operations, incompatible procedures, and a disregard for customer satisfaction and experience are amplified or accelerated by inadequate systems or their unthoughtful application.

TECHNOLOGY CASE STUDY T1

How one prominent high street banking institution failed to keep accurate records of accounts on its systems, continued to give false and misleading information to its customers, and then hid behind an inadequate complaints procedure and the Financial Ombudsman Service.

"Santander's computer says no[1]"

We have traditionally trusted the rigour and accuracy of the accounting systems of our major financial institutions expecting that they will be robust, safe and secure, and we largely accept the information that is provided by them. However as the worldwide economic crisis has shaken consumer's confidence in banks and banking in general then the once unquestionable integrity of banks is now under threat, and with their fallibility exposed to the world consumers are gaining confidence to challenge the information they receive and put our financial institutions under greater scrutiny. For example, the miss-selling of Payment Protection Insurance (PPI) on a massive scale, to customers who did not want or need it. Claimants are each receiving an average of nearly £3,000 in compensation if their claim is successful, and refunding these customers has cost the UK banks a collective total of more than £15bn, following the latest provisions by the major banks.

Background to the case

On 18th September 2009 I became attorney for John Smith's property and affairs as he was experiencing poor health and finding it difficult to cope. At that time I pieced together his financial position which included accounts held with Santander UK plc. (formerly Abbey National PLC), and by

1 Carol Beer is a fictional character played by David Walliams in the TV and radio series Little Britain. She is a perpetually bored and extremely unhelpful woman who works at various jobs requiring the use of a computer, such as a bank clerk, travel agent and hospital receptionist. Upon being approached by a customer with a very reasonable request, she will type this in to her computer and, upon discovering the request cannot be met, she will respond with a bored "computer says no." She is unwilling to use any human initiative or common sense to help her customers, and will then cough at them to make them leave.

visiting the Santander Branch in High Street, Solihull, was able to confirm he had two savings accounts and an Investment ISA. The branch staff helpfully provided documentation (in the form of computer screen prints from their systems) confirming his holdings at that time.

Moving forward two years and after a prolonged illness John subsequently died on 2nd November 2011 and I duly informed all the relevant organisations (including Santander) requesting account balances so that as his Executor I could conclude his affairs and make an accurate application for a Grant of Probate. Once again Santander provided information of John Smith's current holdings (this time from the branch at 33 Clumber Street, Nottingham), which was consistent with the information provided two years earlier, and using those figures I made the necessary application for a Grant of Probate. Upon receipt of the Grant a few weeks later I once again visited the Nottingham Branch to conclude this business with them and once again the account balances were confirmed. A transfer of the funds in the two savings accounts were made into an account under my control, and I was told that closure of the Investment ISA account would need to be carried out at their Head Office and would take approximately ten days to complete.

I then received a letter dated 16th January 2012 (Figure 7.1) advising that the Investment ISA account had been closed on 19th May 2006 (i.e. five years earlier, and three years before I became John's attorney), and that an amount representing approximately half the then expected current balance had been allegedly transferred to another investment account.

Santander

Probate and Bereavement Centre

16th January 2012

Dear XX XXXXXXXXXXXX

Thank you for your recent request.
We can confirm that the above account was closed on 19/05/2006.
The closing funds of £XX, XXX.XX were paid in to account HXXXXXXXX.
Please do not hesitate to contact us should you require anything further.
If you have any questions please give us a call or visit your local branch.

Yours sincerely

Figure 7.1: Probate & Bereavement letter - Santander

So imagine the bewilderment when expecting to receive a sum of approximately twice that amount, having had that amount confirmed several times over a two year period, and at least twice in the preceding four weeks, to receive a brief letter saying that the account no longer exists yet only referring to approximately 50% of the expected balance, and with no supporting explanation as to why there might be a difference. How could Santander think that this would be an acceptable response?

I wrote to the Nottingham branch of Santander on 24th January 2012 expressing my concerns and disbelief as they had been involved with confirming the balance on the accounts, and I was later informed by telephone from that branch that my letter had been forwarded to their complaints department. I duly received a response dated 9th February 2012 from the Complaints Department apologising for the confusion they had caused and blamed the 'inexperience of the staff concerned'. It went on to say: *"Please may I again apologise for the confusion caused as the adviser at the branch should have followed the correct protocol and not provided you with the system copy.* ***As you are well aware the information held here is historical and does not reflect correct balances".***

Firstly, how and why would an investor be *'well aware'* that Santander's systems hold only historical and potentially inaccurate information; and secondly if that is true, then why should I believe any of the information provided by Santander thus far including the closing balances of the other two accounts held by John? In fact, can I be confident that the accounts highlighted represent John's complete holding with Santander?

The letter also contained a cheque for £75 described as "to alleviate any additional expenses incurred by me in resolving this matter", but in doing so they have completely missed the point that there is a need to legitimise the apparent differences in account balances; provide an explanation for the failure of their processes and protocols; rectify the apparent issues with their systems so that confidence can be restored before it can be believed that they are telling the truth and are a credible, robust, and trustworthy financial institution. Santander surely can't expect customers to be 'selective' about the information they choose to believe when receiving what should be factual data about something as straightforward as an account balance, distinguishing between what might be 'historical and inaccurate' as opposed to 'current and factual'?

I telephoned the Santander complaints department (21st February 2012) and spoke to a 'stage two resolution clerk' expressing my concerns that their previous letter did nothing to address the issues I had raised and that it was insulting and inappropriate to be sent a cheque for £75. He undertook to investigate this matter further on my behalf. I heard nothing until mid-March 2012 when a neighbour of John's contacted me saying that correspondence addressed to John at his former address had been received by the new tenants. Two identical letters from Santander Complaints Department dated 24th February 2012 were subsequently forwarded to me (by the neighbour) stating that the account in question was cancelled in 2006 and that as I had received a payment of £75 (which incidentally is a cheque I haven't cashed) they were unable to offer additional payments and referred me to the Financial Ombudsman Service.

I telephoned the Complaints Department on 15th March 2012 and once again expressed my concerns that they had not even attempted to answer the questions I had raised and asked that they respond within seven days. I did then receive a response from Santander in a letter dated 23rd March 2012 which once again did nothing to give me any comfort that there is any rigour or process attached to their investigation, and even less confidence that they understand why this has occurred. They made no reference to the issue of addressing their previous correspondence to John (now deceased) at his former address, and suggested that as they had already offered me £250 (this was the first time I had heard of this offer amount) by way of compensation and that I should return the customer payment form duly completed so that I could receive this payment. Needless to say I didn't do so!

Santander appears unable, or unwilling, or both to address the following issues:

1 How is it that on three separate occasions, over a period of three years, and in two different Santander branches, can it be possible to be given information about an account that Santander subsequently claimed had been closed six years earlier?
2 Although I can't recall the details of the branch staff who gave me the original information at Solihull, the staff at Nottingham were most definitely experienced and long service individuals who I would assume Santander cite as being amongst the most experienced of their branch employees, and it would be troubling to me that two people at Nottingham independently made errors, as well as the original employee at Solihull. This all seems too much of a coincidence.
3 The alleged closing balance of the account in 2006 has no relationship to the account balance as given to me on several occasions (it would be more believable if the figures at least matched), and there appears to have been no attempt to suggest how these amounts might be different (i.e. might there have been a partial withdrawal to another account but what about the remaining funds as there has been no explanation as to the whereabouts of these funds)?
4 Why does Santander feel it acceptable to be selective about which system information they would expect you to believe as a customer? Surely they must accept that system errors undermine the confidence

of customers, so perhaps I should be sceptical of the savings accounts balance amounts too?

5 At the time of registering the POA[2] with Santander I requested that no correspondence should be sent to John's address. This was applied inconsistently throughout this episode culminating in Santander writing to John (now deceased) at his former address. Santander have a complete disregard for accuracy, they regularly spell names incorrectly, apply the wrong titles, and omit inserts and enclosures that are referenced in the documents. Did they really investigate this matter with any rigour and truly establish what had been occurring here?

6 In the final two years of his life I made decisions about John's care and wellbeing based on the assets I believed John had at his disposal, as determined by the account balances I was supplied by Santander. It's likely that John didn't receive the appropriate State assistance for his care expenditure because we believed that he was ineligible for such assistance because his investments in Santander (including the account in dispute) exceeded the savings threshold allowable.

7 Finally, having had previous experience of my own mortgage account being the subject of a bungled staff fraud at a Building Society during the eighties I'm only too aware that these incidents take place yet rarely get brought to the public's attention. It's not too fanciful to consider that John's seemingly 'dormant' account now operated by an attorney was targeted by an unscrupulous member of staff or an accomplice, which could account for the inconsistencies in correspondence indicators; inaccuracies in accounting; and uncertainty about the account closure date etc., Santander owe me an explanation for their behaviour and need to address these concerns.

Santander is no stranger to high profile computer glitches:

> August 2010: Alliance & Leicester customers have found themselves unable to access their bank accounts online as a result of system problems incurred by Santander. Santander was integrating Alliance & Leicester (A&L) with Abbey and Bradford & Bingley, the two other UK banks it owns, but suffered problems during the process which began when it started upgrading the customers' accounts. Santander insisted that the problems were affecting only a "small number" of the five million A&L customers being transferred to its systems but was unable to give an indication as to when the online services would be running again.

---

2 A Power of Attorney (POA) allows someone to make decisions on your behalf, should there come a time when you lack mental capacity to do so yourself.

> During December 2010 up to 35,000 people could have received other customers' details on bank statements. A printing error led to pages from other customers' statements appearing on paperwork sent to current account holders. As a result, recipients were sent details of their own transactions and other people's as well. The bank apologised, but said there was no added risk of fraud as a result. A Santander spokesman was quoted as saying *"We want to reassure customers that the risk of fraud on their account has not been increased because of this error and that this is a one-off incident."*
>
> In May 2011 staff at some Santander branches were unable to access some customer accounts owing to software problems. The bank said that 38 of the 1,400 branches across the country were affected when a software changeover caused the computer difficulties. Although banks suffer relatively regular server problems which can affect their online banking operations, a UK-wide issue with computers in a branch network is unusual. Staff were unable to access certain account information for customers who visited branches.

At the point of writing this case (June 2013) the issue is still with the Financial Services Ombudsman for adjudication (and is covered elsewhere in a different case study), although Santander have now admitted to the FSO that *"Although it is acknowledged by the bank there was an error by staff in providing incorrect information this appears to have been caused by the issue with the bank's computer systems"*. This raises yet further doubt over the validity of the information received from Santander, and ultimately whether all John's holdings with Santander have been accurately identified.

To date Santander have made no attempt to respond to me directly or to answer any of the questions or allegations put to them, and they appear content to hide behind a cloak of secrecy not really understanding the impact this has on customer confidence[3].

So what can we learn from this case about the processes involved?

This case chronicles the events surrounding the closure of savings and investment accounts following the death of the account holder, and the subsequent issues of inaccuracy of systems and the interpretation of those

3 In the Annual Review for 2013 the Financial Ombudsman reported that "too many financial businesses still seem unable to sort out problems themselves, without the ombudsman having to get involved".

systems by the bank staff. It highlights the importance of accuracy, transparency, and rigour.

1. **Failure to keep accurate records** - The Banks admission that the information held on their systems is historical and does not reflect correct balances. Can they be happy at declaring this to customers?

2. **Barefaced Denial** – and no attempt to give a credible explanation for this situation. It would be hard to explain how the account information had been available for over six years yet in the incorrect format without undermining their credibility as a robust financial institution. However, an explanation is required.

3. **Blame the computer it has no employment rights** - The apparent ease with which computer error (or more accurately systems error) can be cited as the cause of a problem as if that makes it acceptable as clearly the computer can't answer back in its defence. The computer has become the 'fall guy' or scapegoat for process or administrative errors.

4. **Hiding behind procedure** – and the ability to 'tough it out' and take no action, no willingness to really address the problem. Hoping that the complainant is 'worn down' by Santanders ineffectiveness before their shortcomings are exposed.

5. **Disrespectful attituide** – The hollow platitudes reinforcing their committment to customer service yet they can't even respond in a timely way to correspondence, or apologise when they write in error to a deceased account holder.

6. **Hand-off to the Financial Ombudsman Service** – the apparent lack of consequences in not handling genuine customer complaints in a professional way, and the convenience of transferring the problemto the FOS.

7. **Timescales to resolve** – at the time of writing this case it is still uresolved and is with the Financial Ombudsman Service awaiting adjudication. It is now twenty-one months since John died and this issue was raised with Santander, so if it is a systems error then how many other customers have been affected by this during that time?

QUESTIONS:

- How can prospective customers assess the effectiveness of a financial institutions processes and systems prior to becoming an investor and risking their funds?
- Who effectively regulates the behaviour of financial institi-tions and holds them to account?

SELECTED FURTHER READING:

- "Ombudsman swamped as PPI complaints soar". The Times, Wednesday 29th May, 2013.
- "Computer says no". The Economist, 24th July 2010.
- 'Unsafe' deposit box, The Times, 12th April 2014.

USEFUL WEBSITE:

Financial Ombudsman Service
http://www.financial-ombudsman.org.uk/

TECHNOLOGY CASE STUDY T2

This case examines the pervasive trend of using on-line ticket websites and vendors for major arts and sporting events, a practice that is becoming little more than an alternative to lottery gaming sites.

A new form of National Lottery that is on-line ticket purchasing

The odds of making a successful ticket purchase on-line for concerts and events is probably little better than scooping the jackpot on the National Lottery, as most of us that applied for London 2012 Olympic tickets will feel is the case. The only difference being that at least with the National Lottery you get some gratification from the anticipation that builds that you might become rich beyond your wildest dreams, and you quickly experience a sense of closure when put out of your misery when the winning numbers are revealed. So a weird cluster of unsuccessful on-line applications for concert tickets, Olympic sporting events, and BBC radio recordings has left me wondering if this method of ticket purchase is a robust, impartial, and serious business process or just a game of chance.

Background to the case

No doubt like many thousands of other people I applied via a ballot to attend the *'Children in Need – Rocks the Royal Albert Hall'* concert that took place on Thursday 12th November. The attraction for me in addition to it being for a good cause was the appearance of Sir Paul McCartney so I duly registered my interest. I received the 'confirmation of registration' email which included the instructions as to what would happen next; my personal registration number (to be used if I get through to the next stage); and advice that I would hear if I had been successful (or not) by Wednesday 21st October.

Completely unconnected with that application I also received that same day an email update from the BBC about the forthcoming recordings of the

Radio 4 series "I'm sorry I haven't a clue" (ISIHAC)[4]. The email described the details of two planned recordings the first being in London. I duly registered my interest but unlike the Children in Need application only those who were successful in the ballot would be notified by email, coincidently also by 21st October.

Needless to say I received the *"thank you for supporting Children in Need but you were unsuccessful on this occasion"* email on 21st October, and heard nothing more from ISIHAC signifying by default that I had been unsuccessful. Obviously disappointed but rationalising the odds of success I consoled myself that I probably didn't really stand a chance of getting these but at least I had tried!

That evening I heard that Sir Paul McCartney had just announced a concert at the O2 stadium for one evening only and that tickets were going on sale shortly. As an O2 customer I knew of priority booking for concerts at the O2 arena but had never used that facility before. I immediately looked up the O2 website to check what O2 customers had to do to register for priority tickets. I was having problems texting via my O2 service so I registered using the on-line method and received a unique code and eagerly awaited the ballot to open.

On the appointed day my first attempt to book tickets was met with an engaged tone, but subsequent attempts eventually got me through to an operator. I could hardly believe it as tickets were still available and I was able to have a sensible dialogue about seating options. Once I had decided where I would like to sit the operator asked for the priority code, which I duly gave her, only to be told that the code I had given her was invalid. "INVALID"! [Shouts]

Having confined this series of experiences well and truly to the further reaches of my mind, on 27th October I then received unexpectedly another email from Children in Need explaining that there were limited tickets being made available and that the remaining tickets would go on sale on-line from 10:00AM the following day (Figure 7.2).

---

4 ISIHAC is one of Britain's most loved radio shows which has been broadcast since 1972. It is amongst the handful of legendary British audio comedy formats, listened to around the world. Introduced as "the antidote to panel games", it consists of two teams of two comedians "given silly things to do" by a chairman. The show has won several awards and attracted many fans; it is easily one of the most popular programmes on BBC Radio 4.

Subject: BBC Children in Need Rocks the Royal Albert Hall

Great news!

You are one of many people who entered the ballot for tickets to BBC Children in Need Rocks the Royal Albert Hall taking place on Thursday 12th November 2009. Whilst you were not lucky enough to have won through to the purchase stage of the ballot, not all the successful applicants have bought a ticket. We therefore have a limited number of returned tickets in each category available to sell.

Please be aware we are emailing tens of thousands of you with a chance to buy just a few remaining tickets, but we feel this is the fairest way to sell the last tickets.

The remaining tickets will go on sale 10am on Wednesday 28th October. The following link will be activated at this time and will take you to a log-in page:

Etc.

Best wishes,
BBC Children in Need.

Figure 7.2: BBC Children in Need rocks the Royal Albert Hall letter

Keen to avoid once again raising my expectations only to get them dashed, my initial reaction was not to bother. But on reflection given a slim chance I felt it worth the effort yet experienced the following:

10:00	Received holding screen with the message: "Your request has been placed in a queue. Your request will re-attempt automatically every 20 seconds or you can try again by manually refreshing this page. Thanks for your patience during this time".
10:12	A 'run time error' crashed Internet Explorer and I had to reboot my machine.
10:14	Reinstated back to the holding screen (but now I suspect much further down the queue)?
10:27	The original screen carrying the colour Children in Need Pudsey graphics disappeared from the screen. This then defaulted to a black & white screen with the same holding message as before.
10:44	Got through to the subsequent screens, added my unique number and attempted to purchase seats from the available choices only to get the Pudsey graphic once again with the message "Sorry, there are no tickets currently available for this event".
10:52	Gave up!

Table 7.1: Sequence of events

I remained in that 'queue' for the next hour but nothing changed!

London 2012 Olympics

Like so many other sports enthusiasts I was revelling in the fact that the 2012 Olympic Games was being held in London, the first (and likely only) time during my lifetime to be hosted in the UK, so I had decided that I would try and attend some of the events on this special occasion. In March 2010 (857 days to the opening ceremony) I registered my interest on the London 2012 website so that I could be kept up to date with the ticketing process and make the ticket applications at the appropriate time.

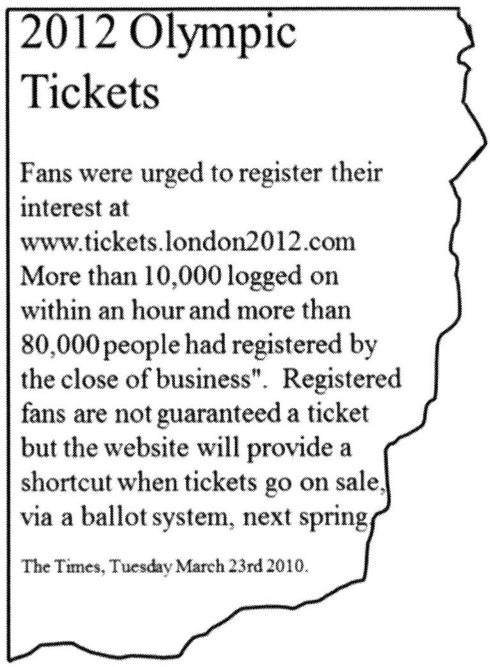

2012 Olympic Tickets

Fans were urged to register their interest at www.tickets.london2012.com More than 10,000 logged on within an hour and more than 80,000 people had registered by the close of business". Registered fans are not guaranteed a ticket but the website will provide a shortcut when tickets go on sale, via a ballot system, next spring.

The Times, Tuesday March 23rd 2010.

Figure 7.3: Olympics tickets newspaper clip – The Times, March 23rd 2010.

Over the next twelve months LOCOG (The London Organising Committee of the Olympic and Paralympic Games) sent a series of promotional emails with the intention of keeping people interested in the forthcoming event and provide additional insight to behind the scenes articles informing of progress with preparations, venue achievements and details of the calls for volunteers etc.

Almost one year later applications were opened for tickets and I duly applied. Although we would have liked to attend some of the more popular and showcase events we deliberately avoided those and medal ceremonies as it was always likely that the opening ceremony, key athletics track and field events, and sports where UK has some dominance (swimming and cycling) were always going to be oversubscribed. Therefore we chose some minor sports where there were many qualifying rounds, and where the events took place in open or large arenas thereby affording a larger viewing capacity (shooting, badminton, equestrian eventing). With 466 days to the opening ceremony we received our confirmation of ticket application email which included our reference number (to be kept safe as it would be needed in future correspondence).

Alongside the rest of the nation we entered the nervous period of waiting to see if the tickets we had requested would be fulfilled. Everyone was anxiously accessing their credit card statements on-line to check if any debits had been made to their cards thereby signifying your application had been successful, as we did too and for once we would have been happy to see this transaction appear on our credit card statement.

On 24th May 2011 430 days to the opening ceremony we received an email (Figure 7.4) with the subject "Important London 2012 Olympic Games ticket application information"

Subject: Important London 2012 Olympic Games ticket application information

Thank you for applying for London 2012 Olympic tickets. As you will be aware, we have started to allocate tickets and are now taking payments from Visa credit and debit cards, as well as banking cheques and postal orders. The vast majority of payments will be taken by next week (31 May), with the entire process completed by 10 June.

We will contact you before 24 June to let you know if you have been successful and, if so, which tickets you have been allocated.

Second chance sales

There will be another chance to apply for tickets – we are calling this 'second chance sales'.

If you have not been allocated any tickets in the initial process, you will have the first chance to apply for tickets. This will be followed by a further chance for those who were allocated some or all of their ticket request.

Second chance sales will include tickets for lots of great sport including Basketball, Beach Volleyball, Boxing, Canoe Sprint, Cycling (women's mountain bike), Football, Handball, Hockey, Taekwondo, Volleyball, Weightlifting and Wrestling. So there are plenty of other chances to be part of the greatest show on earth.

Etc.

Best wishes,
The London 2012 ticketing team

Figure 7.4: Important London 2012 Olympic Games ticket application information email.

During this time the press was full of stories of those having made multiple and high value applications being successful, but the majority of people I knew were experiencing disappointment (as were we).

Three weeks later 406 days to the opening ceremony, now expecting we had been unsuccessful our fears were confirmed on receipt of the following email (Figure 7.5).

Subject: Your Olympic Games ticket application

We would like to thank you for applying for London 2012 Olympic Games tickets.

Due to overwhelming demand for tickets, we are sorry that you have not been allocated the tickets you requested. We can confirm that we have not taken any payment from you.

Demand for tickets greatly exceeded supply in the sessions and price categories you applied for. Where sessions were oversubscribed, we undertook a random ballot to allocate tickets in the fairest way possible. We had applications for more than 20 million tickets, seeing huge demand across many sports. Two-thirds of all price categories were oversubscribed and went to ballot.

Exclusive opportunity

We would like to invite you to take advantage of an exclusive opportunity to purchase some of the remaining tickets, in advance of those customers who were allocated tickets in the initial application phase.

From 6am on 24 June until 6pm on 3 July 2011 you will be able to request some of the remaining tickets on the London 2012 ticketing website.

These tickets will be allocated on a first come, first served basis. They cover a great range of Olympic sports including Athletics, Basketball, Football, Handball, Hockey and Volleyball. Download the full list of available sports.

During this second chance sales window you will only be able to submit one application, and you will be able to apply for a maximum of three sessions. Once you submit, you will receive an email confirming your application. We will then advise you which tickets you have been allocated within 24-48 hours, subject to successful payment. All payments will be taken between 4 and 7 July 2011.

We very much hope you will take advantage of this exclusive ticket offer so you can still be part of the greatest show on earth.

If you have any questions regarding your Olympic Games ticket application, please visit or frequently asked questions.

Etc.

Best wishes,The London 2012 ticketing team.

Figure 7.5: Olympic games ticket application email.

I immediately checked the website to see what tickets would be available but none of the sports we had identified originally were listed, and many of the two million tickets were for football (which I had no desire to attend), so rather reluctantly we declined to take advantage of what was described as an 'exclusive offer'.

Diamond Jubilee Concert

Now 2012 was not only the year of the London Olympics but also the year of the Diamond Jubilee of Queen Elizabeth II, and to mark this significant achievement there was a series of events, pageants and celebrations taking place around the country including the Diamond Jubilee Concert[5].

The Diamond Jubilee Concert was to be held on Bank holiday Monday 4 June 2012 as part of the extended weekend celebrations to mark Queen Elizabeth II's Diamond Jubilee (i.e. 60 years on the throne). The event is located outside Buckingham Palace on a stage specially constructed around the Queen Victoria Memorial including a series of one-off collaborations featuring artists such as Elton John and Sir Paul McCartney.

10,000 free tickets for the concert were made available to the public, with applications possible, by post or online, between 7 February and 2 March 2012. After the application period closed, successful applicants were then drawn by random ballot. A total of 1.2 million applications were eventually received, 240 for every available pair.[6] Concert ticket holders were given access to the palace gardens for an afternoon picnic before the main event. They were served cold hampers with a British themed menu specially designed by Heston Blumenthal. Tickets for the Diamond Jubilee concert were sent to the successful applicants at the end of May 2012.

Once again the method of choice for ticket application was an on-line ballot.

---

5 Ten years earlier, the Queen celebrated her Golden Jubilee with two concerts - one classical and one pop - also at the Palace. Party at the Palace and Prom at the Palace received more than one million applications but there were only 12,000 tickets available for the two concerts. In 2005, there were two million bids for tickets for Hyde Park's Live 8 show, attended by 205,000 music fans.

6 BBC News, 17 April 2012.

Subject: The Diamond Jubilee Concert 2012 – Ticket Application

Thank you for applying to enter the Ballot for a pair of Diamond Jubilee Concert tickets. Your application has been received.

We will email successful applicants by the end of March 2012. Please remember to check your spam or junk email folders.

Please note that unsuccessful applicants will not be notified.

You can review the Ballot Rules and the Terms and Conditions again, plus the answers to a number of frequently asked questions at **www.bbc.co.uk/diamondjubilee**.

The Diamond Jubilee Concert will be broadcast live on BBC ONE and Radio 2 on Monday 4 June 2012.

Please do not apply again! Only one application per person is permitted regardless of method of application.

Figure 7.6 The Diamond Jubilee Concert 2012 – ticket application email

As with the earlier on-line applications of this type the no-news wasn't necessarily good-news, and our application was once again unsuccessful.

London 2012 Olympic Games tickets reprise

Clearly I was disappointed at not being allocated any of my choices for London 2012 and it's fair to say that there was a considerable backlash in the nation against the organisation of the ticket ballots with disappointed people outnumbering those who were successful by at least 4:1. Canvassing a wide circle of friends and colleagues almost all were returning the news that they were unsuccessful and LOCOG were receiving increased bad publicity for creating an overwhelming demand that it couldn't satisfy.

And finally, during May 2012 LOCOG announced that further tickets for London 2012 were being released and that for two weeks a succession of sports would be featured each day and that priority would be given to those that had participated unsuccessfully in the previous applications processes. My motivation for this was extremely low, but with 74 days to go to the opening ceremony we had the opportunity to purchase up to four tickets from the sports available, and one of our original choices (shooting) was available!

So what can we learn from this case about the processes involved?

This case describes a series of applications made for event and concert ticket purchases on-line. Its purpose is not to lament what might be described as appalling bad luck in obtaining tickets but to examine how this now common process of ticket purchase performs and the impact on end users of this process. It shows how this method, while no doubt enjoyed by vendors and event organisers alike (as it maximises ticket sales and ensures sell-out events and the greatest possible return on ticket sales), if allowed to prevail could generate significant levels of disappointment as witnessed by those not able to share in the experience of the London 2012 Olympics. Although my experience might not be statistically significant, to be unsuccessful in applications for tickets in all five of these events does make you question this process of ticket purchase.

1. The need for feedback loops and progress indicators

You don't really know how well you did or how close you really came to buying tickets. Waiting in-line at a box office you get a sense of progression through the queue, you know that there are tickets for sale and can witness people being successful. If they sell out before you reach the head of the queue you at least have some feedback on how close you came. Now I'm not advocating that standing in-line is a better method, but some of the characteristics of this approach give you some visual and practical clues and feedback on how well (or not) you fared in the process.

As a method of purchase this is still not above suspicion and threatens to be a 'black art' as second market ticket vendors still appear able to access tickets in vast quantities minutes after the tickets are released for purchase thereby making them available for re-sale at inflated prices.

Indications of how you are progressing along the application system is something that could be built into an on-line system. It's a bit like Disney giving you a clue that from this point in-line you are 20 minutes from the ride. In the on-line method the negative assumption is usually applied, i.e. if you hear nothing by this date then you were unsuccessful.

2. Broadband/network speeds/refresh rates.

Whether imaginary or not I can't help but assume that by living in a rural community where Broadband speeds are woeful (i.e. on average around 0.25MB), then this reduced performance (speed) must be disadvantageous and reduce the likelihood of competing equitably with others who enjoy much faster connection speeds. If so, then I'm never likely to be successful in a competitive first-come-first-served (FCFS) scenario.

I'm reliably informed by friends who know better about the technical configurations than I that there are a host of competing factors that will really determine if network speed will be a contributory factor, including; the design and size of the ticketing system where all the demand aggregates, and how the demand is balanced across that system; the amount of data that might be shipped back and forth between you and the system (unlikely in this type of transaction); or apparently the two teenagers downloading videos and music in their bedrooms at the same time could be a constraint!

More likely (and this does chime with rural locations) is the contention ration applied at your local BT exchange for DSL services (typically 50:1), i.e. 50 homes or offices contend for access to the uplink, so it's not just your own teenagers you have to contend with, it's the 100 others too!

3. The mental attitude to approach this

As I buy my National Lottery ticket I probably subconsciously suppress any thoughts of winning as statistically I know that it's unlikely that I will do so. Does this allow me to accept the outcome more readily and therefore not be dissuaded from buying a ticket in future? However, in this lottery process I know that entry isn't limited or restricted (except by my own financial constraints), so my chances of being included in the draw are not diminished. So all the anxiety of a FCFS process is removed, I know what I'm entering, I can witness the outcome of the winning numbers (the draw takes place live on television), and I can check the outcome directly (I match my numbers to the winning numbers).

My mental approach to a ticket purchase process is that it is not a lottery or ballot, and therefore subconsciously a different set of behaviours have been embedded. To recognise it as a game of chance would alter my approach (and reduce my expectations), but might this ultimately just result in the same long-term outcome as with the National Lottery, that I now don't take part?

4. Choosing the right method for the right occasion

It's not always entirely clear if what you are entering is a 'first-come, first served' (FCFS) process; or a distribution based on geographical spread and other factors; or a chance allocation based purely on some random number generator that applies an algorithm to allocate tickets. There was much criticism of London 2012 Olympics ticket allocation as it completely ignored the existing mechanisms in place within sporting bodies to use them or their membership to allocate tickets (in much the same way as Wimbledon does for championships through Tennis Club memberships).

5. There is no apparent appeal mechanism to challenge the allocation (lack of transparency to the process)

It's not always entirely transparent as to what method of ticket allocation is being deployed which leads to a complete lack of transparency. A mix of methods, 'ballot' and first-come–first-served (FCFS) is often used but what determines your ability to get selected is completely random, or is it?

QUESTIONS:

- What level of feedback or additional information would make an applicant comfortable that their application is being considered?
- What are the prerequisites for such schemes to work successfully?

SELECTED FURTHER READING:

- *"Take That: websites crash as reunited 'man band' sell one million concert tickets in a day"*. The Times, Saturday 30th October 2010.
- *"One Deception*: ticket scams rake in £3.7m". The Sunday Times, Sunday 8th June 2014.

USEFUL WEBSITE:

http://www.bbc.co.uk/showsandtours/

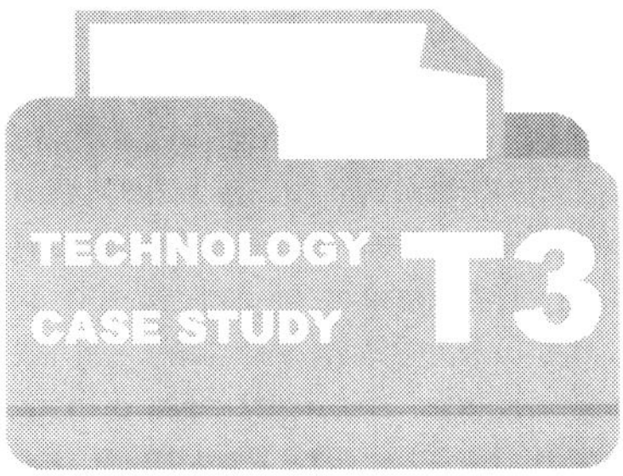

Examples of the problems experienced by users when engaging with technology and in particular the difficulties faced by the old or the technically challenged..

User Interface

It was just before 7 o'clock on a Saturday morning when the telephone woke me from a deep sleep following a rather late and disturbed night. As I answered in a half comatose and shocked state to hear my elderly father in a panic I immediately feared the worst! Establishing if I was 'awake yet' he launched into a lecture on how a message had appeared on his television screen and that he didn't know what to do! Once my brain got over the initial shock of him being perfectly okay but just having problems with his television, I realised what had happened.

A few weeks earlier he had been complaining that some of the regular TV programmes he enjoyed had 'disappeared', and he could no longer find a number of the channels he liked to watch. I asked him if he had 're-tuned' when the 'new service message' appeared on his screen. "What new service message" barked the reply! When I had the opportunity to check the TV settings I established that the 'new service alert' option had been disabled when the unit was installed, and that he had been unaware of any service upgrades for three years, slowly losing channels and services during that time. It was then that I enabled the alert feature, thereby allowing him to accept new or changed services as they became available, and this was the first time there had been a service change since then.

This little incident made me realise just how alien current day technology is to someone who has limited exposure to it, and the way we take for granted menu structures, binary selections modes, multi-purpose keys and buttons, and words such as 'select', 'enter', and 'cursor'. It's no coincidence that programming video recorders (VCR's) has become the butt of so many jokes, and those new entrants to this market make a virtue of the simplicity of programming and use. Similarly, trying to remotely visualise the TV menu structure and layout of my fathers handset in order to guide him through the accepting of the new service option, over the telephone, was indeed a challenge, and gave me a whole new appreciation of remote help-desk operations!

Continuing this theme, from personal experience I like using maps and prefer to get a mental picture of a journey and how it relates to the physical landscape, and more specifically a mental 'shape' of the journey (i.e. down, across, down again, keep left of the city etc.). This certainly helps when you are faced with commands such as 'Eastbound' or other such directional instructions, especially when you are driving and unable to examine the map. So the use of Satellite navigation (SATNAV) has been a challenge. Its adoption, in my case, has been episodic, cautious, and thought provoking. I had used it some years ago in a rental car in the US, and previous use improved confidence. However, I like to get a context for where I'm going but the small screen (even on the built-in versions) is too small to show the complete journey at a sensible scale, and the detailed version too limiting. You can no doubt select preferences but the instruction manual is longer than a Harry Potter novel. I tend to find SATNAV works best for me switching it on when I'm approaching my destination and the possible combinations or alternative routes it could offer are limited, and the margin for error therefore reduced. However, I did once enter the postcode of an organisation I was visiting only to end up at the local Postal Sorting Office, as this company publishes a postcode relating to the sorting office rather than their own site!

As a frequent promoter of IT to help solve business problems and improve efficiency and effectiveness I understand the benefits of Radio Frequency (or wireless) devices. I applaud the flexibility and mobility they promote, be it instantly passing an order to the kitchen for service in restaurants, or checking stock room inventory when a customer asks for an item not available on the sales floor. But as a user and recipient of the service (or lack of service), I'm acutely aware of how incongruent, in some of these situations, the application of technology can be.

On a regular visit to Porto (Portugal) I had time to visit a well-known 'coffee house' known as the 'Majestic Café'. It boasts a long heritage, fantastic patisserie, traditional values, starched aprons and quality service; you could say "a tradition of excellence"! It was all going well until the waiter taking my order reached for an electronic device 'slung' from his waist and then avoided any further eye contact for the remainder of the transaction as he was transfixed by scrolling through menus, the rapid tapping of his pointing device on the glass screen, and repeatedly having to reaffirm what I had just ordered as he wasn't really listening to me but concentrating hard on the screen and the device. Not only had the old world character of the Café been shattered, but also it felt like I had been in some way ancillary to the whole event. Not a great customer experience!

As 'chip and pin' is now embedded in the UK[7] (i.e. the use of a personal identification number to validate the use of a credit card instead of signature verification), the technology is once again taking over. If you pay by card it

7 Chip and Pin was a decade old in May 2013.

can now be a completely 'dialogue free' transaction (although in some petrol stations I can see how this would be an attraction!). As customer familiarity grows with the devices (and these are many and varied), you can insert your card, and follow the instructions on screen, entering PIN, validating card type and transaction amount, and finally removing your card on command, all in complete silence, giving the attendant yet another excuse to avoid any interaction! Taking this one stage further, when paying for a meal in dimly lit restaurants you are now expected to accept the transaction amount, confirm that you want to give a gratuity (by using the function keys), insert the amount of the gratuity and press enter, accept the new total and press enter, accept the card type (toggle and enter), a total of twelve key stokes on my last count! How long before someone decides what a great opportunity this affords to collect customer information, feedback, socio economic grouping and much more?

What can we learn about the processes involved from this case?

It doesn't matter how fast the processor or how clever the application, if the user interface device is 'unusable' then it is worthless. Clearly many of these devices are designed by engineers – for use by engineers, so what about the rest of us? Human-computer interaction (HCI) can't be left to engineers alone and requires that we develop more user centric design principles when building such interfaces. Have you ever wondered why we only use a fraction of the features available to us on our video recorders? Reduced complexity would be a good starting point.

QUESTION:

- If you were assessing user interface devices such as those described within the case, what would be your main criteria for choosing between alternative technological options?

SELECTED FURTHER READING:

- The term HCI was popularised by Card, Moran, and Newell in their seminal 1983 book, *The Psychology of Human-Computer Interaction*.

- *'Airlines to cut waiting time by axing obsolete security checks – Ministers agree to make systems user-friendly'*, The Times, 28th October 2012.
- "Pass the plate? End of the collection is nigh". The Times, Friday 17th August 2012.

USEFUL WEBSITE:

http://www-01.ibm.com/software/ucd/designconcepts.html

TECHNOLOGY CASE STUDY T4

How by having more information channels available to us this increases complexity and in fact we have less reliable information available to us!

The more information we have the less information we have

It's a truism that we live in the 'information age', a phrase that is meant to convey the positive aspects of a society in which we have easy access to an unlimited source of information. It's used to be distinct from previous 'ages' described as 'industrial' or 'agricultural', and is generally considered to be progressive rather than regressive. We might today have access to greater volumes, but I would argue we often derive less value, as much of what we receive is duplicated; translated (with a spin); or even fabricated! We rely on an ever more sophisticated mechanism for collection and analysis but at the risk of continuity and provenance of the data being compromised. At a time when suppliers and vendors should know more about me as a consumer than ever before they act as if they know nothing.

Driving on the M1 Southbound I came across an electronic overhead sign that read:

TO M6 VIA M69
17 MILES
15 MINS

The intention of this sign was to inform motorway users that it would take 15 minutes to reach the M6 motorway should they travel the 17 miles by going via the M69 which connects both routes.

By being able to travel this 17 mile journey in 15 minutes assumes that your speed must be averaging just over 60 mph (i.e. approximately a mile per minute). Ordinarily this would have been very useful information, but at that particular time the overhead gantry speed signs were flashing '40' MPH, and the actual speed, due to the volume of traffic and congestion at a major intersection of two motorways, was less that 10 mph. It made me reflect on the incongruence of these signs, and question what was the point of an 'informational' device that is clearly giving incorrect information.

What I really needed to know was the estimated time of arrival (ETA) under the road conditions that prevailed at that time and surely the sign should be dynamic and take its inputs from what is actually happening on the motorway in order that it gives accurate and helpful information?

The immediacy and 'always on' nature of information these days when you have constant access to it as opposed to the natural time delay until the next time you fire-up your laptop, has heightened my awareness to the inappropriateness of some of the information we receive. Three examples:

Amazon sending me special offers to purchase Dan Browns latest book when I had already pre ordered it from them several weeks earlier and was expecting it to be shipped automatically when available. So although Amazon can tell me what books *'others who also bought this book'* have purchased they can't recognise what I have already purchased. Or Pink Elephant Business Parking at Heathrow Airport sending special offers for parking but not recognising that my car was already in their safe keeping at Heathrow T5 Business Parking having been pre-booked several weeks earlier and their number plate recognition system had automatically matched my arrival at the car park to the pre-arranged booking.

But the most annoying incident was when trying to purchase foreign currency from Travelex on-line using my Netbook computer. I got to the part of the transaction that uses 3D security but the pop up screen requiring me to enter my VISA security details was 'pinned' in a fixed position on the screen. Scrolling down didn't reveal the foot of the box containing the 'send' button. After aborting the first transaction I realised that I could change the zoom level on internet explorer to show more content in the screen and hence reveal the whole box. On repeating the process at the pop up screen I changed the zoom level to reveal the button, only then to get the unhelpful message that my 'card could not be processed'. Could not be processed now, for ever, or was this because I had aborted the first transaction, or was there a problem with my card? Typical of on-line sites these days there are no telephone numbers published for you to make an enquiry so I rang a 24 hour Visa number to find out. Several calls later and only having threatened to cancel my card did I discover that Visa had rejected the transaction as what appears to me as quite normal card behaviour had conformed to a pattern typical of card fraudsters, i.e. that I had made a small transaction (£4 cardholder not present transaction to Birmingham Library for a document search), and was then trying a much larger transaction (to purchase foreign currency) so they had put a 'stop' on my card, very useful as I was just to depart to the US on vacation! What is the point of the security number, and the additional 3D security if it isn't to validate my identity? How long before the validation requires validation and then further validation, and how do you know if your typical card use imitates fraudulent usage patterns?

What can we learn about the processes from this case study?

Now for those of us who have worked in operational IT roles we can no doubt rationalise these situations with simple explanations. In the motorway example the two systems are probably quite separate and rely on an operator sitting somewhere in a control room, or worse two operators in two separate control rooms, relying on a cerebral connection between the motorway conditions and the messages that need to be displayed, but this didn't happen. For Amazon and Pink Elephant an extract of those clients who had already placed orders or bought their services should have been run and extracted from the mailing list, but once again this didn't happen. And finally a set of rules applied to a purchasing transaction procedure should also be matched with all the correct security information having been provided - but once again it didn't.

No matter how you view these incidents they are the subject of process or service failures, and when viewed through the lens of the customer or end user they just don't work, albeit for all manner of rational reasons be they technological, human, procedural, or design. Their consequences, while in these examples might initially appear minor, I believe could have far reaching ramifications potentially for both the end user/customer or the organisation providing the goods or service. The motorway sign we now no longer trust or believe, is the one we ignore that tells us of fog ahead that has caused an accident we are hurtling towards.

I approached both Pink Elephant and Amazon to get their feedback. Pink Elephant didn't respond but Amazon replied as follows (Figure 7.7).

From: "Amazon.co.uk Customer Services"
Date: Mon, 23 Aug 2010 10:51:37
Subject: Your Amazon.co.uk Enquiry

Dear Customer

Thank you for writing to us to bring this to our attention. First of all, please accept my apologies for this situation.

From your email, I understand that you have received an email for the item which you have already placed order.

Please understand advertisement (recommendation) emails were sent by our system automatically and I am sorry that it was incorrect in this instance.

I have forwarded the message to appropriate department further to make sure it doesn't happen again to you or to other customers.

Customer feedback such as yours helps us to continue improving the selection and service we provide. We appreciate the time you've taken to write to us.

If you have any other suggestions for us or would like to make a comment at another time, simply send us an e-mail. To do this, you can visit our Help Desk at the following URL:

http://www.amazon.co.uk/contact-us

We look forward to hearing from you. Thank you for shopping at Amazon.co.uk.

Warmest regards

Amazon.co.uk

Your feedback is helping us build Earth's Most Customer-Centric Company.

Figure 7.7: Amazon Customer Services email
Note the ease with which systems were once again blamed.

QUESTION:

- What is the role of technolgy in developing the customer experience?

SELECTED FURTHER READING:

- 'Learning from problems' (Chapter 13). Johnson, R., Clark, G., Shukver, M, (2012) 'Service Operations Management' (Fourth Edition), Pearson

USEFUL WEBSITES:

http://www.highways.gov.uk/
http://www.amazon.co.uk/

TECHNOLOGY CASE STUDY T5

In this age of identity fraud this case highlights examples of the problems with user authentication and the security of passwords which continues to be an issue even with experienced users of technology.

Identity crisis

Our increasing use of computers has heightened the importance of how we identify ourselves to computer systems *(identity authentication).* I was horrified when a quick count of unique user names, passwords, and PIN's I am required to have in use to access all my on-line accounts and memberships numbered in the hundreds! An obvious consequence of having this many (in an attempt to avoid too much reuse) is the inability to operate safely and securely and at the same time observe the security advice to not write them down but commit them to memory. This is made even harder when a preferred or regular 'user name' isn't available and you are forced to adopt an automatically generated alternative. If you are lucky, or named 'Xavier', 'Yolander', or 'Zenah', it might contain some letters that are meaningful to you, but these are usually random and system generated with an alpha numeric mix in upper and lower case characters. Some systems also force you to change the password on a regular basis and won't allow you to reuse any of the previously used passwords, or parts thereof, or repeat numbers in sequence, or use full stops, underscores, or other symbols, or even letters in alphabetical sequence (ascending or descending).

Having just changed laptops I realised how dependent I had become on the machine to automatically insert passwords when it recognises the initial character of a valid user name. Yet it took nearly fifteen minutes to remove any trace of personal data from an on-line airline check-in transaction for a flight using a publicly accessed computer in a hotel, this taking longer than the transaction itself! So now I'm reduced to a listing of accounts with user names, passwords, i.e. a directory of what I have to remember, but where do I store it, and do I dare take it anywhere with me? This 'PIN and password blindness' drives some unusual behaviour. I know of one person who used to embed her ATM PIN within a fictitious telephone number in her address book as a way of remembering what numbers to use. So it should be no surprise that the most frequent calls made to computer help desks is password related, especially when the user returns to work following a vacation!

Research conducted during 2005[8] suggested that adults on average had two PIN's and eight usernames to remember, and less than 60% of respondents could remember two of them unprompted. One in four had twice this many and some have 45! It would be interesting to see if this trend had increased, especially following the introduction of Chip and Pin card transactions and the growth of Broadband, internet usage, and on-line transactions.

When speaking to a group of South African retailers in Cape Town we discussed the likelihood of using biometrics at the point of sale, a move that apparently many South African retailers are quietly supporting, as are the Banks in an attempt to counter ATM fraud and customer authentication. The use of fingerprint identification is being seriously evaluated in order to remove the use of PIN's. This was all looking promising until an unwitting bank official made a bullish statement in a newspaper article that fingerprint identification would make it difficult for the ATM criminals, as *"it would mean that they would have to chop off a person's finger to gain access to their money"*. In a country that has experienced some of the world's highest crime rates and personal attacks you can imagine that there is a nervouesness about this method of authentication.

On-line registrations

Registration is a prerequisite of using many on-line services these days, and nearly everything you enter into, such as travel loyalty schemes, supermarket discounts, cashless parking, all have an on-line element to them that requires that you first register, often including your payment details (i.e. credit card and bank account numbers), generating even more user names and passwords. Just reflect on how many of your Christmas gifts this year will require on-line registrations for guarantees, or after sales service, as they incorporate a 'software key' that you have to access on-line to enable use of the product.

A recent change of job brought this '*password scrabble*' to a head for me. The number of 'registrations' that use an email address as a proxy for username forced a string of changes. This was a real test of my recall of 'passwords' and even memorable events; places; and the meaningful security question prompt, especially for those less frequently used or dormant accounts. So frequently used is my mother's maiden name, first school, road I grew up in, favourite place, the name of my pets, that they must now cease to be secure, especially as you increasingly run the risk of your bank records or patient medical records being on a computer disc that is 'lost in the post',

8 Research conducted by 'Teamspirit', a financial services marketing company, May 2005.

or on a laptop stolen from the unattended boot of a Civil Servants car!

I noticed that the instructions on a tax form enthusiastically promotes the use of an on-line alternative and encourages you to *"Register for the on-line service at www.hmrc.gov.uk and select Self Assessment under do it online"*. What they conveniently omit is that in order to register you are first issued with a 12 digit alpha numeric code. Then you need a 'Unique Tax Reference' (i.e. a 10 digit number). As I didn't have a UTR, or any correspondence containing same, for security reasons the Revenue would need to post this to me, with apparently a ten-day lead time (heaven forbid that someone might steal my code and pay tax on my behalf)! I would then have to request a PIN, which required yet another posting from the revenue, and another ten day delay. In total somewhere between 14 and 20 days just to register. Surely this severely undermines the principle of convenience, speed, and ease of operation that an on-line offering is meant to promote, whilst adding to a growing list of identification devices.

What can we learn about the processes from this case?

We appear happy to run the risk of increased security issues for the perceived convenience and cost effectiveness that digital transactions bring. Our 'on-line' persona comprises a combination of secret codes, numbers, and phrases, yet despite our best attempts at securing the technology through encryption, it is the user that is the weakest link. The anonymity of using cash in transactions is once again becoming rather appealing!

QUESTIONS:

- The most usual prompts used by sites to remind you of a password you have forgotten are: name of dog, favourite colour, and mothers maiden name. How many of these do you use?
- What level of security should consumers expect of websites they use frequently?

SELECTED FURTHER READING:

- 'E-commerce needs better authentication strategies'. Financial Times, 19th September 2007.
- 'The end of the cash era'. The Economist, 17th February 2007.

- 'Identity parade – It's best for governments not to know too much'. The Economist, 16th February 2008.
- 'Fingerprint scanner could help in battle to end online banking fraud', The Times, 7th June 2008.
- 'Britons put digital safety at risk with pets for password'. The Times, Monday October 21st 2013.
- 'Consumers have to protect themselves on-line'. USA Today (Money), 22nd May 2014.

USEFUL WEBSITES:

http://www.cifas.org.uk/ (**CIFAS** is the United Kingdom's fraud prevention service).
http://www.ico.org.uk/for_organisations/data_protection/registration/data-protection-registration (Information Commissioner's Office)

TECHNOLOGY CASE STUDY T6

This case explores the challenges of the limited bandwidth available to many parts of the UK and the two tier system of broadband access that excludes many from the services now available via this technology.

More eBay and email, shopping and Skype

In the nineteenth century there were no televisions, aeroplanes, computers, or spacecraft; neither were there antibiotics, credit cards, microwave ovens, compact discs, or mobile phones. There was however, an Internet.

During Queen Victoria's reign, a new communications technology was developed that allowed people to communicate almost instantly across great distances, in effect shrinking the world faster and further than ever before. A worldwide communications network whose cables spanned continents and oceans, it revolutionised business practice, gave rise to new forms of crime, and inundated its users with a deluge of information. Romances blossomed over the wires. Secret codes were devised by some users, and cracked by others. The benefits of the network were relentlessly hyped by its advocates, and dismissed by its sceptics. Governments and regulators tried and failed to control the new medium. Attitudes to everything from newsgathering to diplomacy had to be completely rethought. Meanwhile, out on the wires, a technological subculture with its own customs and vocabulary was establishing itself.

Does all this sound familiar?

Source: Tom Standage (1998) Victorian Internet. The remarkable story of the telegraph and the nineteenth century's online pioneers. London. Weidenfeld & Nicolson.

In 2010 the then UK Prime Minister (Gordon Brown) promised 100Mbps speeds to support bandwidth-heavy services[9], yet 11% of homes don't yet receive the 2 Mbps speeds most of us already pay for. I'm constantly amazed at how we think the UK is an internet ready nation when so many applications already rely on (and assume) that reasonable speeds are already being provided.

It's good to know I'm not alone, as a 'Tweet' I read recently asked *"why does the web work better on my Blackberry while hurtling 300 kmph through France on the Eurostar than in central London? Contention rates?"* I concur as how was it possible that I got almost a perfect service out in the Italian countryside at a friend's Umbrian farmhouse on my '3' wireless broadband dongle but can't even reach the '3' network eight miles from the centre of Nottingham?

I despair at the constant stream of advertising material I receive either on-line or by post offering me 'unlimited' services and broadband based facilities – *'More eBay and email, shopping and Skype'*. The vital missing ingredient is the necessary broadband bandwidth to make all these services work, yet despite this we continue to receive promotional material and literature from our existing broadband supplier (BT) who know they can't provide the service!

"With BT Totally Unlimited Broadband you can use your broadband whenever you like, for as long as you like, with no limits and no extra charges. Unlike some other broadband suppliers we'll never slow you down – even at peak times". Which bit of 'totally unlimited' don't they understand? With average download speeds of around 0.5 Mbps it's hard to see how the new and additional services offered by BT can be delivered, and it's impossible to run most YouTube clips or BBC iPlayer without it refreshing every 10 seconds making it impossible to watch. As BT now launches its new Broadband sports services this is yet another service I will be unable to receive yet indirectly will be subsidising through my Broadband rental charges.

So what can we learn from this case about the processes involved?

Despite the widespread adoption of Broadband facilities there are still large swathes of Britain, espececially rural areas, that are not adequately served with Broadband and despite the inexorable advance of Brodband based services there is a two-tier nation emerging where those that have poor or limited access will be disadvantaged by being unable to access applications and services that require a fast connection to make them useable. As the economics of implementation dictate that infrastructure investment will be prioritised by large communities of users then rural areas will remain disadvantaged and run the risk of virtual disconnection.

---

9 The Times 23rd March 2010

QUESTION:

- As timecales slip for the introduction of rural Broadband solutions what is a realistic target for the introduction of 20MB broadband to support businesses and households in rural communities?

SELECTED FURTHER READING:

- *"Broadband speeds third higher than a year ago"*. The Times, Thursday 17th August, 2012
- *"Broadband delays leave rural areas in the slow lane for two more years"*. The Times, Friday 5th July 2013.
- *"Broadband 'blunders hit taxpayers"*, The Times, Thursday 26th September, 2013.
- *"Normal life is impossible without broadband"*, The Times, Monday 30th September 2013
- *"Slow internet puts brakes on Tech City"*, The Sunday Times, 11th May 2014.

USEFUL WEBSITE:

http://www.official-documents.gov.uk/document/cm76/7650/7650.pdf (Digital Britain, Final Report, June 2009.Department for Business Innovation and Skills).

TECHNOLOGY CASE STUDY T7

This case highlights how despite good intentions a reasonable system can be disrupted by supporting elements that are not adequately monitored or controlled, and will have an impact on millions of users if it is allowed to prevail.

Electronic Vehicle Licensing (EVL)

The Driver & Vehicle Licensing Agency (DVLA) introduced Electronic Vehicle Licensing (EVL) in 2004 enabling customers to pay vehicle excise duty online and by phone. However, customers still have the option to tax their vehicles via the Post Office.

On trying to relicense my vehicle I was precluded from using either of the EVL methods (on-line or telephone) as my vehicle insurance that had been renewed just three days earlier was not showing on the Motor Insurance Database (MID)[10]. When enquiring of my insurer why it appeared on the EVL system that my vehicle was uninsured I was told that DVLA won't accept the information from the electronic insurance file for 14 days prior or after the date of tax renewal. The reason given was that it prevents those renewing just to tax their vehicle and then cancelling the policy once this has been done. What I don't understand is how that is any different from the traditional method of producing paper documents (i.e. Insurance and MOT certificates) which could still be cancelled after taxation has taken place.

A quick straw poll of friends and family[11] suggests that for at least 36% of us our insurance renewal dates coincide with our tax renewal dates (i.e. within 14 days) as policy changes and switching of insurers often takes place in conjunction with a change of vehicle, therefore rendering this method unusable for all those who are in this position. However, two respondents reported they had deliberately renewed their vehicle licensing for six

10 The Motor Insurance Database (MID) is the central record of all insured vehicles in the UK. Managed by Motor insurance Bureau (MIB), the MID is used by the Police and the DVLA to enforce motor insurance law ensuring that vehicles driven on our roads are insured at all times.

11 In canvassing responses from family and friends I used the voting buttons (a Microsoft Outlook feature) which apparently doesn't work if the recipient is using an Apple application, interesting in itself.

months (rather than twelve months) in order to stagger future insurance and vehicle licensing renewals so they could take advantage of EVL.

Buried within the MIB website it does say:

> *"Please note that motorists may not be able to use EVL if they have recently changed their name and/or address, changed their insurance company or any details of their vehicle. There may also be problems verifying insurance cover if the tax and insurance are both due at the same time."*

The DVLA responded by saying:

> *"It seems that this is all a question of timing. DVLA has access to the insurance industry systems and are reliant on insurance companies updating the information on policy renewals in a timely manner to ensure we are able to access the information. It isn't correct that DVLA won't accept the information, as soon as the insurer updates the MID we are able to access this".*

The MID only records the expiry date of the current insurance period. Once that current period ends the insurer has to update the database with the new insurance period and although insurance cover may have been agreed with an insurer a few days or weeks in advance of expiry of existing cover, the information is not necessarily sent to the MID until the current policy expires. This can take anything from a matter of days to a few weeks, depending on the insurer concerned.

So what can we learn about the processes from this case?

1. It makes sense that a task as frequent as relicensing your motor vehicle should be made as simple as possible and is ideally suited to an on-line process. However, in an attempt to have a superior method of renewal that is efficient, immediate and convenient, it relies on an inferior method of data transfer from the insurance companies to the MID. Given the frequency that this activity takes place (there were 34.6 million vehicles licensed for use on the roads in Great Britain on the 30 June 2012. Of these vehicles, 28.7 million were cars. The all vehicle figure represents a 0.5% increase on the quarter 2 2011 figure)[12], then it would make sense to improve this.

---

12 The statistics are derived from data held by the Driver and Vehicle Licensing Agency (DVLA), which administers vehicle registration and licensing records in Great Britain.

2. It demonstrates a fundamental lack of understanding of the processes at work here and the behaviours of the customers as it's perfectly legitimate (and natural) for around 36% of us to have insurance policy renewal coinciding with vehicle licensing renewals. So this is a process design that excludes a large percentage of its potential users. The Vehicle Licensing renewal documentation actively promotes the EVL method in the knowledge that approximately 36% of genuine motorists wanting to comply will have no choice but to visit the Post Office.

3. What might now be considered a mature system (it's been in operation since 2004) still relies on a fragile feed of data from subscribing motor vehicle insurers. I suspect that adoption of this method of relicensing would be reduced if first time users who were unsuccessful might not use it again.

QUESTION:

- Who promotes the view of the motorist (i.e. the cutomer) when processes about relicencing are being designed?

SELECTED FURTHER READING:

- *"Switching from paper to on-line might save Government £70bn"*. The Times, Monday September 2nd, 2013.
- *"Number is up for the windscreen tax disc"*. The Times, Tuesday August 26th, 2014.
- *"Computer pile-up as drivers queue for digital car tax.* The Times. Thursday October 2nd, 2014.

USEFUL WEBSITE:

https://www.gov.uk/government/publications/vehicle-licensing-statistics-q2-2012

Afterword:

On 1st October 2014 the Driver and Vehilce Licencing Agency (DVLA) scrapped the traditional paper disc displayed on widscreens in favour of digital records. On the first day of operation the website was receiving 6,000 visits a minute and crashed under what was described as "unprecedented demand".

This short case highlights how careless operations, incompatible procedures, and a disregard for customer satisfaction and experience are amplified or accelerated by inadequate systems or their unthoughtful application.

Last chance to avoid the new penalties

If you're sending Her Majesties Revenue & Customs (HMRC) a Self-Assessment tax return, you can do it online using the secure service HMRC provides. HMRC claim many advantages to filing or sending your tax return online instead of by paper, including automatic calculations, faster processing and later deadlines:

- it's convenient, safe and secure - your account is encrypted, and protected by your chosen password and a unique User ID
- you get an instant acknowledgment as soon as HMRC receives your tax return
- your tax is worked out automatically, so you know what you owe or are owed right away
- HMRC can repay any money you are owed more quickly than if you send a paper return
- the deadline for online returns is later than for paper returns
- you can complete your tax return at your own pace, saving it as you go
- you can tailor your return, completing the right pages for your circumstances
- you can store your completed return online and print out a copy for your records
- you can view your Self Assessment payments and any amounts owed online
- if you're self-employed, you can view liabilities and payments for your business taxes too
- you can amend your contact details or use the secure email channel to ask HMRC a question
- you can pay by Direct Debit - it's safe and secure, and you're less likely to miss a payment deadline
- (Source: HMRC website)

Yet having registered on-line with HMRC for self-assessment tax returns through the Government Gateway[13] system, waited seven days for an activation code, received the appropriate code and ten digit reference number, and completed my return on-line and subsequently received the calculation of the tax owed by me for the year in question, then why do HMRC send me a letter dated 10th January (Figure 7.8), received 18th January, entitled *'Last chance to avoid the new penalties'*, which is a reminder to those that haven't sent the 2010-11 paper tax return to do so before 31st January 2012 in order to avoid paying £100 penalty?

Tax Reference xxxx xxxxx
10th January 2012
Issues by HM Revenue & Customs

Dear

Last chance to avoid the new penalties

If you haven't sent in your 2020-11 paper tax return you must now file online. You must do this by **31 January 2012** to avoid paying the £100 penalty for filing late. Remember you will get even more penalties if you are more than three months late.

Before you can file online you will have to register to use our online service. As soon as you enrol we will send you an Activation Code. This can take up to **seven working days** to arrive so please **do this now**. Go to **www.hmrc.gov.uk/online**

Here are some of the benefits of filing online.

- It is easy and secure
- You can do it anytime you like, save what you have done and go back to it.
- You will get instant confirmation that we have received your tax return
- It works out the tax for you and tells you how much you owe

Please do not file a paper return after 31 January online deadline. Please file online instead or you will get the £100 penalty **and** further daily penalties from 31 January.
If you need help to get started go to **www.hmrc.gov.uk/sa** or phone the Self-Assessment Helpline on **0845 900 0444.**
Go online and be on time.

Figure 7.8: Last chance to avoid the new penalties – HMRC letter

13 The Government Gateway is the centralised registration service for e-Government services in the UK.

Now you could just take the view that you know that you have made the necessary return and can prove same from your correspondence, but having gone through an extensive process of registration and subsequent dialogue with HMRC why do they still send you erroneous correspondence which not only has an associated cost of production and postage, but raises additional questions over the robustness of HMRC's processes and the accuracy of their records, or even your personal tax calculation.

So what can we learn from the processes in this case?

1. It gets passed off as a simple computer error as if that makes it an acceptable action.

2. It decreases confidence in HMRC and their ability to run an effective operation.

3. If nothing else HMRC should demonstrate good housekeeping. In these times of austerity then avoiding the unnecessary expenditure of sending inappropriate and pointless correspondence is important, as collectively this will amount to a significant cost.

4. Receipt of this letter could be the catalyst for additional queries and calls to be made to an already overstretched HMRC department to understand why this letter has been sent (especially as it threatens penalties), and HMRC have a culture of applying charges and penalties automatically which only get removed if YOU can prove they are inappropriate (i.e. guilty until proven innocent)

5. It demonstrates that they don't have an integrated approach. I might concede that if only days apart between filing on-line and receiving this reminder there might be a legitimate timing issue, but there was almost six weeks between the on-line filing and this reminder for a paper return, enough time to ensure this doesn't happen.

6. It erodes the benefits of the online systems.

7. This is counter to tactics allegedly deployed by other departments of HMRC where by using 'nudge' (behavioural change) techniques they tell none or late tax payers that others in similar situations to theirs are paying, which galvanizes them into action. All this does is confirm that the Revenue don't have a clue about your individual tax position and your ability or willingness to pay.

8. Like so many other letters sent in error it becomes noise and you start to ignore them, in some cases fatally!

QUESTION:

- What can you expect from HMRC and what is reasonable for them to expect of you?

SELECTED FURTHER READING:

- 'HMRC - Your charter' (Published by HMRC).

USEFUL WEBSITES:

http://www.hmrc.gov.uk/
http://hmrcisshite.blogspot.co.uk/

CHAPTER EIGHT
The Design of Processes with the Customer in Mind

8.1 Introduction

What follows in this chapter is a series of case studies depicting how processes don't always appear to be designed with the end-user in mind. This 'outside-in' view allows us to examine a diverse range of processes and witness how organisations in the pursuit of their own objectives can ignore the customer requirement.

The customer case studies comprise:

C1. Do the crime in a neighbouring police manor – the Police will never catch up with you: The roles that instinct, perception and learned behaviours take when engaging with unfamiliar processes. This case illustrates the dysfunctional processes operated by Britain's Police forces when collaboration is required across forces, and emphasises the importance of challenging the processes when they appear dysfunctional.

C2. Eat, drink, and be merry for tomorrow we will send the bailiffs round: This case describes the challenges faced by someone growing old while dealing with a series of medical complaints (one of them terminal), and the challenges faced with the rigid and inflexible operating processes that agencies, service providers, and support services insist on following.

C3. The self-service Krypton factor: How Self-service has become a code word for 'bad service' or even worse, 'no service' at all.

C4. Café Culture – a question of line balancing: This case highlights the need to understand the concept of line balancing when providing production-like processes in a fast-food and drink environment.

C5. Your call is important to us: The efficacy of the call centre is directly proportional to the efficacy of the organisation it supports. So before you buy a product or service from an organisation contact their call centre.

C6. e-billing, you know it makes sense: The inability of organisations to provide services that are suited to their customers and the assumption that everyone has an 'on-line' capability thereby discriminating against non on-line users.

C7. It's with my Solicitor for safe keeping but I don't know where to find him: It's likely that most people labour under the illusion that documents lodged with their solicitors are in safe hands, but a recent experience has given me a different perspective.

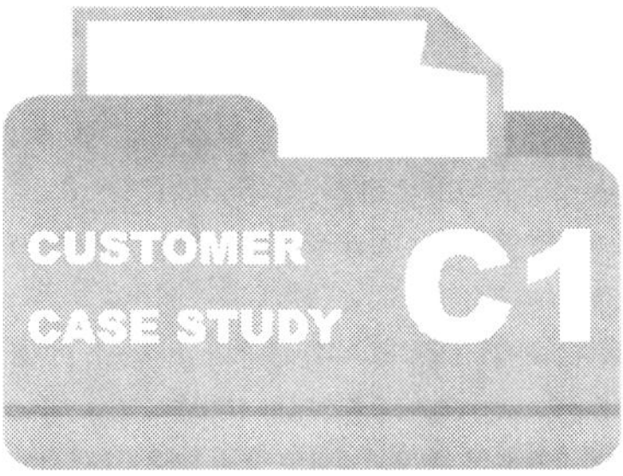

The roles that instinct, perception and learned behaviours take when engaging with unfamiliar processes. This case illustrates the dysfunctional processes operated by Britain's Police forces when collaboration is required across forces, and emphasises the importance of challenging the processes when they appear dysfunctional.

Do the crime in a neighbouring police manor – the Police will never catch up with you

I recently discovered something I suspect the criminal fraternity have known instinctively for some time, that is if you are going to commit a crime then do it in the manor of a Police force outside where you live. Now the obvious conclusion here is that by doing so, you might not be known to a foreign Police force and hence avoid recognition (and therefore capture), but while this might be true what I didn't appreciate is that neighbouring Police forces don't have tried and tested processes and protocols to ensure that this divisional divide of responsibilities is seamless, in fact they generate sufficient confusion and doubt between themselves that any would-be criminal is highly unlikely to have their collar felt.

Background to this case

On balance I'm grateful that I have had very few occasions in my life to need to call '999' (911 in the US etc.) to access the emergency services. My expectations embellished by crime drama of this rare event is that my call would not only be time-stamped and recorded, but more importantly that it would kick-start a series of well-honed processes that are designed to protect the innocent, defend the law abiding, and seek out the perpetrators of crime. Introduced in 1937 the 999 service is just celebrating 75 years of use in the UK (2012) and of those calling the emergency services 52% are connected to the police, 41% get through to the ambulance services, 6% go to the fire brigade, and 1% are for the coastguard and cave and mountain rescue services[14].

---

14 Source: BT, *Cable & Wireless*

However, while driving home one evening, a caravan towing motorist kindly ruined my day by abruptly switching lanes in congested traffic and in so doing reshaping the front nearside wing of my car as his caravan scrapped down the nearside of my vehicle. To make matters worse as I shuddered to a halt he drove off without stopping, it's what the police describe as a 'non-stop RTC'.

My instincts were firstly to get his registration number (and I had the presence of mind to check that both the number on the caravan matched the number on the towing vehicle), and secondly to try and stop his escape by somehow blocking his path with my car, but he now had the advantage of being in-front of me and the congested traffic meant I couldn't get around him to stop him driving off without potentially causing a further accident. With the perpetrator having fled and my car now blocking rush-hour traffic at a busy motorway junction I moved off to find a safe refuge where I could take stock, assess the damage and call 999. What I didn't do before I moved my vehicle, and I now know this to be critical, was to enlist the help of any adjacent motorists who might have seen what had happened and could act as independent witnesses.

As the incident happened in Oxfordshire the Thames Valley Police Force became the primary force managing the investigation and was the recipient of my 999 call. As no one was injured and my vehicle still driveable I was asked the relevant details and told I could proceed on my journey and instructed to report to a Police station of my choice and to take along with me my documents (driving licence, insurance etc.), and to make a statement of the incident. I duly reported to a Police station that evening in Nottingham (where I live) but was unable at that time to see a uniformed member of staff so was interviewed by a Police Constable two days later at my home. I had been careful not to use my car in the interim period so that I could preserve evidence (i.e. paint deposits from the caravan on my car etc.), thereby providing as much information as possible. During the statement collection the PC was able to establish the registered keeper of the other vehicle via the Police National Computer (PNC) although she didn't reveal it to me, but did confirm that the registered address of the vehicle owner was somewhere in the South East of England (i.e. thus involving a third Police constabulary).

Inter-force collaboration

A month passed by and I heard nothing more from either Thames Valley or Nottingham Police so I contacted the PC who had initially taken my statement (i.e. at that time the only named contact I had), and she expressed some surprise that I heard nothing but agreed to investigate why I had not been contacted. Nottinghamshire Police maintain that the necessary administrative processes were completed in full and sent to Thames Valley Police (electronically) on the day of their collection (24th October). Thames Valley however maintains that they have no way of receiving 'outer-force actions' electronically other than by email, and that the relevant documents were not received at their offices until approximately one month later (21st November), and that they were 'actioned' upon receipt. With both forces denying any wrongdoing and each blaming the other for the delay I was forced into the official complaints procedure with each force simultaneously to drive out some answers to the issues I was raising – as both forces couldn't possibly be telling the truth!

Despite Nottinghamshire's initial robust and steadfast denial of there being any issues with how they handled the case from their perspective, the complaints process did force a closer examination of the facts which has subsequently highlighted that error messages had been returned to the originator of the email sent to Thames Valley suggesting there had been a problem with the transmission of the email traffic between Nottingham and Thames Valley. Despite these error messages the Police Constable in question did not take any action to either attempt to resend the documents or contact Thames Valley to establish that they had been received, consequently the case stalled.

Nottinghamshire Police have since conceded that their officer acted irresponsibly by not making further checks as to whether the email documentation had been received by Thames Valley Police when error messages had been flagged on the system. Nottinghamshire Police have since issued local guidelines to all their officers to hopefully avoid incidents of this nature in future, as extracts from correspondence between the forces concerned show:

From: Nottinghamshire Police
To: Thames Valley Police
Subject: RTC documentation

NOTTINGHAMSHIRE POLICE PROUD TO SERVE

It has been conceded that the RTC documentation was ultimately received by Thames Valley from Nottinghamshire by email on 21/11/2011 in order that you could undertake the relevant enquiries into the RTC. There was clearly a failing by our Nottinghamshire Officer in not checking that when the email with documentation attached originally sent on 24/10/2011 had arrived with you. The complaint matter against Nottinghamshire has been locally resolved with learning issues being identified around our failings.

Etc.

Figure 8.1: Nottinghamshire Police email #1

NOTTINGHAMSHIRE POLICE PROUD TO SERVE

From: Nottinghamshire Police
To:
Subject:

Dear Dr Poulson

Following our recent discussion regarding your complaint please see the below email, the main text of which has appeared on our internal Operational Notice Board. This Notice Board is accessed by Officers across the Force area and obviously advises as we discussed to hopefully prevent a similar experience to that experienced by you occurring in the future.

Emailing information/documents to outside agencies
"When Officers are emailing information/documents to outside agencies, including foreign forces, best practice is to ensure that the information has been received by a follow up phone call and to record the name of the person confirming receipt. This is particularly important when documentation relates to investigations. If such documentation is sent by post it should be by recorded delivery in order that there is an audit trail."

Figure 8.2: Nottinghamshire Police email #2

The subsequent delay in sending the statements between the two forces has given the perpetrator of a non-stop RTC the latitude to deny that an accident took place; has allowed him to fabricate counter allegations; and evade the timely inspection of his vehicle which would have undoubtedly revealed the scars of the two vehicles having collided thereby providing unequivocal evidence that there was in fact a collision, which the other driver involved has denied.

Management of the investigation by Thames Valley Police

As the incident happened in the Thames Valley area they become the primary force managing the investigation. Despite their primacy they failed to take control of the investigation, apparently being content at the non-receipt of any supporting documentation from Nottingham for as long as one month after the incident. A telephone conversation with their ACJ

Manager (Traffic) at Thames Valley claims that receipt of the documentation from Nottingham Police would serve as the trigger to recommence activity on the investigation and that no action would have been (nor in fact was) taken until this had been received. Notwithstanding Nottinghamshire's errors, the consequence of a failure to adequately monitor progress in this case allowed the error in Nottingham to go undetected and was exposed only when I made enquiries as to the progress of the investigation, and on that basis nothing would have happened if I hadn't intervened.

Clearly this procedure is inadequate as the failure to identify the missing statement in this case demonstrates, and while Thames Valley Police were quick to blame Nottinghamshire they did nothing to either identify that a statement was missing nor took any corrective action to secure it. Thames Valley Police response to the official complaint has quite skilfully avoided the very issues that are at the heart of this complaint. What I learned from the Nottinghamshire Police episode was that if I had believed their initial response on this matter it would have concealed that they had in fact failed to successfully pass the necessary documentation to their Thames Valley Police colleagues when they said they had. So despite their misplaced confidence it took the allegations of non-receipt from another force to ultimately expose their shortcomings. Thames Valley's response to my complaint is little more than a chronology of events that fails to address the issues raised in the initial complaint, and it places a disproportionate and unfair emphasis on Nottinghamshire Police shortcomings in order to deflect attention from its own.

'Working in partnership to make our community safer' [15]

Our Values

To foster the trust and confidence of our community, we will:

- Treat everyone fairly and with respect
- Act with courage and integrity
- Take pride in delivering a high quality service and keeping our promises
- Engage, listen and respond
- Learn from experience and always seek to improve.

15 Headline from 'Our Aims & Values', Thames Valley Police Strategic Plan 2011 - 2014

I would hope that Police Officers from whatever force are alert to the behaviour of people trying to evade detection when involved in a crime. Failing to stop at the scene of a road traffic accident could similarly be the actions of someone trying to flee the crime scene in the hope that: (i) they can escape detection, (ii) avoid being breathalysed, or (iii) are driving an unsafe or illegal vehicle. These reasons should have been a consideration in this case. That being so I would have expected that the pursuit of the third party who failed to stop at the scene of this accident might have been more rigorous and exacting than to rely on a written request for information (now some five weeks after the incident); without the pressure of being interviewed in person by an investigating officer; being given time to fabricate a counter allegation; and without the benefit of subjecting his vehicle to an inspection. His subsequent statement did of course place him at the scene of the accident, and paint residue deposited on my vehicle from his caravan could have been easily matched thereby proving a collision had occurred, but Thames Valley did not follow this through. Why?

It's hard to reconcile that on the basis of the counter allegation alone the investigating officer concluded that this was believable enough to nullify my original statement; even though I had immediately stopped at the scene and dialled 999; that I was interviewed in person by an officer within 48 hours of the incident (I presented my documents at a local police station on the day of the accident); and the damage to my car was inspected by the officer and photographic evidence obtained. I completely understand how without independent witnesses or other forms of evidence the retrospective apportionment of blame might well be more difficult to assess. However, securing the available evidence and then determining what (if any) action can be taken are two quite separate steps. The failure to secure the evidence enabled the third party to deny a collision had ever taken place and therefore make it difficult to prove. So I can only conclude that the investigating officer must believe that I had obtained the damage to my vehicle in another incident not connected with this one; or had covertly taken paint samples from the third-parties caravan and applied them to my own vehicle to feign a collision with that vehicle at that time in that place; and had wilfully wasted Police time by calling 999 from the scene of a fictitious accident!

Albeit not confirmation of blame, proof that there had in fact been a collision would go some way to discredit the third parties allegations and prove his statement that there had been 'no accident' as unreliable. It also confirms he was either fleeing from the scene because he was aware that he had caused an accident, or if unaware was driving without due care and attention. So on the word of someone who fled from the scene of an accident Thames Valley Police concluded that there was in fact no accident to investigate (despite the clear damage to my vehicle as examined by Nottinghamshire Police). Yet upon renewal of my insurance policy E-Sure still increased my premiums despite there being no claim made by me (nor of course the third-party as he has attested that there was never an accident), this allegedly as a precaution to guard against the third party making a claim at a later date (the so called 'no-fault penalty'

Escalation to the Independent Police Complaints Commission (IPCC)

Thames Valley Police deny any wrongdoing yet have failed to address the issues raised in the original complaint to them and still need to respond to:

(i) Why their suspicions were not aroused when someone fails to stop at the scene of an accident and that their investigations should have taken that into account,

(ii) Why they didn't interview the third party in person, was this because the third party wasn't local and this would involve another Police force,

(iii) Why the third party's vehicle wasn't inspected for evidence of damage (or repair) rather than relying on the driver's word alone that there was no damage,

(iv) Why they didn't examine the evidence provided and match this with the pattern of damage to my car (as it would have shown that the statement was inconsistent) and,

(v) Why was I not given the opportunity to respond to the counter allegations and demonstrate how the pattern of damage to my vehicle could not have been caused in the way the events were described by the third party?

The response from the IPCC will be covered in a separate case study.

So what can we learn from this case about the processes involved?

This case describes the situation surrounding a relatively minor motor accident in which the offender drove off from the scene without stopping. Its purpose is not to question the decision by Thames Valley Police not to pursue the offender, nor the morality of those causing the accident, but to examine how the processes at play in this case were influenced by the varied interests of the actors involved. It shows how it was poorly managed across three police forces and how the inter-force practices don't actively work together.

1. **The fragility of the inter-force working and the cooperation between forces**

   Despite the British Police being organised into constabularies I had believed that they operated in cooperation and that they would have standard processes that operated across forces to reflect best practice and efficiency when operating inter-force. However, it transpires that forces, although governed largely by the Law and PACE (Police and Criminal Evidence Act), operate in an autonomous way. Consequently they don't see the service as a homogenous unit but separate forces leading to hand-offs, divisionalisation, and silo operations. This manifests itself in:

   - Poor/broken systems of communication and protocols across forces
   - Unclear management of the case (who has primacy) and shouldn't they manage it better?
   - Decision making processes of officers (determined by the need to involve another force) and therefore the easy option is taken

2. **The importance of obtaining an independent witness (over anything else)**

   Hindsight is a wonderful thing and the experience of this situation has led me to realise that one of the most important things I could (and should) have done, above anything else, was to secure independent witnesses who could attest to the fact that the third-party did in fact abruptly switch lanes and in doing so ran into my vehicle, then drove off without stopping. Unfortunately, I believed that to quickly report the incident to the Police and avoid further disruption to other road users was the most important. However, without the benefit of having independent witnesses then subsequent claims on insurance policies, or pursuit of the perpetrators, become almost impossible and then becomes their word against yours which results in a stale-mate.

3. **How do other agencies in the process (i.e. Motor Insurance companies etc.) reinforce the importance of securing a witness?**

Interestingly, a quick analysis of the literature of a number of top insurers, including the company I was insured with at the time of this accident, only list securing independent witnesses as approximately fifth in the actions you should take immediately after being involved in a road-traffic accident (see appendix one), and mention no advice on what to do when the third-party fails to stop although they do say that it's an offence not to stop!

4. Perception – the role I thought the police would play in the process

What is clear is that our individual perceptions of how a process might be conducted, and the roles that the actors involved might take, does influence our participation and ultimately our satisfaction with the outcome. In this case my perception was that the Police were the 'defenders of the innocent' and as the innocent victim of a crime I would be shepherded through the intricacies of the process and didn't expect to have to mediate between forces and expose inherent flaws with inter-force working. However, their emphasis throughout was all about how to minimise the workload on themselves and to put their needs first ahead of that of the victims needs.

5. Instinct or learned behaviours

There is a reason why you repeat and rehearse the safety procedures when travelling by aeroplane – it's so that you do them instinctively in the event of there being an issue and that you can recall your learned behaviour.

Having had this experience I would now act differently if I encountered a similar situation, as my learned behaviour would now tell me to prioritise securing independent witnesses over everything else as I now know that the success of subsequent police prosecutions and successful insurance claims relies on having these, and that without them you have little chance of making successful claims against the offending driver. Of course it has also taught me that if I had been the perpetrator of this accident then denial, counter allegations, and the ineffective processes of the Police would ensure I wouldn't be detected!

6. The desire to make a local remedy rather than address the wider issues (Local resolutions were preferred to a wider investigation)

Once Nottinghamshire Police had admitted liability in not handling the correspondence correctly in this case there was a renewed vigour by them to see the complaint designated as a 'local resolution', that is a fast track method to expedite it off their to do list and to 'close' the complaint presumably being able to report that the complainant had been satisfied with the outcome, which helps with their complaint resolution rates. This resulted in the remedy for the broken processes being applied to Nottinghamshire Police only, and was a clumsy procedure for checking that correspondence or email had been received by another force.

7. **Having to use the 'official complaint' mechanisms to get a sensible dialogue with both forces**

The only way to get the attention of Nottinghamshire Police (and Thames Valley Police) and be taken seriously was to enter into the complaints process, as all other attempts to escalate the issue internally had completely failed.

QUESTION:

- Is not the failure to stop at the scene of an accident a criminal offence?

SELECTED FURTHER READING:

- 'Paying the no-fault penalty'. Troubleshooter, The Times, 13th October 2012.
- 'Plebgate cost grows', The Times, Tuesday 1st October 2013.

http://www.justiceinspectorates.gov.uk/hmic/wp-content/uploads/crime-recording-making-the-victim-count.pdf

USEFUL WEBSITE:

http://www.ipcc.gov.uk/ (Independent Police Complaints Commission)

Afterword:

November 2014 saw the publication of the final report of an inspection of crime data integrity in police forces in England and Wales. The report *'Crime-recording: making the victim count'* was produced by Her Majesty's Chief Inspector of Constabulary. Her Majesty's Chief Inspector of Constabulary (Thomas Winsor) said the presumption should be that victims should be believed. The report summary and conclusions included:

Victims of crime are being let down. The police are failing to record a large proportion of the crimes reported to them. Over 800,000 crimes reported to the police have gone unrecorded each year. This represents an under-recording of 19 percent. The problem is greatest for victims of violence against the person and sexual offences, where the under-recording rates are 33 percent and 26 percent respectively. This failure to record such a significant proportion of reported crime is wholly unacceptable.
Even when crimes are correctly recorded, too many are removed or cancelled as recorded crimes for no good reason. Of the 3,246 decisions to cancel, or no-crime, of the crime records that we reviewed, 664 were incorrect. These included over 200 rapes and more than 250 crimes of violence against the person. Offenders who should be being pursued by the police for these crimes are not being brought to justice and their victims are denied services to which they are entitled.
In over 800 of the 3,246 decisions we reviewed, we could find no evidence that the victim was told of the decision to no-crime their report. Victims may be under the impression that their crimes continue to be recorded and investigated when they are not.
We were reassured to find little evidence of the misclassification of crime. Our audit showed that 96 percent of crime records reviewed were classified correctly, either at the time of initial recording or subsequently.

CUSTOMER CASE STUDY C2

This case describes the challenges faced by someone growing old while dealing with a series of medical complaints (one of them terminal), and the challenges faced with the rigid and inflexible operating processes that agencies, service providers, and support services insist on following.

"Eat, drink, and be merry for tomorrow we will send the bailiffs round"

I never anticipated the process minefield I would be entering when I became responsible for an elderly relative, who through a combination of poor health, loneliness, and depression became reclusive, had turned to drink, and completely lost control of his personal affairs. Apart from the distress of seeing someone you knew as being a smart and independent worldly individual who enjoyed life, being reduced to a frail and dishevelled frame, I was even less prepared for how bad the processes we operate in our society actually are, how obviously inflexible, irrational, stupid, dangerous, and so obviously not fit for purpose. As the population continues to grow and the life expectancy lengthens[16] we have a growing elderly population, so the impact of what is discussed in this case will only get more acute and visible over time.

---

16 During the last century, there were peaks in the numbers of births after both world wars and a longer baby boom during the 1960s. Over the next 25 years people born just after World War II, now aged in their 60s, will continue into the oldest ages, reaching their late 80s by 2035. The 1960s 'baby boomers' currently in their mid-40s, will reach their early 60s around 2025 and by 2035 will be in their early 70s.

As these birth cohort's age they will contribute to the continuing ageing of the UK population. In terms of increases in the number and proportion of older people in the UK population, the percentage of persons aged 65 and over increased from 15 per cent in 1985 to 17 per cent in 2010, an increase of 1.7 million people. By 2035 it is projected that those aged 65 and over will account for 23 per cent of the total population.

Source: ONS Population ageing in the United Kingdom its constituent countries

For the purposes of this case let's refer to my relative as 'John Smith'. It's hard to know where to start on this sorry tale but perhaps I'll just describe it as it happened.

The background

On first being alerted to John's situation I had to fight my way through correspondence that was almost knee deep in the hallway of John's bungalow in a Birmingham suburb. Analysis of the letters he had received was both interesting and distressing from a process perspective. Almost all of it had been unopened and so it was reasonably easy to arrange in date order and to piece together the chronology of the correspondence. My immediate concern was for the number of threatening and rather hostile letters indicating the instruction of bailiffs, court orders, or threats to 'cut-off' supplies', and in one instance from an electricity utility company (EDF) an identical letter that had been sent eleven times, each letter exactly the same as the previous one except for their date of posting. What would compel an organisation to send exactly the same letter on the eleventh occasion when the previous ten occasions had had no impact at all? I was to learn that utility companies appear particularly bad at understanding anything that falls outside what they might describe as their 'normal' operating procedures, but what constitutes normal?

Severn Trent Water Limited

A quick triage of the correspondence sifted out that which was of no importance (i.e. marketing leaflets, menus from local Chinese take-a-ways, and free advertiser newspapers), on-going informational and low priority mail, and then the critical or time dependent. There was no shortage of threatening and overbearing letters gradually escalating in severity with a hardening of language as they progressed through the stages. I was drawn particularly to a Telemessage (formerly known as a Telegram) from Severn Trent Water Limited, the water utility company for John's bungalow. The Telemessage followed on in chronology from the previous *'Notice of Court Action – Unpaid Water Services Bill'* (which was edged in black ink making it appear rather funereal); this followed on from the red edged 'Unpaid Water Services Bill'. This matter had been passed to a debt recovery agency so I called them immediately to say I was now handling John's affairs and that I would be settling the bill. To put all of this in context the outstanding amount was £49.67p.

As requested in the Telemessage I then also called Severn Trent Water Limited and explained the situation and that I wanted to pay any outstanding amounts on John's behalf but they refused to entertain any discussion with me as this was not my account and then quoted 'data protection' as the reason. What I couldn't understand was that all I wanted to do was to clear the debt, and I couldn't see how in any way that would breach any data protection issues. I was then told to write to Severn Trent Water Limited to give further information as I also wanted any correspondence from them to be sent to me directly as John hadn't got the capacity at that time to deal with this. I duly wrote to Severn Trent Water Limited using their on-line forms facility on their website (Figure 8.3)

To: customer.relations@severntrent.co.uk
Subject: Ref: Mr John Smith – Account Reference 3456565678

Dear Sirs,

Further to my telephone call earlier today, I was asked to confirm in writing that Mr John Smith is currently unwell and at this time is unable to manage his affairs. Consequently, he has not been able to respond to your correspondence or pay outstanding water services bills. I'm currently organising power of attorney so that I can manage his affairs on his behalf until he is fully recovered. Please advise how we can resolve these issues.

Yours sincerely

Figure 8.3: Email to Severn Trent Customer Relations

The automated email response read as follows:

From:
To:
Subject:

SEVERN TRENT WATER

Thank you for your enquiry, your details have been submitted to the relevant department and we will reply to you within the next 10 working days.

Figure 8.4: Automated email response from Severn Trent Customer Relations

I never did receive a reply to this email but did discover some time later that Severn Trent Water Limited had responded, but to John directly, thereby completely ignoring the very content of the letter and not even affording me the courtesy of informing me of their actions. It took the intervention of a personal friend who is an Executive at Severn Trent Water Limited to take up this case on my behalf and to allow me to make the necessary payments and to get them to review their procedures to be able to recognise that there are legitimate circumstances when payment for water services might be made from someone other than the account holder.

Birmingham City Council - 'Meals on wheels'

For just over a year John had been in receipt of a 'meals on wheels' service, a daily hot lunchtime meal delivered directly to his home operated at that time by the local Birmingham City Council Social Services Department. This way we could be assured that he was receiving at least one hot meal a day. I had been impressed at the conscientiousness of the delivery staff who would telephone me if they were unable to complete their delivery, for example if for some reason John didn't answer the door when they arrived, and this gave me some comfort that they were acting responsibly and recognised the importance of keeping other interested parties informed with what was happening.

However, from the unopened correspondence I was to learn that the monthly charge for this service (approximately £110) had not been paid for over a year, and that Birmingham City Council had instructed a debt collection agency to recover the debt (at that time over £1400). This had been ongoing for some time and as each successive monthly invoice was unpaid it was transferred to a debt recovery agency that delighted in sending threatening letters suggesting all sorts of draconian measures to recover the money. At the point of my intervention they numbered at least eight in total.

I enquired of Birmingham City Council as to how it could be possible for John to run up such a debt without it being investigated, or at least flagged to me, as their drivers would immediately contact me for a host of other reasons, so why not this reason? Their response was that they would never just withdraw a service to a user (in this case regular meals) as they know their users are probably dependent on them. Cynically, I suspect this is to avoid the potential of newspaper headlines that someone in their care had starved to death because the service was withdrawn as a bill wasn't paid. While an admirable sentiment not to withdraw their services because of non-payment they obviously thought that the threat of bailiffs and debt recovery agents knocking on the door to sequestrate your assets was in some way the lesser of two evils (Figure 8.5). This was not a monetary issue as John had the funds but had just lost the ability to manage them.

Debt Recovery Agency

Notification of Intended Court Action

Creditor: Birmingham City Council
Amount due: £99.20
Account number: 909087987676654

You have failed to respond to previous correspondence and the amount above remains unpaid, so please note the following:

- Failure to respond to this notice could result in Solicitors being instructed.
- Should proceedings be issued they may include a claim for interest from the date of our clients invoice, accruing at the rate of 8% per annum together with court fees and legal costs from the date of issue.
- We hereby give you this last opportunity to contact this office to either pay in full or make arrangements to pay. Phone us now on 0871 3841050.
- Do not ignore this notice, as this account will be passed to solicitors within 14 days.

Reference number must be quoted when making payments and on all correspondence and is especially important when making payments to HSBC Bank.

Figure 8.5: Notification of intended court action.

Lasting Powers of Attorney (LPA's)

To help John I needed to take control of his personal finances to ensure that he had access as required to the funds he needed to live on, but also to ensure that all of his standard charges and bills were, as far as possible, managed directly thereby removing the possibility of him running up any debt. The Office of the Public Guardian (OPG) was established in October 2007 and is an executive agency of the Ministry of Justice. Its remit is to support and enable people to plan ahead to prepare for their health and finances to be looked after should they lose capacity in future, and to safeguard the interests of people who may lack the mental capacity to make certain decisions for themselves. The OPG's core functions are to:

- register Lasting Powers of Attorney (LPAs) and Enduring Powers of Attorney (EPAs);
- supervise Deputies appointed by the Court of Protection;
- maintain the registers of Deputies, LPAs and EPAs and respond to requests to search the registers; and

- investigate complaints, or allegations of abuse, made against Deputies or Attorneys acting under registered powers.

As of August 2012 there were 804,005 LPAs and EPAs on the register. This is broken down as follows[17]: LPA: 430,078 and EPA: 262,610.

The process to obtain an LPA was relatively straightforward however it did take a little longer than I would have liked, but once complete I had hoped it would give me the wherewithal to operate John's bank and building society accounts and get his financial affairs in order. Unfortunately as shown here these institutions aren't as prepared as they could be to work with attorneys on their clients behalf. However OPG is trying to work with these organisations to improve the stakeholder management (see fig. 8.6).

Stakeholder engagement – relationship management

We continued to build on the success of our model of stakeholder engagement throughout 2011/12. We value the support and commitment of key organisations and individuals in achieving our objectives to increase the number of people applying for and registering LPAs and to support Deputies effectively in their role. The Strategic and Operational Policy Stakeholder Groups continued to meet to assist us in meeting these objectives. These groups have been particularly helpful in supporting us to raise awareness and recognition of the MCA and providing valuable feedback on our proposed new fee structure contributing to its successful implementation.

We have also continued working with financial institutions so they can appropriately support customers acting as Attorneys or Deputies. A small working group has drafted a document outlining the various kinds of third party authorisations. Financial institutions will then be able to use this document to adapt their training and internal processes. This will be published early in 2012/13. We would like to thank Age UK, the Alzheimer's Society, British Bankers' Association, Building Societies Association, Law Society and Solicitors for the Elderly for being part of the working group that has driven this project forward.

Source: April 2011 – March 2012 Office of the Public Guardian Annual Report and Accounts

Figure 8.6: Extract from Office of the Public Guardian Annual Report & Accounts 2012

17 This only includes the cases which are currently 'live' and does not include applications which have been registered and later cancelled. An example of why an application could be cancelled would be due to the Donor or Attorney passing away. This total does not include EPAs which have not been registered but which are still in use. EPAs are only required to be registered once the Donor has lost or is starting to lose capacity. Whilst the Donor still has capacity the EPA can be used by the Attorney without it being registered with the OPG. This is in contrast to LPAs where it would need to be registered with the OPG before it can be used.

A document "Guidance for people wanting to manage a bank account for someone else" (for consumers in England & Wales) was published but this focusses more on the public than it does the financial institutions.

Lloyds TSB

John had banked with Lloyds TSB for over forty years and the majority of his regular financial transactions were (and could) be administered through the existing accounts he had with them. Despite the initial ease with which I was able to register the LPA with Lloyds TSB for the ongoing administration of John's affairs, it didn't proceed without issues. The bank appeared to have a dysfunctional view on how it allows an attorney to operate another account especially if the attorney is not themselves a customer of Lloyds TSB.

Despite placing 'No Correspondence Indicators' on John's accounts Lloyds TSB were incapable of suppressing the correspondence to John's home and continued to send some of his correspondence. This included replacement credit cards when I had specifically agreed that they should not re-issue them as John was incapable at that time of keeping the PIN (Personal Identification Number) secure, or even remembering it!

It was convenient for me to operate John's accounts by using Lloyds TSB Telephone Banking Service so that I could pay bills, transfer money into an account that allowed him access to funds locally via an ATM, and to set-up and monitor Direct Debits. The Telephone Banking processes were applied haphazardly and on occasions the operator couldn't access the relevant authority for me to operate John's accounts, so refused to help. Similarly, I was told to pretend to be John when using telephone banking as it was easier for them and I would have full authority to undertake all the transactions!

Despite their advanced analysis of transactions occurring on customers' accounts they failed to spot an unusual transaction pattern of ATM withdrawals where it appears John had been pressurised under sufferance to make withdrawals from a local shop that levied a hefty transaction fee each time funds were accessed.

Even after John's death closing the accounts became a fiasco of being passed between branch and head office to get this resolved with branch staff having different understanding of their own organisations processes and procedures.

Council tax payments by Direct Debit – Birmingham City Council

I had paid John's previous council tax payment on his behalf and made provision for correspondence to be sent directly to me so that upon the next renewal I could handle it directly. The current renewal notice arrived at my home address and I proceeded to arrange payment via direct debit, so following the instructions on the renewal form I telephoned the customer service department to set this up.

During the call I explained that I was setting this up on John's behalf for whom I have power of attorney, so the operator insisted on going through a series of security questions: the full address of the property; how the last payment was made; the amount on the current bill and so on. Having answered these all correctly I was then told that I couldn't set up the direct debit over the phone as I wasn't the account holder (i.e. the council tax account holder), despite me having answered all the questions correctly and by prior arrangement the current bill having been sent to my address directly.

I enquired why and was told *"because those are the rules"*. I recognise that might be the case but then enquired what 'the rules' were trying to protect? This request was met with a degree of hostility and a sarcastic response that *"well it's no use debating it as we won't take it"*. I once again asked please (for my own understanding) explain to me what is being protected by you insisting on my sending a mandate (which of course the bank will honour – as they would any other instruction from me) for which there was no real explanation other than to quote 'the rules'. I then asked that if I hadn't said that I was doing this on behalf of John but made out that it was John making the call this would have been accepted, to which the operator answered 'yes'!

'Sorry you're leaving us' - the growing trend of the appropriately named 'erroneous transfers'

The complications caused by the appropriately named 'erroneous transfers' where a dubious authority is obtained from an account holder to transfer their account to another provider. Once the process is underway (be the authority obtained legitimately or otherwise) then the only way of reversing this is to transfer away from the new service provider back to the original one. Commission based door to door salesmen working on behalf of Utility companies who prey on unsuspecting individuals in their home in order to get them to switch energy and utility service providers are making matters worse.

This isn't just an issue for the elderly; I too recently fell victim to the powers of erroneous transfers, when upon receiving the ubiquitous 'sorry you are leaving us' letter (see fig. 8.7) which determined that E.ON had without any real authority passed away my account to Southern Electric. However, as time proved that Southern Electric had no authority to request our electricity account and had acquired it in error, they couldn't bill me for the period it was in their charge. Neither could E.ON, so it cost them both!!

e·on

Sorry you're leaving us

We've just heard that you'd like to leave us and we're very sorry we're going to lose you. Please call us free on **0800 197 3937** (if you haven't spoken to us already), to talk about finalising your electricity account so we can make sure that the transfer goes smoothly. We're here 8am to 8pm Monday to Friday and 8am to 1pm Saturday.

If you don't know that you've entered into an electricity contract with another supplier and want to stay with us, we'll do everything we can to keep you. But please call us today, as there's not much time to try and stop the transfer.

We look forward to hearing from you soon.

Yours sincerely

Customer Transfer Team

Figure 8.7: Erroneous transfer letter – E.On

So what can we learn from this case about the processes involved?

This case describes the challenges faced by someone growing old while dealing with a series of medical complaints, and the challenges we faced with the rigid and inflexible operating processes that agencies, service providers, and support services insist on following. Its purpose is not to call for a completely integrated health strategy or a fundamental overhaul of the National Health Service (albeit that might be beneficial), but to examine through a series of incidents why we make processes that could (and should) be relatively simple and straightforward be as difficult as possible and in doing so create more problems and issues.

1. **Methods of communication:** It's clear from the correspondence received that despite the escalating severity of language and threats of all manner of punishments most of the postal communication reflects the mindless approach by organisations to continue with a strategy of communication that clearly wasn't working. How many more letters would EDF have sent before realising that it was not resolving anything, a process that wasn't working for them or John?

2. **What constitutes 'normal':** Recognising when situations are outside what might be considered 'normal' and require a non-standard treatment, is important to service providers and should be part of their capability to detect those. Clearly, this is a skill as yet lost on Utility companies and banks despite the growing population that is entering this category. What provisions are they making to monitor the appropriateness of their processes to the population they serve, and how do they design-in the flexibility required to handle this?

3. **Lame excuses:** Let's blame this thing called 'data protection' – it's suitably vague, sounds semi-official, and probably creates enough of a smoke screen to deter the less persistent of enquirers. It's in a similar vein to describing it as a 'computer error' as if somehow it's perfectly reasonable that the computer makes an error and you have to put up with it; but unlike blaming a colleague or another department it can't answer back so is a 'safe excuse'.

4. **Appearing to be the person you are helping:** My learned behaviour now tells me that it would have been far easier, expedient, and probably less hassle for the banks and other service providers if I had just passed myself off as John when either on-line or by telephone and in fact Lloyds TSB actually suggested that is what I should do! Processes of this type have to be designed to accommodate friends, relatives or attorneys to easily assist in the support of those in their charge. I understand the need to safeguard confidentiality and security, but any process that prefers that you fraudulently impersonate the account holder rather than operate the lawful and correct procedures, is reinforcing a behaviour that can only makes things worse.

5. **Lasting Power of Attorney:** Despite attempts to train and inform staff of the benefits of LPA's and how the attorney can support the donor, there appears to be a low level of understanding as to how these should operate and each organisation appears to have a unique way of addressing these.

QUESTION:

- How can we ensure that service providers understand how their 'one size fits all' approach only fits where it touches, and how this needs improvement to satisfy a wider range of consumers?

SELECTED FURTHER READING:

- 'New help for people who have to manage an account for someone else' (April 2013). Jointly developed by the Office of the Public Guardian (OPG), the British Bankers Association (BBA) and the Building Societies Association (BSA), working in collaboration with the Law Society, Alzheimer's Society, Solicitors for the Elderly and Age UK. For the first time, banks and building societies have a consistent approach to apply to policy and process in support of third party mandate holders.

USEFUL WEBSITE:

Office of the public guardian:
http://www.justice.gov.uk/about/opg

How Self-service has become a code word for 'bad service' or even worse, 'no service' at all.

The self-service Krypton factor

Self-service is an everyday part of our lives. When it works well it is hardly noticeable, but when it doesn't work it really goes horribly wrong! Two recent experiences with 'self-service' car parking proved just this.

I arrived at Rugby rail station without any prior knowledge of the major building works taking place (I later discovered this was due to the addition of a new platform and this had totally disrupted station operations). Unfamiliar with the site layout I did battle with the assault course of temporary traffic lights to find a car park. Being midday the station car parks were very busy, but I did find a space at the furthermost point from the station buildings. I parked and then had to walk back 200 yards to the 'Pay and Display' dispenser. The fee for the minimum parking duration (24 hours) was £6, and the machine only took coins; no notes; and no credit cards. Having just over £3 in coins I had to look for an alternative way to pay. Adjacent to the pay and display machine was a 'pay by phone' advert describing how by calling one of the two numbers listed you could pay by phone, and included the encouraging statement confirming "all major credit cards accepted".

I dialled the second of the two numbers provided as it was designated as being 'operator assisted'. Having never used this system before, and limited time before my train departed, I thought this would be a quicker and more successful choice. I was greeted with an automated recording explaining that this service was temporarily unavailable! So reluctantly I resorted to the 'automated option'. To save time, or so I thought, I started walking back towards my car, during which I commenced the 'registration process'. Having no prior knowledge of the vendor I didn't really want to 'register', especially as this required that I enter my credit or charge card details, but as the car park was unattended and therefore self-service, I had no option!

Part way through the process I was asked to enter a 4 digit location number. Location number! Frantically looking around to find a number I ended up running back to the pay and display machine to get the number. As I haven't yet mastered the equivalent of breaking the world record for the 200m dash I was unable to enter the number in time before the system ejected me from the process. I then restarted the registration from scratch, and just in case I required any other information I remained in the vicinity of the pay and display machine until asked for my vehicle registration number! Now I'm really good at remembering the registration numbers of vehicles I owned 20 years ago, but as for the current vehicle it could be anything. In the absence of a ticket to display as proof of payment, the parking information explains how the accuracy of entering the correct number into the system is vital, as it was the only method by which the parking attendant would know if you had paid the fee (Parking attendant, where are they when you need them?).

Once again I had to sprint the length of the car park to my car. Then followed the laborious task of having to enter a seven digit alpha numeric registration number in to a mobile phone keypad. The phones multi-function buttons require confirmation that you actually mean, for example, the letter 'L' by confirming with the number (3) from the audible instructions you receive after each key, this to distinguish from the letter 'J', 'K', or the number '5' all served by the same key selection! If this is your first time using this method it is most confusing.

By this time having registered, requested the appropriate parking duration, and then headed off for the station, I had missed my train! In the 1h 20 minutes wait for the next train I had time to reflect on the fact that I didn't have any form of receipt, a prerequisite for us business travellers. I later noticed that one of the two text messages I had already received from NCP (National Car Parks) included the one liner 'for receipts go to **www.ncp.co.uk/fastpark**.

Of course, the privilege of using this 'self-service' payment method had also attracted a 40p fee, and twenty four hours later (having retrieved my car and travelled some 200 miles from that car park) I received another text reminding me that I could extend the parking time automatically by "calling this number". I'm sure that for the regular traveller using Rugby Station the system, once you are familiar with it, works well. However for the casual user, and I don't know when I will next have to travel via Rugby station, if ever, it wasn't a great customer experience.

If that wasn't bad enough just a couple of days later when parking at Grantham Station I had another disappointing self-service experience. The nearest pay and display parking machine to where I was parked was out of order. The next nearest, in the adjacent parking area, would accept neither my American Express card nor a HSBC Switch/Maestro card. I then proceeded to the next nearest point of payment, which was the station ticket office, where I purchased a parking ticket along with my travel ticket. As I had to park at the furthermost point from the station, and the time taken from the aborted attempts to pay at previous machines was lengthy, I did not have time to return to my car to display the ticket. I informed both the parking attendant and ticket clerk of not being able to 'display' the purchased ticket, and was assured that they would liaise to ensure I was parked appropriately. Of course, upon returning to my car that evening I had received a fixed penalty parking ticket for not displaying a valid ticket!

Central to my defence when writing to then GNER (Now East Coast Mainline) to get this penalty suspended was that a prerequisite of an effective and 'fit for purpose' self-service Pay and Display parking system must be the adequate provision of working payment machines that accept valid forms of payment in the vicinity of where you park. A defence I'm pleased to report that was successful!

What can we learn from the processes in this case?

Self-service should not be a code word for 'bad service' or even worse, 'no service' at all. This cunning plan to let your customers do all the work, and at their expense, should not be condoned by the discerning customer!

1. There is a trend to shift the work (and expense) in undertaking processes from the vendor to you (the customer) in the name of improved efficiency, and 'self-service' is disguised as being better for the customer despite it involving more time and effort on your part rather than that of the vendor.

2. Cinema ticket purchase on-line not only attracts an additional booking fee (thereby making it more expensive for you to supply the labour), but also any benefit is lost when you have to queue at the kiosk in the cinema foyer to print and collect your ticket. Of course you can now print your own ticket at home (once again at your cost) which is marketed as a convenient way for you to avoid the queues in the foyer!

3. Self-checkout in retail is a great alternative when you only have a few items in your basket, but increasingly the number of goods that are on restricted purchase or require a supervisor to assist with promotional codes, bar codes for special items, or queries about payment cards and discounts, reduces the efficacy of these devices.

QUESTION:

- As a consumer, what do you expect from an organisation in return for undertaking the task or activity for yourself (i.e. self-service), or do you just accept that this is the way it is now?

SELECTED FURTHER READING:

- 'Former hockey star stole £450 from Sainsbury's in self-service scam... by scanning all his groceries as loose onions' (Daily Mail, 2nd October 2013). http://www.dailymail.co.uk/news/article-2439872/Ex-international-hockey-player-stole-450-Sainsburys-self-service-scam-scanning-groceries-loose-onions.html?ito=feeds-newsxml

USEFUL WEBSITE:

http://www.link.co.uk/Pages/Home.aspx (LINK ATM Network)

CUSTOMER CASE STUDY C4

This case highlights the need to understand the concept of line balancing when providing production-like processes in a fast-food and drink environment.

Café Culture – a question of line balancing

A combination of business and vacation travel afforded me the opportunity to fuel my voyeurism of retail and service outlet processes in diverse locations such as Melbourne, London, San Francisco, Sydney and Hong Kong. What is immediately apparent is that café culture is ubiquitous; high streets everywhere dominated by vendors of freshly brewed coffee. However, regardless of location, chain, or vendor, what also appears universal in the execution of their business is the complete lack of understanding that there is a relationship between taking and fulfilling your order!

As a customer you are forced to adopt the fast food service model of *Select è Pay è Collect*, where the process is meant to benefit from the division of labour and plays out in series rather than in parallel. Most establishments now operate this production line method where you are corralled into line to give your order to barista #1 at the register, during which you choose what you want and they take your order *(Select)*. They then take your tender *(Pay)*, and pass on your requirements to baristas #2 and #3 to complete the order *(Collect)*. All well and good you might think, but have they ever considered the problem of 'line balancing'[18]?

Most don't use the register (i.e. the place the order is captured), to pass the order down the production line. Instead they rely on a quaint 'shorthand' that has emerged for your 'skinny latte, decaf, double shot with Mocha to go', that gets scrawled onto the side of the waxed paper cup with a thick black indelible pen and sometimes this will also include your name to avoid any confusion as you *collect* (and it makes them appear more customer friendly). The cup then becomes your order docket in this process, which often can't be read by those making up the order, and completely

18 Assigning numbers of operators or machines to each operation of an assembly line so as to meet the required production rate with a minimum of idle time.

breaks down as a process if the customer decides to drink 'in', whereby they switch to using 'real' crockery. An alternative approach is to call out aloud the order in the hope that barista #2 is able to tune-in above the music, remember, and then accurately fulfil the order, especially as they are likely to be mid-way through the previous order while doing this.

Closely-coupled retailing: Has anyone studied the relationship between the length of time it takes to capture an order, versus the time taken to prepare the drinks? How often have you got 2 or 3 baristas taking orders (at say sub one minute per transaction), and only one barista making-up the orders (at say 2-3 minutes per order)? Once you have ordered and paid you are hostages to the process with no alternative but to soak up the experience of your bespoke order being prepared to your exact specification! Then add to this mix the purchase of food, loyalty schemes, and this all becomes a real mess! The reaction of most establishments to more customers arriving is to increase their capacity to take orders, leaving the poor barista preparing the drinks to fall even further behind. Why do they choose these busy times to merchandise their stock, and if all you want is that Mozzarella and Tomato Pannini to go (without any hot drinks) you also get caught up in this dysfunctional production process? *"Sorry about the wait"* becomes the chant of the flustered barista as they hand over a double mocha with extra cream, and then all those awaiting drinks eagerly look at each other to establish ownership. And the poor customers who ordered their drinks for consumption on the premises are still waiting!

McDonalds drive-thru have now started to deploy members of staff with portable hand-held devices in the drive-thru queue in order to increase the flow of orders taken. Great idea but as the queue is still linear in every other respect (i.e. payment and collection) then unless the capacity to put-up the orders has similarly been enhanced then there is no real benefit and it becomes an exercise in deception.

One 'Bakery and Coffee Company' outlet I recently frequented proudly displayed the heritage of the establishment as "trading since 1906". I think some of its original customers could still be awaiting their order. Finally, in the interest of 'balance', I did come across one female barista who demonstrated beyond any doubt the ability of the female of the species being able to 'multi-task'! Not only could she remember several orders, but would also prepare the drinks, and take payment apparently simultaneously. No line balancing problem here!

So what can we learn from the processes in this case?

The simple concept of line balancing is integral to service delivery especially where the activities that make up a process have been sub-divided between a number of operators. The ability to understand the relationships between the activities and their work content and dependency, is crucial in providing an efficient and effective operation.

QUESTION:

- Is there a mismatch between the performance of the service processes and the task for which they were designed?

SELECTED FURTHER READING:

- Operations Management (Fifth Edition) Slack, Chambers, Johnston (2007), Pearson Educational. Pg. 211-214.

USEFUL WEBSITE:

http://www.iomnet.org.uk/Home.aspx Institute of Operations Management

CUSTOMER CASE STUDY C5

The efficacy of the call centre is directly proportional to the efficacy of the organisation it supports. So before you buy a product or service from an organisation contact their call centre.

Your call is important to us

I know it shouldn't, but my heart sinks whenever a call centre is involved in a process, as you just know in advance that there is going to be something about it that irritates you. Whether it's the singing lilt of the operators voice, or the endless *'Vivaldi Four Seasons'* music on hold, punctuated with the repeated messages about how important my call is to this organisation as it leaves me waiting eternally for an operator, or the mindless questions you get asked to confirm your identity despite already having gone through an extensive menu choice and entered your sixteen digit account number and date of birth, only to get a recorded message saying *"this office is now closed. Our opening times are….."* Two of my recent exchanges with call centres have done nothing to improve this view, however they have served to make me think about the inappropriateness of these mechanisms, the inability of operators to ever really be able to answer the query I put to them with the information they have available to respond, or the impossible task they have of trying to make up for poorly designed business processes.

Moving a mobile contract from one service provider (BT) to another (O2), along with the transfer of an existing telephone number, as I tried to do recently, must be a standard transaction in these days of mass mobile usage. However, what was supposed to be a simple process didn't turn out that way, and involved me making six calls to the O2 call centre. I replaced my existing 'BT' SIM card with the one provided by O2, and then waited the requisite twenty-four hours before trying to connect to the network. When the time elapsed the connection couldn't be made. I called O2 'Customer Services', and having gone through the obligatory security exchanges I informed the operator that my mobile phone service wasn't working. Obviously reading from a screen of information about my account the call centre agent rejoiced in informing me that everything was "OK" with the account! Clearly everything wasn't OK as I couldn't use the phone (having gone to extreme lengths to explain how I had to use a different phone to make this call to them)! Despite this, the agent was insistent that everything was in working order when I repeated the explanation that the phone didn't work, and yet he appeared incapable of understanding that, despite what his system was conveying, the phone would not connect to the network. A week and a further five calls later (each time speaking to a different operator and having to explain in full the content of all the previous calls), we established that the SIM card O2 issued had not been set up correctly and if I had ignored their advice (and processes) and just kept the original SIM in my phone all would have been well – so why was I ever sent a new SIM? Luckily they were empowered to make an account adjustment for the loss of service for one week (but only after I prompted them), but I haven't yet plucked up the courage to look at my account statement to see if a credit was actually applied, especially if that means further calls to the O2 'Customer Services'.

Utility companies have regularly become the focus of ridicule as a result of the growing trend of using overseas call centres. The dash to outsource these call centres has invoked a substantial backlash to the use of non-native speaking agents, based in some far flung location, trying to adopt English colloquialisms in an attempt to match and pace local accents, which also includes the use of dialects and slang. Yet when Indian call centres ground to a halt amid emotional scenes of grief-stricken fans mourning the death of the Bollywood film star Rajkumar, causing much disruption to UK based companies and their customers, our love affair with overseas call centre outsourcing began to wane. UK banks are now positively promoting the use of UK based call centres, and Nat West positively differentiate themselves by advertising UK based call centres 24/7. HSBC 'Premier' customers get a differentiated service by being directed to UK call centre operators, obviously recognising the need for a premier service for premier customers. So what does that say about the rest of their customers who have to endure overseas call centres? If this wasn't bad enough, the Austrian Justice Ministry have set up call centres in prisons employing convicted fraudsters and hired them out to private companies. It might just be worth checking that your bank isn't amongst those companies taking advantage of this 'captive audience', and that you could be handing over your personal banking details to a fraudster on the payroll. It brings a whole new meaning to the term 'cell phone'!

E.On (formerly Powergen) continue to send me correspondence regarding an unknown account, quoting an account number that, when referring to their records, shows that the account doesn't exist. I can, and do on a regular basis, confirm that there is no account with these details at this address. I'm not entirely sure that the operators believe that I could possibly be in receipt of any correspondence so addressed, with an account number containing insufficient digits, but I enclosed the originals as proof (if any should be required) in a letter to their 'Customer Service Manager' over six months ago, needless to say I haven't received an explanation, apology, or even a reply. Yet despite their constant mantra of this being an invalid account, they seem unable to stop producing correspondence for it! It is inappropriate to brand these call centres as 'customer service'. From my own personal experience I consider they are inherently flawed and wonder if they really do have a chance of providing a positive customer service. You never speak to the same person twice, thereby having to repeat the nature of your enquiry in full before the next operator can try and help. The nature of your call is often to complain when you are not satisfied with something, often as a result of poor processes and procedures, and invariably the operators are not empowered to construct solutions. I suspect that the efficacy of the call centre is probably directly proportional to the efficacy of the organisation it supports. Unfortunately, the lasting impression of the caller will be impacted by the service they receive from the call centre. So before you buy a product or service from an organisation, contact their call centre.

So what can we learn from the processes in this case study?

1. The elaborate mechanisms to establish the identity of the caller can make it unfriendly and overly complicated, and be an assault course for the caller. Barclays Wealth & Investment Management has recently deployed a voice biometrics solution to automatically confirm the identity of Barclays customers. By engaging in a 20-30 second natural conversation the biometric system can compare the customer's voice against their unique voiceprint on file. If the identity of the caller can't be verified then the process switches to a conventional knowledge-based authentication process.

2. The information available to the operator is usually truncated or insufficient to handle a more detailed enquiry which results in another call or a hand-off to another department or function.

3. The very nature of an 'in-bound' call centre makes the likelihood of speaking to a single operator unrealistic, and speaking to a different operator and having to explain in full the content of all the previous calls is tedious. Clearly there is a need to engineer call centre processes to ensure either a single call can complete the transaction, or devise a way to connect the caller to the operator that dealt with the original call.

4. Empower call centre operators to make account adjustment or take other action to rectify poor service.

5. A recent reversal in trend has seen more call centres revert to 'on-shore' rather than the 'off-shore' variety that had been in vogue over the last ten years. This is largely to address the issue of native speaking agents but is also a reaction to the erosion of labour arbitrage advantages that had previously been enjoyed by off-shore facilities.

6. A premier service for premier customers is admirable, but that doesn't mean your ordinary customers require a sub-standard service.

QUESTION:

- If you have a choice of requesting information on-line or speaking to someone at a call centre which do you choose?

SELECTED FURTHER READING:

- *'British Gas under fire for using more call centres in India'*, The Times, 8th March 2008
- *'Do you want to buy any double glazing? I'm calling on my cell phone'*, The Times, 25th March 2008.

USEFUL WEBSITE:

www.nuance.com/voice-biometrics.

The inability of organisations to provide services that are suited to their customers and the assumption that everyone has an 'on-line' capability thereby discriminating against non on-line users.

e-billing, you know it makes sense!

Virgin Media Inc. provides fixed and mobile telephone, television and broadband internet services to businesses and consumers in the United Kingdom. My father, aged 83 years old, subscribed to one of their TV services. Virgin Media insist on sending him a monthly paper bill and charge him £1.75 per month for this (which on an annual basis is a levy of almost 10% of the rental cost). As he pays by direct debit and has a fixed monthly charge he neither wants nor requires a monthly bill and would prefer that they don't send or charge him for it. You can avoid the monthly charge by registering for e-billing (i.e. an internet based service) which enables you to look up your bills on-line and receive emails and marketing literature from Virgin Media, but as my father isn't a silver surfer[19] he is actively excluded from this option. His existing paper bills carry the message:

i Paper bills

Getting your bill in the post costs £1.75 a month. So, to save money, just switch to e-Billing and you'll be saving £21 a year.
See back of page 1 for details.

Figure 8.8: i-Paper bills notice.

19 Silver surfer refers to the trend of ageing people who are tackling using the internet and computers and not the comic strip hero!

I contacted Virgin Media on his behalf some time ago to get this arrangement changed and suggested that they were actively discriminating against customers who didn't have an on-line capability. They agreed to suppress the bills and not charge him. Despite this promise it never happened so I registered on-line on my father's behalf using my own email address to allow him to avoid getting the paper bills and the associated charges.

Even when I was going through the registration process the system required a 9 digit account number suggesting you read if from your printed bill, however only an 8 digit number appears on his correspondence. I then had to ring Virgin Media, run the gauntlet of their IVR system, to eventually talk to an operator who told me that you have to add a zero before the number! I asked him how I would have known to do this as it wasn't mentioned anywhere and he just laughed and said "you wouldn't"!

I'm sure Virgin Media would consider themselves 'customer centred' however this scenario is, I believe, a great example of not only a poor attempt at understanding their customers, but also an appalling attempt at building processes that work.

What can we learn from the processes in this case?

1. Adopting pricing mechanisms to encourage customers to switch from paper bills to an on-line method is legitimate as there will be a higher cost of providing paper bills than the on-line alternative, so the avoidance of the paper bill surcharge appears as a reasonable reward for adopting the alternative method. Of course the apparent incentive is really a tactic to open up an email marketing channel as not only does e-billing give you access to your account and billing details it also enables Virgin Media to email you regularly with offers and promotions[20].
2. It is however discriminatory behaviour towards people like my father who don't have on-line access to these facilities, and therefore the legitimate wherewithal to avoid the surcharge, which at approaching 10% of the total service costs seems inflated.
3. The ability to opt for no correspondence or receive only an annual statement at reduced costs were his preferred options, so as customer behaviour will naturally find a way to avoid what will be seen as an unnecessary surcharge for using the system, then registering a valid email (despite it not being the account holder's) will have the same

20 During August 2013 Virgin Media sent five emails to my father (i.e. to my email address), four of which were promotional advertising forthcoming programmes or related offers. Only one of the emails contained information relating to billing.

effect. So despite the slight inconvenience to me of receiving pointless marketing communication from Virgin Media my father is now able to enjoy his Virgin Media TV services without the billing surcharge. Of course the penalty for Virgin Media in not being able to satisfy this demand is that they are operating under the illusion that they are marketing to my father, when in fact they aren't.

4. Of course the very provision of a cable based TV service is an on-line capability and what would be really effective is if Virgin Media could provide the account status and billing information using the very technology (i.e. via the TV service) they are providing without the need to add additional technology layers to the mix!

QUESTION:

- Is it reasonable that customers who don't use on-line methods of communication are financially penalised for not doing so?

SELECTED FURTHER READING:

- *'The keyboard is mightier – The internet has created a new networked generation'*, The Times, 11th August 2006.
- *'The trouble with computers'*, The Economist, 8th September 2007.
- *'Beware high cost of using cheques'*. The Sunday Times (Money), 25th May 2014.

USEFUL WEBSITE:

Virgin Media: http://store.virginmedia.com

Afterword:

Not long after this case was written my father sadly passed away. A subsequent task for me as his Executor was to cancel services such as Virgin Media. It was ironic that as Virgin Media took instruction from me about my father's death, and then sent the return packaging required for me to return the Virgin equipment to my home address (rather than the address at which the service was registered), and that I then returned the Virgin Media equipment as requested, that they then asked for proof of my identity by requesting I provide an original utility bill prior to refunding the £10.20 rental credit my father was due. It's hard to see what risk Virgin Media were attempting to mitigate at this point in the process by insisting on having sight of an original utility bill? I did request that they return the utility bill once the transaction was completed as if they consider it as proof of identity then I would sooner it was in my safekeeping rather than theirs. Needless to say at the point of writing this case it was never returned!

It's likely that most people labour under the illusion that documents lodged with their solicitors are in safe hands, but a recent experience has given me a different perspective.

"It's with my Solicitor for safe keeping but I don't know where to find him"

A local Solicitors had ceased trading upon the retirement of the senior partner and although provisional arrangements had been made by them to keep important documents they were holding on their client's behalf in safe and secure storage elsewhere, there was no provision for establishing how to access them.

John had some years earlier made a will which was held for safe keeping with this now retired solicitor. John was not enjoying good health and had let his personal affairs lapse and I had been drafted in to help. When going through his correspondence I came across a letter from his solicitors giving notice that they intended to cease trading upon the retirement of a senior partner, and that John should contact their offices to either collect his will or make arrangements for storage elsewhere. The letter was dated six months earlier than when I found it and was the only correspondence received from them on this matter. I immediately telephoned the number on the letterhead but the number was now disconnected.

Unable to make contact directly with the John's solicitor I was advised by my own solicitor to contact the Legal Complaints Service[21]. With the mission *'Resolving complaints about solicitors'* the Legal Complaints Service (LCS) worked in conjunction with the Solicitors Regulation Authority in its role as a regulator of the solicitors' profession. As the solicitors in question had ceased trading I was unable to exhaust their own internal complaints procedure but LCS were able to act on my behalf. Fortunately LCS were able to make contact with the solicitor at a private address and establish what arrangements had been made for the secure storage of documents left in their charge. From this it was possible to trace the new location of the documents and via a firm of Chartered Accountants, retrieve the will and make alternative arrangements for its ongoing secure storage.

21 The Legal Complaints Service was a body that formally investigated complaints about solicitors, which was superseded by the Legal Ombudsman in 2010.

What can we learn from the processes in this case?

1. One written letter to John informing him of the change in circumstances with no follow-up to that original letter doesn't seem like the actions of a responsible professional solicitor, nor is it a robust process. The fact that John didn't respond did not raise any further action on the solicitor's part.
2. No obvious provision had been made to handle requests from former clients, for example forwarding addresses or contact details for storage related enquiries. Arrangements should have been made to make this information available to The Law Society and other professional bodies that would be an obvious point of contact for those seeking information.
3. Were it not for the services of the LCS I would have had great difficulty in tracing the whereabouts of the document storage so that it was possible to retrieve John's will.
4. It was suggested by one professional contact that John should make another will rather than search for this original (something that defeats the whole point of making the provisions in the first place).
5. We take for granted that professional services such as solicitors will operate robust and secure processes especially where legal and other important documentation is concerned, and trust them with our most important and valuable documents and possessions, but as this case demonstrates it is not an assumption we should make at all.

QUESTION:

- Who should check that these provisions have been made and who should that information be registered with?

SELECTED FURTHER READING:

- Complaints against solicitors and other lawyers. Standard Note SH/HA/3762. Last Updated 6th March 2013. Author: Catherine Fairbaim.

USEFUL WEBSITE:

The Legal Ombudsman www.legalombudsman.org.uk

CHAPTER NINE
The Behaviours of People in Processes

9.1 Introduction

What follows in this chapter is a series of case studies describing the behaviour of people within processes. It depicts how people are largely unpredictable, difficult to organise, and inherently selfish. It also explores issues with tackling organisations through complaints procedures, ombudsmen and arbiters.

The behaviour case studies comprise:

B1. Would you like help with packing your bags: Is this just a UK phenomenon that groups raising funds are allowed to terrorise shoppers at the checkout on the busiest shopping day of the week?

B2. Now wash your hands: So why do we think that the sort of people who would avoid washing their hands after going to the toilet; dispose of their chewing gum in the urinals; or forget to turn off the taps after use (three regularly occurring notices in male toilets); will alter their behaviour because of a notice giving them instructions to do so?

B3. How do you complain about the complaints process: How bodies such as the Financial Ombudsman Service and the Independent Police Complaints Commission are being used to arbitrate on an increasing level of complaints that aren't being resolved directly with the originating institution.

B4. Help us to be as good as we can: While I recognise the value of such data gathering, it only becomes useful if the feedback actually modifies behaviour, changes attitudes, or results in an improvement of processes.

B5. The world's favourite airline – what price loyalty?: Do loyalty schemes really build loyalty?

BEHAVIOIUR CASE STUDY B1

Is this just a UK phenomenon that groups raising funds are allowed to terrorise shoppers in supermarkets at the checkout on the busiest shopping day of the week?

Would you like help with packing your bags?

It was a busy Saturday morning at our local supermarket, and uncharacteristically forced to shop at the weekend we battled our way through the hordes towards the checkout. Oh what joy as we rounded the last aisle to view all 35 checkouts with long lines and the approach aisle invisible for a sea of people.

So was this just shear weight of shoppers? Well not entirely! As we made our way up our line towards the checkout we could see the angelic faces of two children, a boy and a girl, accompanied by a harassed adult. The boy obviously bored and preferring to be with his friends playing football rather than trapped in a supermarket, kindly stopped picking his nose when the checkout assistant asked *"would you like help with packing your bags"*? Now what do you say? From the 'T' shirts being worn by the kids (and their adult minder) they were raising funds to fight the proposed closure of a local pre-school nursery. Clearly not wanting to offend them when our turn came around we timidly responded *"yes please"*!

It was at this point that I took up a position behind the kart (i.e. the furthermost distance from the little angels) so that I could avoid any possible temptation of a Basil Fawlty like 'clip to the head' as our little helpers happily put any thing in any bag, tipped upside-down goods you would want to stand upright, and disregarded the fragility of items like flowers and greetings cards. The girl inspected every item as if she had never seen them before, poking her fingers through the packaging to examine the texture of the Broccoli (very educational)! Her limited stature meant that on average five items was all she could handle per carrier bag. Then followed the double handling as the obviously stressed adult was trying to combine the part-filled bags thereby compounding the problem. It didn't help though when struggling to get a French Stick (i.e. a long thin bread loaf) to balance upright alongside other items in a half empty bag, she solved the problem by 'folding it', thereby breaking it into two halves, so that it could be packed 'efficiently'! Thank goodness my wife was with me and able to cautiously supervise operations while making the children feel as if they were adding value and earning our donations. Unfortunately they were just making the lines longer, elongating the transaction times, and raising the blood pressure of shoppers.

What can we learn from the processes in this case?

How can both the needs of the charity and the needs of the customers be met without causing such disruption?

QUESTION:

- Is this just a UK phenomenon that groups raising funds for good causes are allowed to terrorise shoppers at the checkout on the busiest shopping day of the week?

SELECTED FURTHER READING:

- *'Stores that drive customers nuts'*. The Sunday Times, 5th February 2006.

USEFUL WEBSITE:

http://www.customernet.com/ The Customer Service Network (CSN) are a leading independent customer service excellence organisation.

BEHAVIOIUR CASE STUDY B2

So why do we think that the sort of people who would avoid washing their hands after going to the toilet; dispose of their chewing gum in the urinals; or forget to turn off the taps after use (three regularly occurring notices in male toilets); will alter their behaviour because of a notice giving them instructions to do so?

Now wash your hands

There is a wonderful scene at the beginning of the Blues Brothers[22] film where Jake Blues is being released from the 'Joliet Correctional Center'. He is escorted to a collection point at which he is reunited with his personal belongings. He ignores the sign on the wall informing inmates **'when waiting for clothes stand on the line. Do not move beyond the line at anytime'.** Blues disregards this advice crossing the line as he approaches the counter, only to be pulled back by his two burly minders. When required to sign for the return of his possessions, now having learned his lesson, with both feet now firmly rooted behind the line and someway from the counter, like a tree being felled he falls forward, makes a human bridge with his stiffened body to place his 'mark' on the receipt.

I can't watch this film without being reminded of the inability of people to follow instructions or observe the protocols given as part of the services they are receiving, so this case focusses on the behaviour of 'customers' rather than the service providers. Unfortunately, unlike Jake Blues, their minders are not in attendance to help them observe the rules!

I'm intrigued, and constantly amazed by, the mistaken belief that the public will *'toe the line'*, and abide by the rules or conventions, or more practically to observe lines painted on floors, roads, and walkways in the forlorn hope that they will be observed. *[For the avoidance of any doubt, 'line' is being used here to denote a visible mark or symbol often painted upon a surface, as opposed to the American interpretation of a queue of people.]*. The airport baggage collection carousel being a particular favourite, as this never fails to throw up a

22 The Blues Brothers is a 1980 American musical comedy film directed by John Landis and starring John Belushi and Dan Aykroyd as "Joliet" Jake and Elwood Blues, characters developed from the The Blues Brothers musical sketch on the NBC variety series Saturday Night Live.

succession of people who just can't bring themselves to do something as simple as stand 'behind' a line. The line is designed to keep passengers a little distance from the carousel (for their safety and the comfort of other passengers), yet there are always those who will push in front of you to take up 'pole position' right at the front of the waiting crowds, leaving a trail of destruction in their wake as they clumsily manoeuvre their trolley through the crowds into their position, obscuring everyone else's view of the luggage as it approaches, and then being too close to the moving belt to be able to manhandle their luggage from the carousel without cracking the shins of those standing about them. Ruining the process for everyone else but hey, they are OK!

This preoccupation with lines continues, signs reading: **'Keep back from the platform edge. Passing trains cause air turbulence. Stand behind yellow line'** decorate platforms at many stations, yet passengers continue to stand on the very edge of the platform even when high speed trains pass through the station without stopping, severely compromising their safety, and no doubt testing the nerves of the poor train drivers.

The unattended taxi rank between London's St. Pancras station and Kings Cross, is a joy to behold. At the head of the queue the rank comprises three 'bays' from which you can access a taxi, allowing three simultaneous 'pick-ups' thereby increasing the speed of turnaround and efficiency (in theory)! Despite the bays being clearly marked and numbered, for most it appears beyond their capability to recognise the process and adhere to it. And oh the anxiety if you are fourth in the queue and you are now faced with the dilemma of leaving the security of being at the head of the main body of that queue to take up position at bay #1 in readiness for the next trio of taxis to move into position. You have to hope that those behind you follow your example and move into the shortly vacant bays 2 and 3, rather than squeeze between the barrier and kerb to take the fourth and fifth taxis in line, thereby completely confusing everyone around and 'stealing' the taxi that was meant for you! So much for Disney Corporation designing queues that pass by the place where you join a ride so that you can observe others engaged in the process before you engage in it.

Motoring related examples are, of course, too numerous to list here but these days does anyone adhere to 'lane' discipline as set out in the Highway Code? In particular, joining from the left has become a game of dare; car parking a contest of spatial awareness to see how many parking bays can be occupied by a single vehicle; box junctions a tessellation puzzle (i.e. how many vehicles can you get into a limited space without overlapping); and distance chevrons on the carriageway of the M1 intended to encourage separation from the vehicle in front, have become an open opportunity for other road users to precariously thread themselves between you and the vehicle in front.

So why do we think that the sort of people who would avoid washing their hands after going to the toilet; dispose of their chewing gum in the urinals; or forget to turn off the taps after use (three regularly occurring notices in male toilets); will alter their behaviour because of a notice giving them instructions to do so? And have you ever counted the number of items shoppers have in their baskets when they are in the **'5 items or less'** queue?

I'm always acutely aware when travelling by air of the cacophony of sound as the seatbelt sign is turned off after landing and everyone rushes to release their seatbelt. However, I'm even more amazed by those who have perfected the 'silent' seat belt release, whereby they appear to be compliant but are in fact ready to depart the aircraft prior to landing. My wife was reminded of the importance of these 'rules' as her hand was crushed between a fellow passenger's bag and the armrest of her seat as he attempted to retrieve his overweight hand luggage from the overhead locker before the aircraft had come to a complete halt. He then lost his footing as the aircraft lurched towards the gate dropping the bag on her hand in the process. She was not amused although was badly bruised!

Great idea if it wasn't for the passengers!

Anyone who as an interest in business processes and has spent endless hours in airports will know that the procedures we are forced through when travelling (in particular by air) are laborious and inefficient, and many a time I have redesigned the processes in my mind to be more efficient, traveller friendly, and time saving. So I read with interest the article on a faster way of boarding planes which could save time and money ("Please be seated", The Economist, September 3rd 2011).

The proposal was to board passengers window seats first, then middle seats, and finally aisle seats, and all this by alternate rows as congestion is often caused by passengers stowing their luggage in the overhead compartments so this gives them some room to do so. Of course to many of us this would seem a good way to proceed, and I'm sure I remember Lufthansa undertaking trials of boarding window seats first (although not in alternate rows) more than twenty years ago.

However I fear this approach is fatally flawed as it assumes that passengers have the will and ability to be compliant and disregards completely human nature, and imagine the anxiety of them not being able to stow their luggage in their preferred overhead locker near their seat as the space had been taken up by earlier boarding passengers. It also raises an interesting issue of families being asked to board separately which could be a challenge when small children are travelling.

So what can we learn from this case about the processes involved?

1. What hope then for honesty boxes (also known as an honour box)? Although, I did come across some interesting research recently (Bateson, Nettle, & Roberts 2006)[23] which appears to show that using the image of a pair of human eyes in the signs and notices associated with a honesty box in a university coffee room, dramatically increased (by up to three times) the money collected for drinks taken, thereby providing evidence for the importance of cues of being watched, and the effects on cooperative behaviour.

2. So how do these examples inform those of us that design processes where customers are involved? What is it we assume the customer is capable of when we design processes, or do we have to design for the lowest common denominator? Our assumption that common sense will prevail, is perhaps to abandon that common sense. Despite all the good design principles the everyday operational issues often take control, with the associated consequences.

QUESTION:

- As customers we know what we expect from our suppliers, vendors, and service providers, but do we understand what our behaviour as customers shoud be?

SELECTED FURTHER READING:

- *"Please be seated"*, The Economist, September 3rd 2011.
- http://travel.usatoday.com/flights/2010-07-26-continental-self-boarding-houston-intercontinental_N.htm

USEFUL WEBSITES:

www.bpmi.org Site of the Business Process Management Initiative
www.opsman.org Definitions, links, and opinions on operations management.

---

23 Bateson. M., Nettle. D., and Roberts. G., (2006). Cues of being watched enhance cooperation in a real-world setting. Biol. Lett. (2006) 2, 412 – 414. doi:10.1098/rsbl.2006.0509.

BEHAVIOIUR CASE STUDY B3

How bodies such as the Financial Ombudsman Service and the Independent Police Complaints Commission are being used to arbitrate on an increasing level of complaints that aren't being resolved directly with the originating institution.

How do you complain about the complaints process?

As seen in a number of the cases described earlier sometimes you have to enter the complaints process of the organisation you are dealing with in order to get them focused on the issue you have and how they might need to respond. However, as the aforementioned cases have shown, these are rarely adequate and the processes can be superficial and meaningless unless the organisation has the moral fibre to truly and impartially investigate the cause and reasons for the issue. Having to escalate the issue to a third-party, such as an ombudsman, is for most people a process that isn't second nature, and the very process you are subjected to means that only the hardy (or hard done by) will have the tenacity to see it through to the end. This might be a deliberate function of the design (i.e. a deterrent to dissuade false claims), but it can coincide with a time when people are at their most vulnerable, needy or distressed thereby increasing the personal anxiety. This case compares and contrasts the path through two interactions with ombudsman services and the idiosyncrasies of those.

So to reprise the cases in question:

The complaint with Santander UK plc. was over the mysterious disappearance of an investment account believed to have a balance of approximately £33k which I was administering on behalf of a recently deceased relative. The internal complaints process had failed to address (or answer) any of the questions I had put to them and continued to insist that the account in question had been closed some three years before I had originally enquired about it, despite Santander branch staff regularly accessing information about the balance and making it available to me. Santander made several ex-gratia offers of compensation for my time and inconvenience, but have singularly failed to address the issues central to this case as they are at risk of it demonstrating that their systems and processes are fallible which could generate sufficient doubt for their investors thereby inducing a consumer crisis of confidence, the worst possible outcome for a bank. So once the Santander internal processes had been exhausted the only course of action was to turn to the **Financial Ombudsman Service (FOS).**

In the case with Nottinghamshire and Thames Valley Police, the complaint raised jointly with the two forces had been successful in part by securing a local resolution from Nottinghamshire, but the internal complaints process with Thames Valley had once again managed to generate only superficial and one-sided responses with no real sense that the central issues had been understood or examined. Despite repeated attempts to get clarity on the process undertaken, all attempts had been unsuccessful and therefore the only avenue then available was to escalate this to **the Independent Police Complaints Commission (IPCC).**

The processes of both these organisations were similar, and factors common to both were:

- The prerequisite that you must have exhausted the internal complaint processes of the organisation you have a complaint against before they will enter into any process with you. This is understandable but can often mean you have to pursue an unsuccessful complaint through several stages with that organisation just so that you can exit their process completely in order to enter the process of the ombudsman.

- Both processes require that you apply within a specific and non-negotiable time period following the completion of the organisations complaint process (where any lateness is generally not tolerated).

- They also both require that you complete documentation in a prescribed way (which is difficult to complete with brevity without missing vital evidence or supporting information) and there is little opportunity to deviate from this format. They require that you are able to clearly articulate complex situations, arguments, and disputes with the requisite clarity.

- You have to be specific about the nature of the complaint you wish to pursue, which isn't always as clearly defined as you might think, or it might span several different categories of complaint or appeal. For example: (i) where you have made a complaint but were unhappy with the outcome; or (ii) where you need to make a complaint having experienced inappropriate behaviour; or (iii) where you might have witnessed something inappropriate and need to report it

- You need to be aware that you are entering a potentially lengthy procedure. For the IPCC it was twenty weeks between acknowledgement of my application (which had already taken five weeks) and my complaint being allocated to a casework manager. For the FOS at the time of writing this case (August 2013) I was still awaiting an adjudication some eighteen months after entering their process.

- Should you subsequently discover new evidence or information as part of this complaint process which alters the nature of the complaint, then they don't allow a deviation from the original complaint even if their investigations reveal new evidence, and you would be subjected to a new application (along with the associated waiting time) should you wish to pursue this.

- The decision once made is final and neither party will allow further dialogue about the detail of the complaint, even though the final decision can contain factually incorrect conclusions and information.

- Regardless of the time taken to reach a decision which can run in to years, you are expected to respond to the outcome within one month (i.e. 30 days) and this is non-negotiable. Dialogue is restricted to discussion about whether to reject or accept the decision but no discussion is allowed about the detail of the case.

Financial Ombudsman Service (FOS)

The FOS has official powers to sort out complaints between customers and a financial business and can decide what is fair in each individual case. Every year over a million people contact the FOS about financial problems involving banking, Insurance, mortgages, credit cards and store cards, loans and credit, pensions, savings and investments, hire purchase and pawnbroking, money transfer, financial advice, and stocks, shares, unit trusts and bonds. If the FOS thinks a business has treated you fairly, they will explain why. But if they agree the business has done something wrong, they can order them to put things right. The service is free to consumers.

It took between 27th March and 14th August 2012 for an adjudicator to be allocated to my case. It then transpired that the wrong adjudicator had been appointed and that the case had been transferred to another team. They had backlogs so it would take a few weeks more before any action was taken. There has then been an ongoing dialogue (although at a pedestrian pace) between Santander, the Adjudicator, and myself culminating in the adjudicators view that although Santander had eventually admitted that their systems were at fault, and that this had caused their staff to give incorrect and outdated information, he couldn't safely conclude that monies were owed to the accountholder! The case was then forwarded to an Ombudsman for a final decision who concluded that despite the *"extremely unsatisfactory"* nature of this situation Santander UK Plc. should pay compensation limited to £250. No corrective action was imposed on Santander, nor any apology or explanation recorded, and this allows Santander to continue with their current practices unchecked and essentially undetected without any corrective action being enforced upon them.

Independent Police Complaints Commission (IPCC)

This became an appeal against the process undertaken by Thames Valley Police in investigating the complaint and the role therefore of the IPCC was to review the investigation into my complaint and not to re-investigate the complaint itself. So despite any wrongdoing by Thames Valley Police (aided or not by the actions of Nottinghamshire Police) the ruling of the IPCC was that Thames Valley had acted appropriately in their handling of my complaint, and that there is no appeal against their assessment. On reflection it might have been more productive to have complained under a 'direction and control' issue regarding the operational management of TVP and their general policing standards.

The fact that someone fled the scene of an accident without stopping and was enabled by the inadequate processes of the Police to deny that an accident took place, remains unresolved.

What can we learn from the processes in this case?

1. There is a reluctance to openly investigate what has happened in these cases with a preference for entering a 'local resolution' in order to supress the shortcomings of those involved and reduce any consequences.

2. it's a lengthy and time-consuming process that despite the legitimacy of your situation takes a skilful approach and insightful knowledge of the process to extract any sense of fair play.

3. it's as much about understanding the complaint process as it is the complaint itself.

4. It doesn't necessarily bring closure or satisfaction to your complaint.

5. Failure to observe the small issues escalates into failure with the bigger issues. Witness high profile cases such as Stephen Lawrence, Maria Stubbings, and the Hillsborough disaster.

QUESTIONS:

- How good is your organiation at capturing information about problems and learning from them?
- Why do some organisations complaint processes, though intent on staisfying customers, lead to dissatisfaction?
- How can managers use problems to drive improvement?

SELECTED FURTHER READING:

- http://www.financial-ombudsman.org.uk/publications/ar13/index.html Financial Ombudsman Service Annual Review 2012/2013
- http://hillsborough.independent.gov.uk/repository/report/HIP_report.pdf Hillsborough Report
- http://www.archive.official-documents.co.uk/document/cm42/4262/4262.htm Macphearson Report (Stephen Lawrence
- 'EDF forced to pay £3m in customer complaints fiasco'. The Times, Saturday August 23rd, 2014.

USEFUL WEBSITES:

www.citizensadvice.org.uk/index/aboutus/complaints_policy/complaints_procedure.htm
http://www.which.co.uk

While I recognise the value of such data gathering, it only becomes useful if the feedback actually modifies behaviour, changes attitudes, or results in an improvement of processes.

Help us to be as good as we can

It's fascinating these days to witness our propensity for collecting feedback. I'm sure its originally grounded in 'applied customer service' techniques, but it has now become ubiquitous; made easier by our love affair with on-line interactions it's almost impossible to do anything without being asked for a comment, recommendation, or a simple vote. While I recognise the value of such data gathering it only becomes useful if the feedback actually modifies behaviour, changes attitudes, or results in an improvement of processes.

SMS feedback service – East Coast Trains

East Coast Mainline trains operate an 'SMS Feedback Service' where you are encouraged to text the advertised number to give feedback on your journey. The sign carries a three digit code unique to the train coach you are sitting in which you are asked to include in your text as it helps them to locate where you are sitting and give a speedier response.

I duly sent a text explaining that window seat 55 wasn't working (the chair back would only stay in the reclined position). Expecting some interaction (as the message included a unique reference to this carriage) I received the obligatory response:

"Thank you for your feedback - we hope you have a good journey".

Several hours later, having disembarked from the train I received another text:

"I am sorry for the problems with your seat. I will pass your comments onto maintenance control so they can rectify any problems. Regards East Coast

Thank you for your feedback- We hope that you have a good journey".

Prescription Prepayment Certificate

If you have to pay for a lot of NHS prescriptions it may be cheaper to buy a prescription prepayment certificate (PPC) – effectively a prescription 'season ticket'. The certificate is renewed annually and as part of the renewal process you receive an email reminder. You are forced to complete a completely new application, but as they already hold a unique reference linked with all your personal details I suggested on their feedback form that it would have been easier to have asked for any existing certificate number at the start of the application process so that you could pre-populate the fields automatically, thereby reducing keying error, and improving the customer experience by making the process easier. I received the following response:

Subject: Re: Prepayment Web Application Feedback

Thank you for your feedback about your PPC application. At present, there is no link between the application page and the database that holds patient details. Our IT resource is currently committed to another project that will lead to significant cost savings to the NHS, and so this is necessarily taking priority over other service improvements we would like to make along the lines you have suggested. You can be assured however, that your feedback is appreciated.

Kind regards

Review Officer

Figure 9.1: Prepayment Web Application Feedback email #1

Repeating the renewal process one year later I couldn't resist when being asked for feedback to request again this change to their systems. Once again the response I received was:

Subject: Re: Prepayment Web Application Feedback

Dear Sir/Madam

Thank you for your feedback about your PPC application.

Your feedback is greatly appreciated, and supports our commitment to continual improvement. At present, there is no link between the application page and the database that holds patient details, therefore on-line customers have to complete a new application if they wish to renew their PPC. This is something we hope to address in the future in response to customer feedback and to make our systems more efficient.
As this involves a significant system re-design, it is dependent on a Business Case to justify the investment and competing business priorities across the Authority.

Kind regards

Service Improvement Advisor

Figure 9.2: Prepayment Web Application Feedback email #2.

Mercedes Benz

I understand, and indeed applaud, the attempts by Mercedes Benz to gain customer feedback following interactions with their dealer network. However, I now feel that the well-intended objective has become intrusive, annoying, and is actively reducing my inclination to use Mercedes in future.

I have just received the *'How do we make you feel?'* questionnaire following a regular service on my Mercedes vehicle. It now appears it's expected that these will be completed after every service. Also after each service we are asked to complete a satisfaction sheet before handover of the vehicle keys (being forced to assume everything has been conducted to your satisfaction before you are really in a position to assess that, having not yet been reunited with vehicle). You are then telephoned a few days later and asked if everything is OK, which is helpful as it gives you the opportunity to say if it isn't, but the caller goes to great lengths to stress that this is the call that question (x) refers to when you receive the questionnaire that follows in the post, so be sure to answer it correctly!

The questionnaire starts with the heading *'help us to be as good as we can'*; a great sentiment if only they meant it. It then provides space on the form for you to supply the correct details if the pre-printed details are incorrect. Now for the third time, as with both previous questionnaires, I have amended the incorrect postal address and supplied the correct information. Despite this Mercedes still write to me with an incorrect address, so this tells me that despite asking for the correct information, and me providing it, they don't act on it.

It then gives details of the vehicle model type. Once again this is incorrect, which not only means that they can't keep accurate records, but could also result in vital recall or other safety information not reaching me as they have me listed with the wrong vehicle type. Once again, as before, I have corrected the information but when will they act upon it?

Costa Coffee

It feels like every time I visit a Costa Coffee outlet and use my Cost Coffee Loyalty Card I'm invited via email to provide feedback via an on-line survey (it's probably on-in-three occasions in reality). During the transaction I get a receipt that shows a running points balance achieved from previous purchases as well as giving details of the current transaction.

The on-line survey (Figure 9.3) recognises the outlet at which I made my most recent purchase and asks a series of simple questions about the quality of the products purchased, the service provided, and also the cleanliness of the store. The frequency of receiving these requests can be annoying, and although it recognises the store you visited it doesn't recognise when you have used the 'drive-thru' service as a different set of criteria probably applies to that group of customers as it's difficult to comment on the cleanliness of the store when you don't actually enter it in the traditional way.

Unfortunately you don't get the opportunity to offer any other feedback on related issues, as I would most definitely complain that approximately 50% of my transactions with Costa are at outlets that don't yet accept the Costa Coffee Loyalty Cards (because they are a franchise), so the whole proposition is pointless if it doesn't capture those transactions and reward your 'true' loyalty, nor do they understand my real buying behaviour with Costa.

> Thank you for visiting the Costa at Nottingham - Castle Marina RP Drive Thru on 24/05/2013.
>
> To help us assess the quality of our products and services, we would value your feedback about your most recent experience. If you are happy to respond, **please click here** to complete our brief online survey.
>
> Many thanks,
> Costa

Figure 9.3: Costa Coffee feedback email.

And finally, I noticed this sign on the rear of an 'Npower' truck as it passed me as I was travelling at 65 mph:

'This vehicle limited to 56 mph
Well driven call 0800 xxx xxx'

What can we learn from the processes in this case?

1. We are in danger of self-selecting for these studies by giving feedback when your experience is at an extreme (either very good or very bad), and what do you expect from your participation in the process?

2. It can become 'noise' as everyone is now requesting feedback via email and on-line channels and this ability to make contact directly makes it easier to do so. Or is it really just a different method of marketing to you?

3. However, if you do take part then what do you expect from that? Would it help to know that the seat on the East Coast train had been fixed, or that the software changes had been scheduled for future action?

? QUESTIONS:

- How can managers use value to drive continuous improvement?
- How would you identify what customers value in your service?

SELECTED FURTHER READING:

- *"How was it for you? Patients asked for feedback on their time spent in A&E"*. The Times, Friday 5th October 2012.

USEFUL WEBSITE:

http://www.acrwebsite.org Association for Consumer Research.

BEHAVIOIUR CASE STUDY **B5**

Do loyalty schemes really build loyalty?

The world's favourite airline - What price loyalty?

As a regular business traveller you will do anything to make your passage through the airport and subsequent journey as easy and stress minimising as possible, and over the years my British Airways Executive Club membership has been the vehicle for doing just that. A 'Silver' member continuously for many years I had become accustomed to the rewards for my loyalty to BA by being 'fast-tracked' through security lines, prioritised in wait lists, and accumulating BA Air Miles to use on subsequent flights and having access to the relative comfort of the Executive Club lounges was a significant relief from having to hunt for an uncomfortable seat somewhere in the airport. You feel part of the BA family safe in the knowledge that they will make it as good as is possible, and most importantly they will get you home safely. So, as someone else put it better than I can *"upon seeing the Union Flag clad tailfin as you approach the aircraft you feel you are stepping onto English soil in a foreign land"*, and I really did feel that on a number of occasions when travelling alone on long haul business trips.

In many ways my loyalty to BA has been tested over recent years; their increasing un-competitiveness with other low cost airlines made it difficult to defend choosing BA for European trips (especially when the ticket is being purchased by your employer); and their retreat to a predominantly London based airport regime makes it difficult (or near impossible) to fly from regional airports, as even those flights offered from Manchester often go via Heathrow or Gatwick. My current job role doesn't require that I travel as much on BA routes so I had reverted to 'Blue' Executive Club status and was intrigued to receive the correspondence relating to the new 'Bronze' category as I thought it might have been a first step towards recognising life time loyalty (something I have proposed to BA previously – which I note they now operate), but was further intrigued by the claim that the tier points[24] wouldn't be reset in order to help reach the next level more easily. I telephoned Executive Club to check my understanding on this and was told that this was correct, and that at my renewal date (March 2012) my tier points won't be reset!

Knowing I was about to book two Business Class tickets to fly to Canada I made the booking and during the call with the BA Agent we discussed this once again and she clearly confirmed that this trip would take me close to the tier points required for Silver, even calculating what this trip would earn. So imagine my surprise to find that upon my renewal in March 2012 the tier points had been reset to zero, just what I had confirmed would not happen.

I requested that Executive Club take advantage of the recorded telephone facility they constantly announce at the start of each call with the warning *"This conversation will be recorded for training and monitoring purposes"* and listen to the recording of my conversation with their Agent which clearly includes the discussion about this being a purchase, based on the earned points being added to the current balance. On the basis of the information given during that call I made the purchasing decision (which incidentally was approximately £1,000 more expensive that Business Class seats on Air Canada and less convenient as BA don't fly direct to London from Edmonton).

Despite Executive Club agreeing that the recording does clearly include that conversation and that I was misled by the agent their conclusion and remedy of this situation was to offer their Agent training! I subsequently logged a complaint with Executive Club but I gather this doesn't get investigated or escalated but just recorded. I consider their actions are dishonourable, especially when they have clear evidence of the Agent giving misleading information, the basis on which I made a purchase decision, and I expected nothing more than they honour the commitment made by the Agent.

So what can we learn about the processes in this case?

1. Actions like this do nothing to build loyalty (in fact just the opposite), and although I would normally want to choose BA first over most airline's I do that only because I believe that I'm dealing with a

24 Tier Points on flights help you move up through the Blue, Bronze, Silver and Gold tiers of the Club. When your collection year comes to an end your Tier Points are reset to zero. You will start your next collection year at the tier you have just achieved and enjoy a full year at that tier — unless, of course, you make it to the next tier.

reputable and honourable business, but unfortunately this incident severely challenges my assumptions.

2. Why, having made a big issue of the recording of telephone conversations, wouldn't they use that system to check what had been discussed during the transaction in order to establish the accurate position?

QUESTIONS:

- Is customer loyalty genuine?
- Do you understand the value of your customers? Can you calculate a Net Promoter Score and / or the average lifetime value of customers?

SELECTED FURTHER READING:

- 'Scoring Points', How Tesco is winning customer lotalty. Hunby. C., Hunt. T., and Phillips . T. Kogan Page (2003).

USEFUL WEBSITE:

www.britishairways.com

CHAPTER TEN
Case Study Analysis (outside-in)

10.1 Introduction

The purpose of this chapter is to analyse in detail the findings from each of the twenty case studies individually and collectively, using cross-case analysis. When faced with case studies of varying degrees of intensity and wide in scope it was difficult to assimilate all that was taking place, so initially three logical themes appeared to start to make sense of what was emerging. The three themes were: (i) Our relationship with technology and the impact it has on processes (labelled **'Technology'**); (ii) how processes aren't always designed with the end user or customer in mind (labelled **'Advocacy'**); and (iii) the behaviours exhibited by people (actors) within processes (labelled **'Natural Behaviour'**).

However, once each case had been analysed in more detail it was clear that the three themes, while relevant, weren't sufficient to cover the range of findings, and also there were emerging causal conditions within these themes which further described what was actually taking place. So the original three themes grew to six themes and these are:

- **Technology:** Supporting and enabling business processes
- **Advocacy:** Looking at processes through the lens of the customer
- **Natural behaviour:** What actors and customers do when engaged in processes
- **Operations & Service Management:** Observe good operations management practices
- **Communication:** What and how we communicate within processes
- **Issue resolution:** How we resolve issues when processes go wrong

There is a significant degree of crossover between themes as causal conditions are observed in multiple cases and can be observed from different perspectives. The list of causal conditions included here is provisional but provides a basis on which to observe the advocacy inhibitors; communication blockers; technology breakdowns; issue resolution obstacles; operations and service management imperatives; and natural behavioural traits that make up this process landscape.

10.2 Technology - Supporting and enabling business processes

Technology is now an integral part of most operations and processes and by its very nature it is capable of handling high volumes of data accurately and efficiently which is why its use has grown so rapidly, in addition to the economies and profitability that comes with that. However, along with that increased speed and versatility, appears to have developed a complacency and acceptance that technology frequently goes wrong, can let you down, and often promises more than it delivers, and an undesirable attribute of that speed of processing can be the spectacular rate at which small problems can escalate into large ones. The case studies highlighted numerous examples (***Technology breakdowns***) of how customers were inconvenienced by inadequate or unreliable technology.

- **The technology has to perform as intended:** One of the virtues of computer systems is the ability to accurately process high volumes of data relentlessly and we have all come to depend on its accuracy. We rely on institutions such as banks as having the wherewithal to run efficient and effective computer systems thereby ensuring that their accounts accurately reflect the holdings of their investors and the debt of their borrows. We expect our mortgage repayments to be calculated correctly as we do the interest on our savings. The increased scrutiny banks are receiving since the banking collapse, has highlighted a growing trend of errors and miscalculations that appear to be uncovered and confidence in the bank's ability is severely shaken. The banks and others have to regain the confidence of the shaken consumers and rebuild an infrastructure that is fit for purpose and beyond any reasonable doubt.

- **Unusable interfaces**: Paradoxically there is a danger that as devices become more sophisticated (due to technological advances) the degree of usability is reduced and not enhanced. There is also a danger that a predetermined level of competence or capability of the end user has been assumed by the developers that is not entirely accurate. The user interface has to work for the user using it at the time and not be sufficiently intimidating that it drives people into alternative channels, preferring some personal inconvenience rather than ritual humiliation at not being able to work the ATM, chip & pin device, computer, and parking meter. Some people deliberately choose not to own a personal computer (PC) which many organisations have chosen as their preferred communication device.

- **Blame the computer:** Albeit a self-fulfilling prophecy and preferred to admitting guilt, wrongdoing, or inadequate processes, an operator, clerk or service provider will blame an inanimate object such as *'the computer'* as it's considered safe to do so as it doesn't answer back. As a customer it's hard to immediately challenge and creates time for the operator to construct another line of defence or seek further help. It's delivered as if the behaviour of this 'out of control' technology is quite normal and we should be accepting that this is the norm. There appears to be no cognisance of 'the computer' being under the control of the organisation and therefore ultimately their responsibility, nor that managing the computer systems should be a core competency for any organisation.

10.3 **Advocacy** - Observe processes through the lens of the customer

- The case studies highlighted how frequently the outcome or end result of the processes appeared to fall short of customer expectations, and in many instances ended in complete dissatisfaction. They exhibited little or no understanding of the customer's needs or perspective, and were clearly adopting an 'inside-out' mind-set considering their own needs first in favour of any other. Some of these causal conditions exhibited here can be found in other categories too. The case studies highlighted numerous examples of ***'Advocacy inhibitors'*** in how the customer was not the focus of the process or activity.

- **No single view of the customer:** The absence of a single overview of the processes involved from the customer's perspective, reduces customer service. This was visible where disparate functions, departments, or divisions engage with a single customer or service user (as the focus of attention) but without any unifying coordination. This was most noticeable in the social services domain where coordination of different services (or even elements within the same service) was missing. For example, the provision of 'meals on wheels' while simultaneously instructing bailiffs to enter the home and repossess possessions to offset a debt for the service being provided. In this example a 'service-user' centric approach to process design would have been much more effective for customer and service organisation alike and could have avoided unnecessary debt collection activity. Thankfully not everyday occurrences but in extremes the cases of social services neglect of children in danger from violent parents are regularly in the news.

- **Intra-company myopia:** This is the preference for 'local' or 'piecemeal' arrangements over a holistic approach with no incentive to fix wider issues. This is the *'I'm okay you're not okay'* approach which could be about self-preservation or just laziness, but the outcome is similar in that the end customer encounters a fragmented process and a reluctance from anyone to take ownership for fixing the situation. This was characterised perfectly by the desire for Nottinghamshire Police to 'fix' by way of a 'local resolution' their inadequate processes for working with neighbouring forces. Not only did it fail to address the underlying problem it added yet further layers of bureaucratic administration that will compound the situation in future. It also failed to liaise with the other forces to get agreement or harmonisation to the revised approach so that everyone could benefit from this change. There were no plaudits on offer for doing the right thing for the customer, in fact the only real incentive was to show as 'resolved and closed' an official complaint made to Nottinghamshire Police by a member of the public.

- **Inter-company myopia:** We know that organisations need to collaborate within processes to achieve the desired outcome, but when complimentary organisations and agencies actively avoid working together to harmonise their working relationships in favour of their common customer then this has a negative impact on the customer service. For example, the failure of the Office of the Public Guardian to facilitate, in particular, Financial Services organisations to observe and operate a common method of approach to working with Attorneys when they are acting on behalf of the account holder. Or the inability of DVLA to harmonise system interfaces and updates to ensure that vital information required by one of its systems was made available in a timely way thus enabling a seamless and robust service for the end user. It adds no value to the end user to have to navigate around incomplete or fragile processes just because participating agencies aren't working together adequately.

- **Self-service substitute:** Transferring the burden of a process to the customer and branding it as 'self-service' has become all too common especially where there is little or no advantage to the customer for doing it themselves. At best it's disrespectful and at worst utterly deceitful. Yet witness the myriad of services now heralded as being 'self-service' and the implication is that it's for the customers convenience and benefit. Where it works well and is genuinely beneficial for the customer then it can be extremely satisfying, and there is evidence that suggests that being in control of the process, working at your own pace (perhaps in a less pressurised environment) and at a time that suits you, can be advantageous. However, we intrinsically expect that there is a quid-pro-quo and that we might in return receive goods or services faster, cheaper, or to order by doing things for ourselves.

- Increasingly the success of a self-service process is the closely-coupled relationship with the technology that underpins it. The stakes are higher and this is where the proposition fails when the technology doesn't play its part. It's not so bad if you have choice or can actively avoid the self-service option, but increasingly the self-service proposition is the only option.

- **Customer incapacity**: There is a failure to understand that customers have different levels of capability and it's incumbent on organisations to recognise the limitations of customers and treat them according to their capability or ability. In many of the cases there was no adjustment or compensation made for age, infirmity or disability yet these were often observed when viewing processes that were likely to involve the elderly or infirm. Organisations have to realise that while they might have a target consumer profile, it is likely that the actual range of the population that become customers might not perfectly fit their operating model or processes.

10.4 **Natural behaviour** - What actors and customers do when engaged in processes

Although the initial reason for this category was the behaviour exhibited by 'customers' in the process, for example where selfishness, impatience, lack of awareness, or limited understanding might make their behaviour unpredictable or unreasonable in performing an efficient process, it quickly became apparent that the behaviour of the actors working within the processes (i.e. the bank clerks, baristas, call centre agents, and police officers) was as influential and disruptive to the outcome and was also deserving of similar scrutiny. So this section explores some of the natural behaviours observed by both actors (i.e. those working within a process), and customers/service users and explores how those behaviours (**Natural behavioural traits**) manifest themselves in our everyday processes.

- **'Denial' as a defence mechanism:** Denial is an outright refusal to admit or recognise that something has occurred or is currently occurring. The apparent ease with which both Santander & the officers from two Police Forces denied any wrongdoing even before they had investigated the issue is insightful. Recognising the litigious nature of society these days it's understandable that front-line staff avoid accepting any responsibility, but realistic processes would provide for these incidents to be logged and investigated responsibly without attempting to discredit or intimidate the complainant.

- **The role of 'instinct' and how that makes us behave:** If you don't engage with a process regularly (or ever), then depending on the nature of the process instinct might kick-in and dictate what you do especially when that process is personally stressful or threatening. This is particularly prevalent when engaging with the emergency services (Police, Fire, and Ambulance) and when you might be at some personal risk. We like to think we know how we would react in specific situations but the very nature of instinct is that something from within determines what you do which might be different to how you would analyse a situation or process in an artificial way.

- **How 'learned behaviours' from previous experiences will alter what we do next time:** How we approach a process influences what we do when we engage in that process again. This can be both negative (for example avoiding a process that hadn't previously worked due either to systems issues, or as a reaction to an unsuccessful method such as on-line ticket purchases), or positive by being prepared to avoid any issues next time. We practice the emergency crash procedure in an aircraft whenever we travel by plane, not that we intend to crash but at least if the need occurred you would have some level of knowledge and familiarity about what to do to help you survive a crash.

- **My 'perceptions' as a customer:** Rightly or wrongly we have preconceived expectations of actors and what will happen when we engage with them within a process. This can both enhance and detract from the experience but it will directly impact on your behaviour and how you perform. My misguided 'perception' that police officers would try to help and seek the truth following an accident was seriously misplaced. Sadly this perception meant that I trusted their integrity and fair play which turned out to be a mistake.

10.5 Operations & service management – Observance of good operations and service management practices

Operations and service management is about how organisations produce goods or services and manage the resources which are used in the production of those goods and services. It takes 'inputs' and transforms them into 'outputs' (via processes) so this is at the heart of any organisation or business. The Operations Management discipline is vast and covers all areas of the business, and will be relevant to different processes at different times, but it's essential that the 'core' disciplines are understood and feature in good process design. The 'café culture' case provided a good example of how a process, in this case a barista preparing coffee, failed to observe some of the basic Operations Management principles, in particular the dependencies on other parts of the production process (i.e. it takes at least twice as long to prepare the order as it does to select and pay for it), as without it there will be an imbalance of effort and workload creating queues and unhappy customers.

The case studies highlighted numerous examples where Operations and Service Management imperatives weren't observed, and the classic Operations and Service Management texts[25] generally cite four dimensions of operations processes which are particularly important to observe:

- **The *volume* of their output:** for example a high volume fast-food chain might focus on speed of delivery which is enabled by repeatability and systemization of tasks, made possible by investment in specialist equipment or people to focus on specific tasks, yet this high volume creates a low unit cost. By comparison a low volume yet bespoke sandwich shop will not be able to enjoy the luxury of dedicated staff or specialist equipment as their low volume drives higher unit costs.

- **The *variety* of their output:** Royal Mail has a high variety of service, and will deliver any post or parcel collected anywhere in the UK to almost anywhere in the UK (and the world). To achieve this it requires flexibility in its processes, a vast supporting network and infrastructure, however its cost per kg of post delivered will be higher than say a dedicated document exchange bureau that is limited to exchanging documents between major cities and conurbations and therefore is able to standardise the service and enjoy lower costs than their Royal Mail competitor.

---

25 For example: Slack, Nigel, Stuart Chambers and Robert Johnston (2011) Operations Management, 6th edition, FT Prentice Hall, Harlow.

- **The *variation* in the demand for their output:** the pattern for most working days are around 9-5 with a break around lunchtime in the middle of the day. So imagine a bank branch that gets most of its customers arriving during the busy lunchtime period (as local workers visit the bank during their lunch break) yet this is the time that their own cashiering staff also want to take off for breaks. Understanding the dynamics of customer variation throughout a working day is critical if a good customer service is to be provided so the bank must change its capacity in some way to accommodate this variation and ensure that staffing levels match the demand rather than a normal office working pattern. Failure to plan for this effectively not only impacts on the customer service but can also be costly in additional payments to staff, overtime, and unproductive staff with nothing to do at the slack times. In contrast, a service business that doesn't suffer similar variations can plan and schedule more effectively knowing that the pattern is more predictable thereby resulting in a higher utilisation of resources at lower cost.

- **The degree of *visibility* customers have of the production process:** This is about how visible the operation is to the customer. It's likely that the more direct contact you have with your customer or service user during the process will directly determine the visibility they have of your operation. This is particularly true of 'customer-processing' operations (i.e. apparel, healthcare, retail), than it is for material or information-processing operations. However this can also be influenced by the nature of the channel to your market. For example, a clothing company that would normally have a physical presence in the high street could significantly reduce its 'visibility' by switching to an 'on-line' channel, thereby reducing the level of visibility. However a trade-off for this reduced visibility might be reduced perceived service, as the 'personal touch' of having experienced and professional staff attending to you in person can have a very positive impact, in contrast to an 'on-line' experience that might be without soul, and albeit efficient, is void of personal experiences.

10.6 Communication – What and how we communicate within processes

All processes rely on effective communication by being able to give and receive information (instructions, output, facts and figures, progress etc.) between the participating parties. Three big issues that constantly appeared within the case studies were: (i) the inability to authenticate the identity of the customer or service user (or their appointed representative where appropriate); (ii) that the methods of communication were often completely inadequate or inappropriate for the situation in hand; or (iii) the absence of any feedback loops and progress indicators. As technology is progressively the method of choice for this communication and face-to-face communication is diminishing, then the pressure for the chosen method to work is even greater. The case studies highlighted numerous examples (**Communication blockers**) of how the customer was not the focus of the process or activity.

- **Ineffective user authentication:** We make it difficult (or even sometimes impossible) for customers or end-users to engage in processes if they (or their chosen representatives) can't authenticate who they are. The example from Lloyds Bank was shocking as they advised me as attorney for my relative's affairs to masquerade as him when using their telephone banking system, and, as there was no easy and convenient way of associating me with my relatives account details (as I wasn't personally an account holder at Lloyds), they suggested I pretend to be him. Now I can appreciate it might have been offered in good faith (however inelegant) as a quick solution to a problem they couldn't fix in the short term, but it leaves me feeling that it could have been problematic and extremely messy should things have later gone wrong.

- **Dysfunctional communication methods:** It's clearly an inappropriate method of communication if the conversation becomes one sided and doesn't solicit a response. Yet the inflexibility within processes to adapt and modify the methods of communication that suit the end-user do exactly that. I couldn't believe that EDF sent eleven identical letters (identical in every way except for the date) without considering what impact the previous ten had made to the situation. HMRC sending communications that were completely unnecessary yet their existence then raised new enquiries from the confused recipients. Or being asked to ring a call centre only to find that they don't have the appropriate information and you need to speak to another group and they aren't able to connect you so you have to again wait in a call centre queue to be answered.

- **Absence of feedback loops and progress indicators:** It appears that a consequence of a more automated environment is the absence of feedback or any sense of progression when engaged within processes, especially when engaging on-line as the personal and human interface dimension has been removed. It doesn't always allow questions about 'the process' to be considered. Despite the technology being able to determine and provide status updates, comparisons with other users, and the number of people in the queue (virtually or logically) it doesn't appear to be standard practice to make this type of information available. For example, the on-line ticket purchasing processes provides no feedback as to your position in the queue, number of other applicants, or your likelihood of success, all things that are readily available in a physical box office scenario.

10.7 Issue resolution - How we resolve issues when processes go wrong

Issue resolution is not the act of pacifying a dissatisfied customer, although that will be one of the steps in the recovery process, it's more about discovering the causes of why processes go wrong, which inevitably they do, in order that they can be fixed before happening again. So the emphasis here is on 'prevention' before the event rather than 'cure' after the event. We know that many organisations actively seek feedback from their customers/service users but do they use the information they collect productively and creatively? Evidence from the case studies suggest that they don't and in many situations the outcome is aggravated by requesting feedback and then not acting upon it. The case studies highlighted numerous examples (**Issue resolution obstacles**) of how customers were unable to resolve issues that had been created by inadequate or poorly designed processes, or a lack of adherence by the organisation to those processes.

- **Method of appeals when things go wrong:** Although organisations don't plan on failing they should 'plan to respond to failure' and accept that when it happens they need to be able to reply in a responsible way and handle the complaints of their customers effectively, efficiently, and above all honestly. Too many of the case studies described how complaints weren't handled appropriately and complainants were left with no alternative but to seek legal and other help in pursuing a claim once the internal complaints process had been exhausted. Despite the formation of bodies to support aggrieved customers they are inundated with cases which reflects the growing trend of organisations not taking this seriously and relying on the good offices of Ombudsman and others to undertake the time-consuming analysis and subsequent unravelling of the complaint. Organisations also need to realise that understanding customer complaints is a great source of ensuring the issue isn't repeated or is 'designed-out' of any subsequent processes.

- **Hiding behind procedure or protocol (fictitious or otherwise):** Quoting *'the rules'* or making spurious claims that legislation such as the *'data protection act'* is the reason to avoid being helpful and providing a service, has become all too common. I'm sure there are occasions where these acts are prohibitive, but in the normal course of events processes should be designed to observe the laws that govern the operation of that organisation and industry but should be able to distinguish between genuine restrictions and those that are fabricated in order to provide a convenient excuse for poor service. Often when challenged to give an explanation as to how an act such as 'data protection' is being applied and is appropriate to the case in hand it rarely elicits an accurate or informed response.

10.8 Summary

This chapter brings together the cross-case analysis from earlier chapters (seven, eight and nine), and highlights the causal conditions observed. It opens with the three original themes that emerged from the initial grouping of the case studies: (i) Our relationship with technology and the impact it has on processes (**Technology**), (ii) how processes aren't always designed with the end user or customer in mind (**Advocacy**), or (iii) the behaviours exhibited by people (actors) within processes (**Natural Behaviour**). The groupings are then extended to include the wider issues identified through the cases, namely: (iv) the need to observe good operations and service management principles (**Operations & Service Management**); (v) what we communicate within processes and how we do that (**Communication**); and finally (vi) how we resolve issues when processes go wrong (**Issue Resolution**).

PART THREE:
‘Upside-down’

CHAPTER ELEVEN
Process detox

11.1 Introduction

I started this book by stating that I believe organisations don't deliberately set out to design and operate poor processes and nothing I have researched or written here or elsewhere changes that view. I do however believe that most organisations are predestined to operate poor processes, and as this research has shown it's woven into their DNA. So they will need help if they are to avoid the many pitfalls that will lead them to operate poor processes, either for themselves (inside-out), or their customers (outside-in). To make matters worse this is often overlaid by the desire for 'quick remedies' through the piecemeal adoption of technology regularly influenced by fashion (i-phones, i-pads and alike) and before we know it we have a plethora of sub-optimal IT commitments in part determining how we work but with no real coordinated vision and at the same time only partially take advantage of the incumbent technology we already have and end up with the worst of all worlds.

So why 'Process Detox'? Well in much the same way as rehab (rehabilitation) requires that there is a deliberate act and that an alcoholic, drug abuser, or someone with an eating disorder must actively want to change the way they live, then an organisation must actively want to *'kick the poor process habit'* and be prepared for the withdrawal symptoms it will no doubt endure while going through this journey. As with alcohol, drug, and food abuse it's unlikely to be reversed without help, so it follows that for most organisations this will not happen without intervention. So the purpose of this chapter is to help practitioners and organisations alike with those interventions by providing insight, and by whatever path you arrived at this point in the book, whether by the inside-out route, or alternatively outside-in, you should be able to learn from the findings of both parts and inform your approach to suit the conditions you will no doubt individually encounter.

This final chapter starts by building on the work described in part one (chapters two, three, four and five), which was brought together in the case study analysis 'inside-out' (chapter six). The research set out to determine:

- How key architecture decisions are taken
- What are the conditions under which commodity adoption takes place?
- What is the influence of commodity work business processes in that decision-making?

This culminates in what I have described as the ***'seven characteristics of commodity process adoption'***. Despite the original focus of the research being to assess commodity process adoption the findings are equally applicable to all process change activity especially with the 'inside-out' focus. This is supplemented with some practical insights gained from this study that could inform the way managers and practitioners might approach similar situations.

It then builds on the case studies from part two where the technology, behaviour and customer focus issues were examined (chapters seven, eight and nine), and these are brought together and examined in case study analysis, 'outside-in' (chapter ten). The research set out to determine:

- Our relationship with technology and how it influences our actions within processes, especially when it goes wrong
- When processes don't satisfy the end users requirements why that is?
- The behaviours of people in processes and why they act as they do.

This led to the development of what I have labelled as the **'Process A.C.T.I.O.N Framework'.**

I then go on to introduce the new concept of **'Process Smart'** building on the work of Dr Howard Gardner, which looks at the skills and capabilities required of practitioners who work with business processes and is the subject of ongoing research. **Methodological contributions** are documented and the chapter ends with some final **conclusions.**

11.2 The seven characteristics of commodity process adoption (Inside-Out)

In all four cases described in part-one the actors involved adopted a 'structured' approach to decision making following an ordered progression from recognition to resolution, as opposed to an anarchic approach. The findings of this research are therefore predicated on there being a structured approach to decision making and cannot assert that the same outcome would be observed if an anarchic approach were adopted. The research identified that there is a need to understand the closely coupled relationship between process logic, decision logic, and alignment logic. Their relationship in many ways is similar to the well-known 'fire triangle', i.e. the components of fire being fuel, heat, and oxygen, where by removing one side of the triangle results in it collapsing (no fire). The commodity process adoption is much the same. The three sides of the triangle, as illustrated in Figure 11.1 represent the process logic, decision logic, and alignment logic, and all three sides need to be in place (i.e. facilitating commodity process adoption) in order for there to be a sustained adoption of a commodity business process. Each is dependent on the other two.

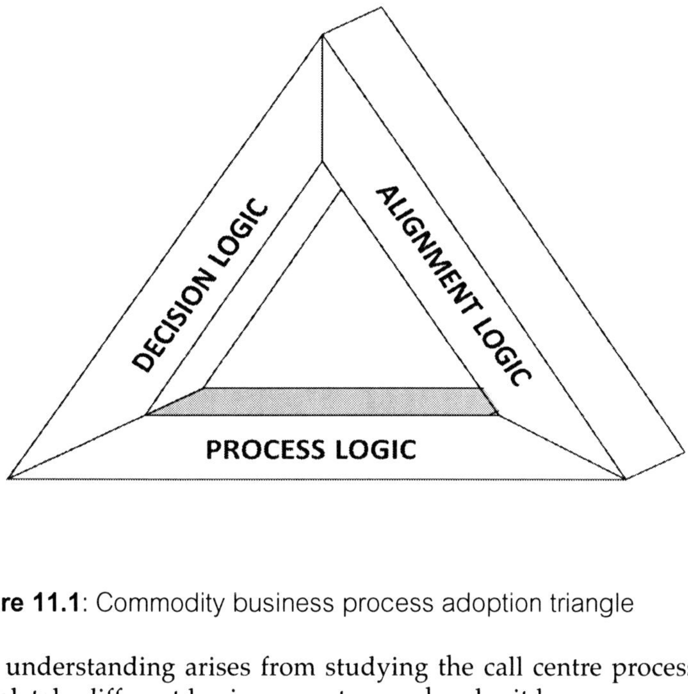

Figure 11.1: Commodity business process adoption triangle

This understanding arises from studying the call centre process in four completely different business ventures whereby it became apparent that even where the components and characteristics of a process might be commodities (i.e. they are not specific to any particular business, are readily obtained, and are more or less equally valuable to any number of businesses), alone this is not sufficient to determine that a commodity process is adopted. The differing conditions under which any decision was made, and the alignment of the different actors in the network, is of equal influence and importance. For example, a strong desire by the actors in the network for a process to be a commodity will not succeed without the components of that process being facilitative, and the conditions under which the decisions are made being supportive to such a commodity approach. Similarly, just because the CEO orders a commodity approach it does not mean that it will be a successful commodity adoption if (i) it does not have the support of the actors involved, and (ii) the process does not have characteristics that are supportive of commodification. Therefore, the components and characteristics of a process not only have to be ***facilitative***, but also the conditions under which the decision is taken have to be ***supportive***, and it has to be ***seen*** to be a commodity by the actors in the network.

This research has demonstrated that commodity business process adoption operates in a dynamic context and not a steady state. It is necessary to conceptualise the dynamic nature of the process, decision, and alignment logics over time, as the characteristics move through different states (facilitating - inhibiting), decision-making at multiple levels in the organisation, and at different times, with different actors in the network. All of which make commodity adoption problematic. Evidence from the process logic findings has highlighted two critically important process characteristics that influence commodity business process adoption, as follows:

ONE: Processes are similar in the core but have a surround that is specific.

The activities at the core of the processes examined were broadly similar, for example in all four cases calls are received, information is exchanged, and details passed to and received from other processes. However, despite this common 'core' there appears to be a 'surround' that is specific to a process, in a particular situation, at a particular time. This was highlighted in examples from the Mail Order case where the uniqueness of its situation (i.e. a mix of outsourced call centre, in-house warehousing, and third-party logistics) made for a situation that was distinctive to those circumstances only, and despite the 'core' elements being broadly similar the context or 'surround' was anything but typical. By using clear terminology (via Activity Record diagrams) some of the descriptive uncertainty can be removed.

TWO: The characteristics of a process differentiate it from any other processes.

The 'surround' as described earlier contains situational and other characteristics that distinguish the process in question from other processes. These characteristics are diverse and unique to a particular situation, but those observed can be usefully grouped into the four categories: (i) *'informational and knowledge'*, which considers the amount and level of information and know-how that is contained within the process and passed between other processes; (ii) *'culture'*, the norms, value and beliefs of the organisation, and how they compare with those of other organisations; (iii) *'administrative inheritance'*, which recognises that organisations start from what is easily accomplished and that they have to accommodate legacy systems, procedures, and processes; and (iv) *'assets, governance'*, which recognises the impact asset specific investments organisations make to support processes, and the issues of governance associated with processes. This is not intended to be a complete or exhaustive list, but is representative of the characteristics observed in these situations. The surround cannot be ignored as it informs the subsequent decisions made, and influences the interests of the actors in the network.

Building on the underlying theory of actor networks, evidence from the alignment logic findings has highlighted two critically important factors that influence commodity business process adoption, as follows:

THREE: The significant difference in the alignment of actors in a network.

The alignment logic recognises the difference in interests of actors in a network. Actors need not always be human individuals but can be non-human entities, and the inscriptions and translations that take place between them emphasise those differences. Throughout the case studies there were numerous examples of how actors (companies, individuals, software products, project teams, managers, and suppliers etc.), had embedded interests within their policies, terms of trading, contracts, products, literature, and procedures, which informed their actions, decisions, and behaviour. An understanding of this variety is key to recognising the inevitable differences it will generate, and that a single or unified view of any situation is seldom automatic.

FOUR: A commodity process has to be seen to be a commodity by the actors in the network.

The strength of any inscription (or irreversibility) must be sufficient to resist the challenges of translations from actors that are not aligned. Therefore, even when a process has facilitating characteristics it will require the alignment of the actors in the network to be such that it is also 'seen' by those actors to be a commodity. The inscription / specialisation framework highlighted the range of interests that could exist when considering the components of a process (i.e. people, technology, know-how, structure and plant & machinery), and the desire for an aligned-commodity (or 'black-box') situation where high inscription and low specialisation components coexist, thereby facilitating commodity adoption. The strength of an inscription can equally legitimise non-commodity alternatives such as the insistence of using BeingWell own staff in the Customer Service call centre. The irreversibility of the inscription to use BeingWell staff was such that it gave this approach a legitimacy that was sufficient to see off any other approach. The research also highlighted how 'hierarchical' and 'intermediate' governance can be used as a mechanism to translate actors in a network.

This research has collected detailed information on the logic surrounding commodity business process adoption across four independent business ventures within one UK retailer, over a five-year period. This work has made a significant contribution to the understanding of the logic required to go about adopting commodity business processes. Such detailed accounts are still rare.

Above all the research shows how adoption of a commodity business process cannot be taken for granted and that the conditions for adoption and the logic applied must be supportive. Three key decision-making conclusions from the study can be drawn.

FIVE: The mix and variety of the decisions taken compounds the differences between processes.

The decision logic has demonstrated that the different conditions under which decisions are made i.e. environments, focus, criteria, uncertainty, and time, and how each of these impact on the decisions taken, as well as what is included and excluded from the decision focus, increases the variety thereby compounding the differences. Every new project appears as a unique situation and is therefore treated differently. Therefore, given all the legitimate *differences* that exist, in even a quite regulated and discrete process such as a call centre, it is not unreasonable to expect that the outcome of a particular business decision might not always conclude that a commodity process would be appropriate.

SIX: Decisions regarding processes take place at multiple levels within a business

The research has shown that decisions take place at multiple levels within a business and that perfect knowledge about those decisions, and why those decisions have been taken, is not always available. For example, decisions are taken at the level of the 'individual', a senior manager or persuasive project team member; at the 'departmental' level, such as in the Customer Service case; or at the 'company' level, as in the Mother and Baby Direct example; and finally at the group of companies level, such as when Group Telecommunications made the asset specific investment in call centre telephony. The outcomes will reflect the rich mix of actors, situations, and contexts. It is not proposed that these comprise a definitive list of levels or types, but that they are indicative of how organisations make decisions about processes.

SEVEN: The closely coupled nature of 'related' decisions and the influence on the final outcome.

The variety and scope of 'related' decisions, i.e. those that don't correlate directly to the process but are closely coupled to it (such as whether to use smart card technology in the Loyalty Card case), are huge and unpredictable and reflect the uniqueness of the context in which a process resides. This uniqueness amplifies the differences between processes, and related decisions have emerged as being important and influential during decision-making and have resulted in a significant impact on the final outcome.

Practical insights

It is worth emphasising some of the practical insights gained from this study that could inform the way managers and practitioners might approach similar situations. Process change will not always be the subject of a rational approach, as it relies heavily on the ability of an organisation to:

- First, clearly identify the work business processes it requires to achieve its business objectives, and in doing so establish the characteristics and components of that process;
- Second, recognise and understand the different conditions under which decisions about business process adoption decisions are taken and the

impacts of those conditions; and
- Third, develop a thorough understanding of the alignment of actors in the network and the significance to the process of inscription and translation activity,

This research has shown that without any formal intervention the dynamic nature of commodity business process adoption makes any sustainable adoption unlikely if left to chance. The configuration of all three of the central logics will at any given decision point rarely be perfectly aligned, however where they are aligned then the likelihood of a sustained adoption of a commodity process is significantly improved. Adoption is more likely where the process logic comprises commodity components, is loosely coupled to other processes, has a high information threshold, and utilises (if required) standard information technology. The decision logic approach would be low in uncertainty, have a choice from many feasible decision schemes, and have adopted a satisficing rather than optimising approach. Finally, the alignment logic would have 'black-box' characteristics (i.e. being highly aligned and a low degree of specialisation), and market governance prevails.

The reality is that when 'real people' are involved then so are their associated prejudices. The adoption of a commodity business process isn't something that all human actors will necessarily do instinctively, why should they? Instead they have to 'learn' to adopt commodity processes, as was demonstrated in the Insurance case. The know-how of commodity adoption is not easily or reliably transferred between actors despite the learning that is available. The research insights generated by the research could easily be developed into practical guidelines for company practice.

For each decision, the call centre requirement showed some unique features. But the subsequent developments show that in fact many of the call centre functions could be handled in a similar way. At the time of the decision, recent history, organisational imperatives and external market supply factors dominated the decision made. In time the functional requirements and basic economics work their way through. Governance of third party organisations proved to be more difficult than originally expected, and opinions of actors can change over time. Interestingly functions initially outsourced were later brought in-house. For many other company functions the movement has been in the other direction.

Organisational variants

"Learning to see the structures within which we operate begins a process of freeing ourselves from previously unseen forces and ultimately mastering the ability to

work with them and change them"[i]. Through the results of this research there has been some insight into the adoption of commodity business processes, using call centres as the focus of the analysis, from the perspective of a single UK retailer. Using the conceptual model of commodity business process adoption as a framework, the model could be applied to different settings (i.e. a different industry or country), or to different work business process such as procurement, business accounting, innovation management, or insurance claims management. Alternatively, different organisational process types could be the focus such as strategic planning, budgeting, and performance management. Building on the findings of this research it would also be possible to investigate how organisations might best approach the design of business architecture in a way that takes advantage of commodity business processes.

11.3 Process A.C.T.I.O.N Framework (Outside-In)

It's impossible to guard against every situation you will come across when developing processes however the repeated occurrence of the causal conditions has led to a set of action strategies that should, if applied appropriately, go some way to avoid many of the bad design decisions made from a customer's perspective. Of course it is important to remember that there is a balance between the needs of the business (inside-out) and that of the customer (outside-in) and that both situations need to be addressed as far as is possible. Built around a slightly contrived mnemonic (but an easy way to recall a simple checklist) the causal conditions are rearranged here to utilise the word 'A.C.T.I.O.N' which helps as a guide to remembering the components of each Action Strategy as follows:

Advocacy – ensures processes are viewed through the lens of the customer
Communication – meaningful two way dialogue with appropriate feedback
Technology – appropriate access and support to enable processes
Issue resolution – simple issue handling when processes go wrong
Operations management - observe good operations management principles
Natural behaviour - what actors and customers do when engaged in processes

In the tables that follow the causal conditions identified in the previous chapter are shown along with a suggested corresponding action strategy for each condition.

Advocacy inhibitors	Action strategies
No single view of the customer: The absence of a single overview from the customer's perspective thereby reducing customer service.	Organisations need to view and design their processes from the perspective of the customer (i.e. often the one place where their focus of attention comes together).
Intra-company myopia: The preference for 'local' or 'piecemeal' arrangements over a holistic approach, with no incentive to fix wider issues.	Try to adopt the *'I'm okay you are also okay'* approach which will lead to an enhanced experience for everyone involved.
Inter-company myopia: When complimentary organisations and agencies actively avoid working together to harmonise their working relationships in favour of their common customer.	Actively embrace these partner organisations and encourage a collaborative approach to process design and ongoing development and management.
Self-service substitute: Transferring the burden of the process to a customer with little or no advantage to them.	Self-service should not be the codeword for 'no' service. Ensure that the end customer benefits from doing part (or all) of the process for themselves.
Customer incapacity: 'one size doesn't fit all' when designing and developing processes.	Understand the variety that exists especially when dealing with the elderly, infirm, or ill, as although a minority (depending on the nature of your business) they equally deserve processes that provide for their needs.

Table 11.1: Advocacy inhibitors and action strategies

Communication blockers	Action strategies
Ineffective user authentication: Making it difficult (or impossible) for end-users to engage in processes if they (or their chosen representatives) can't easily authenticate who they are.	Determine the right way to communicate with customers, substitutes, or attorneys that is meaningful, and to ensure that the process is interacting with a bone fide person who has the authority to act.
Dysfunctional communication methods: Using methods of communication that don't work for the end – user.	Create flexibility in design to cope with multiple scenarios to allow the end-user to engage with the process.
The absence of feedback loops and progress indicators: The absence of timely and accurate information to help a customer understand their progress through a process.	Recognise that the basic need to get feedback on how you are progressing within a process (if at all) doesn't diminish just because the interface is a computer. Information is helpful in determining next steps.

Table: 11.2 Communication blockers and action strategies.

Technology breakdowns	Action strategies
The technology has to perform as intended: Deploying technology that is unreliable and causes problems for both the organisation, and worse its customers, and then taking no responsibility for the resultant issues.	Organisation get the technology they deserve. Take responsibility for the technology deployed within the organisation especially where it 'touches' customers.
Unusable interfaces: Deploying interfaces that don't suit the need or the user and discourage interaction with the organisation.	Ensure that whatever the method of interface is in use by the organisation that it is useable and appropriate for the end user.
Blame the computer: Using the excuse of 'computer error' as the reason for a breakdown in a process whether it be as a result of a technology error or not.	Aim to remove any anomalies in the processes that require a front-line worker to need to give excuses when processes go wrong or when they can't handle the situation. Use these incidents as a learning opportunity.

Table 11.3: Technology breakdowns and action strategies.

Issue resolution obstacles	Action strategies
Method of appeals when things go wrong: Making it difficult to resolve genuine issues of process failure especially when the organisation is at fault.	Plan to respond to failure and accept that when it happens they need to be able to reply in a responsible way and handle the complaints of their customers effectively, efficiently, and above all honestly.
Hiding behind procedure or protocol: Citing rules or laws (fictitious or otherwise) as a reason to avoid doing something.	Aim to remove any anomalies in the processes that require a front-line worker to need to give lame and vacuous excuses when processes go wrong or they can't handle the situation. Use them as a learning opportunity.

Table 11.4: Issue resolution obstacles and action strategies.

Operations and service management imperatives	Action strategies
Volume: The level or rate of output from a process.	Ensure that the desire for low unit costs created from high volumes doesn't skew the process design too much in one direction.
Variety: The range of different products and services produced by a process.	The degree to which processes, products or services are prevented from varying over time (standardisation) has to be tempered with the need to accommodate sensible variety.
Variation: The degree to which the rate or level of output varies from a process over time.	Although stability is easier to manage and generally lower in cost, the need for flexibility should be accommodated within the processes.
Visibility: The amount of value added activity that takes place in the presence of (in reality or virtually) the customer, also called customer contact.	Understand the 'points of visibility' and differentiate between those items that have customer visibility and consequently higher demands, and those which have a lower profile and can be controlled more discreetly.

Table 11.5: Operations and service management imperatives and action strategies.

Natural behavioural traits	Action strategies
Denial as a defence mechanism: The outright refusal to admit or recognise that something has occurred or is currently occurring regardless of the supporting evidence.	Create a safe 'exit' from the process that allows for the calm and non-threatening analysis of the situation which recognises that although uncomfortable for the organisation they might be at fault (and risk).
Instinct: Instinct takes over when I don't know what to do when a process is not encountered regularly.	Consider those processes that would benefit from rehearsal or simulation beforehand just as in preparing to fly in an aircraft.
Learned behaviours: How my previous experience will alter what I do the next time I encounter this situation.	Both positive and negative: How to improve adoption of a system/process by learning from the previous experiences.
Perception: The belief that in a particular situation actors will behave in a pre-determined way.	How do we set reasonable expectations of actors in processes and know what these are?

Table 11.6: Natural behavioural traits and action strategies.

We have seen how when viewed from an 'inside-out' perspective processes favour the organisation, so it follows that when viewed from the 'outside-in' (i.e. through the lens of the customer), then that will have a customer bias. It's difficult to both justify the needs of the organisation and that of the customer (or service user) but that is what we need to strive towards if we are to develop processes that meet the needs of both. These causal conditions and action strategies are meant to be illustrative of what to look out for and suggests possible remedies for those conditions.

11.4 Future Research: 'Process Smart'

From humble beginnings:

It was the summer of 1976 and I had taken the opportunity to work part of the summer vacation at a car dealership not far from where I was growing up. New pre-registered vehicles were delivered to this site as a holding and preparation depot for the main VW, Audi and Renault dealerships in the nearby city. It was after a few days of working there and experiencing how we would misplace car keys and the associated paperwork, and even on some occasions the cars themselves, that it was apparent (well at least it was to me) that there was a complete absence of any process. I realised that it was in the interest of some of my colleagues to ignore this situation as it legitimised their careless approach, however I couldn't just ignore the way we were working.

Over the next couple of weeks I took notes of how we were operating, made counts of vehicles and their movements, logged how many sets of keys were without matched paperwork, and made general observations of problems and issues arising. I compiled the results, came to some obvious conclusions, suggested two alternatives, and made recommendations as to how we could do better. As a naive 17 year old I took my observations to the then General Manager expecting to be kicked out of his office as a cheeky impertinent upstart, yet to my surprise emerged from the meeting with his full support and the responsibility to implement the changes and given just a week to do so. At that time I had no idea that what I had been undertaking was in fact 'Business Analysis', nor did I expect the unrealistic expectations of managers to implement solutions to problems in record time (especially when they had previously largely ignored the problem), but this was to be an important lesson for the future.

Looking back, I now realise that there was in fact an earlier occasion where something similar had happened to me. Our school meals were served in the main dining room which occupied a position to the north of the campus site. Students were timetabled for either first or second lunch sittings, and at each sitting a choice of three menu items was available (usually two hot dishes and a salad). Your time of arrival at the dining hall determined your position in the queue, and in turn whether you had a choice of lunch as portion numbers were limited in each category to reduce waste and therefore choice was further reduced the later your position in the queue. One year the timetabling for our cohort was such that the period prior to lunch was always at a location furthermost from the dining hall, thereby always arriving at the hall later, being further down the queue and receiving reduced or no choice. Our appeals to teachers went unheard as they thought it a case of 'swings and roundabouts'.

It wasn't difficult to simply record on a daily basis our pre-lunch room locations, our positions in the queue and the actual choices available when we reached the serving hatch. Upon presentation of the data the facts were clear which led to a change in the arrangements to ensure that all students had an equal opportunity to get a menu choice. Although I didn't realise it at the time some important lessons were emerging about what I was later to label as 'Process Smart', i.e. having the wherewithal and desire to solve business process problems but in a way that was meaningful, and more importantly the awareness that this is not a skill everyone possess.

So we wouldn't ask a musician to play a Mozart piano concerto at a public performance if we knew that he wasn't an accomplished pianist, nor intimately familiar with the piece and had practiced it many times beforehand. Neither would we ask a footballer to take the crucial match-winning penalty in the final seconds of a vital game if we weren't assured that he was accomplished at penalty shoot-outs, had control of his nerves during a big game, and was probably the best person on the team to succeed. So why then in business do we allow those that aren't 'Process Smart' to design and implement business processes and then be surprised when they fail? Gartner[ii] say that *"Most organisations lack all the skills needed to implement and optimise their business processes"*. How can we guard against that happening and what would a different approach mean for the outcome?

Now it might be more externally apparent and easier to observe if a footballer has natural ball skills or a pianist the dexterity to play difficult pieces of music, but how do you tell if someone has the necessary attributes to analyse a business process and redesign it taking into account all the relevant design criteria? Thinking back to my part-time job at the local car dealership during school holidays, why did I recognise the process failures in what we were doing where others either didn't recognise it or chose to ignore it? More importantly, why did the manager allow me to change the processes so readily without any real credentials for doing so? This has troubled me for over thirty five years and has been reinforced throughout a career that has been centred on business processes and the way organisations operate. Being a good manager or the top salesperson, or worse someone who is underutilised but available to undertake the task, isn't good enough.

So why is it that some people understand processes and their importance, their constitution, design etc., and others quite simply don't? The theory of multiple intelligences (MI) was first developed in 1983 by Dr. Howard Gardner, professor of education at Harvard University. It suggests that the traditional notion of intelligence, based on I.Q. testing, is far too limited. Instead, Dr. Gardner initially proposed eight different intelligences to account for a broader range of human potential in children and adults. These intelligences were: (see also Appendix Three).

- Linguistic intelligence ("word smart")
- Logical-mathematical intelligence ("number/reasoning smart")
- Spatial intelligence ("picture smart")
- Bodily-Kinesthetic intelligence ("body smart")
- Musical intelligence ("music smart")
- Interpersonal intelligence ("people smart")
- Intrapersonal intelligence ("self smart")
- Naturalist intelligence ("nature smart")

The theory of multiple intelligences has strong implications for adult learning and development. Many adults find themselves in jobs that do not make optimal use of their most highly developed intelligences (for example, the highly bodily-kinesthetic individual who is stuck in a linguistic or logical desk-job when he or she would be much happier in a job where they could move around, such as a recreational leader, a forest ranger, or physical therapist).

Notwithstanding Dr Gardner's views that the testing and subsequent scoring of the intelligences is fundamentally inconsistent with the major tenets of the theory, he does concede that tests could be appropriate but only when they are assessed in ways that are 'intelligence fair', that is to examine the intelligences directly rather than through the lens of linguistic or logical intelligences. For example, he suggests that the way to assess spatial awareness might be to allow people to explore a terrain for a while and see whether they can find their way around it reliably, perhaps even when they have to enter or exit at an unfamiliar point.

Developing the work of Dr Gardner, the challenge is to explore ways to determine what 'Process Smart' comprises and how best to test for that capability. I hope it will be possible to profile what good 'Process Smart' looks like and apply that to situations and people who undertake work where the design of processes is key. In short to try and avoid organisations entrusting process design to people who don't really have the appropriate 'Process Smart' skills to do so. Watch this space.

11.5 Methodological contributions

Two principal methodological contributions are discussed here. Firstly, the use of Strategic Choice Approach (SCA) as a research framework to reconstruct the decision logic used within the case studies with hindsight, as told to the author by those involved. The traditional use of SCA is to provide a framework for decision-making by building incremental progress towards a final decision by examining alternative ways of managing uncertainty. The four central themes (shaping, designing, comparing, and choosing) are supported with a variety of techniques to assist in the decision making process. However, in this study the technique was used to *record* the decision-making activity applied to the problem in focus by interviewing actors involved in the original projects. Using the information made available, supplemented by archival records, documents, and direct observation, the decision making process was recreated in each case in a way that captured all the relevant data while providing a complete 'chain of evidence'. This methodology could easily be 'packaged' so that a research student could follow the method and continue this research in other industries or processes.

Secondly, the unique combination of Activity Records, SCA, and Actor Network Theory, in order to analyse the logic of commodity process adoption. The three complimentary techniques provide a holistic approach to understanding the process, decision, and alignment logics at play in commodity adoption. Activity Records provide an explicit visual and narrative description, which reveals the structure of the activity (particularly hierarchy and boundaries), while providing processual context. For example, it has been used by its inventor to document cultural difference in Navajo communities; the recording of the decision logic applied using SCA as discussed above. Finally, the insight provided by Actor Network Theory of the inscription and translation activity of actors in the network.

11.6 Conclusions

Inside-out

It is concluded that despite the apparent similarity of situations on the surface, and the expectation that broadly similar processes located in the same overall business context would adopt similar solutions in terms of commoditisation, governance, and resourcing (architecture), key inside-out architecture decisions of this nature are taken: (i) in a variety of business contexts, (ii) at varying levels within an organisation, (iii) where the views of the actors involved (as to whether each element could be treated as a commodity) can be wide ranging, and can change over time; (iv) in an environment where imperfect knowledge and know-how transfer exists; and (v) where there is no mechanism to recognise when capability has been achieved in a process activity.

The conditions under which commodity adoption is most likely to take place are where (i) the process logic comprises commodity components, is loosely coupled to other processes, has a high information threshold, and utilises standard information technology, (ii) the decision making is low in uncertainty, has a choice from many feasible decision schemes, and the decision makers have adopted a satisficing rather than optimising approach, and (iii) the actors are highly aligned, specialisation is low and market governance prevails.

The influence of a commodity work business process alone is not enough to ensure that the decision to adopt a commodity is achieved, and requires the support of both the decision logic and alignment logic for a successful and long lasting adoption to take place.

Outside-in

It is concluded that despite what might appear natural, obvious, or common sense rarely prevails especially when it comes to business processes. When observing processes through the lens of the customer there is much to suggest that organisations ignore their requirements; make it worse by applying technology badly; they disregard the way people naturally behave (especially during an emergency); they regularly fail to observe the good principles embedded within operations management; they communicate badly and despite soliciting feedback then don't handle complaints well and can often end up including an ombudsman or regulator.

The 'outside-in' requirement is most likely to be satisfied where: (i) Advocacy inhibitors are addressed and the organisation makes the customer (or service user) the focus of its operations, (ii) Communication blockages are avoided through regular and effective exchange of information in a method acceptable to the customer including feedback loops (both ways) and regular indicators of progress; (iii) by ensuring that the technology is robust and fit for purpose. Organisations get the 'IT' they deserve but this shouldn't be inflicted on the customer too; (iv) Accept that things can and will go wrong but remove any obstacles that stop the customer gaining a fair resolution by taking responsibility; (v) understand the importance of the four 'V's (volume, variety, variation, and visibility) and how these essentials of Operations Management shouldn't be ignored and (vi) recognise that when people are involved then anything can happen (and usually does). Recognise what drives us habitually and be prepared for unusual behaviour.

NOTES ON CHAPTER

i SENGE, P.M., 1990. *The Fifth Discipline: The Art and Practice of the Learning Organisation*. New York: Doubleday / Currency.

ii Gartner Report "Eleven steps to take before staffing business process management projects with internal or external resources" http://www.gartner.com/newsroom/id/767412)

APPENDIX ONE
What to do if you have an accident

Extract from Insurance Company guidelines following a road traffic accident

Accidents happen – even to the most careful drivers - and while we hope that you are never unfortunate enough to be involved in a road traffic accident, we know that it can help to be prepared. So here we offer some guidelines on what you should do if you do have an accident, with the aim of helping you deal with the incident at the time, as well as reduce the stress of making a claim afterwards. It's a good idea to print these guidelines and keep them in your car, along with a notebook, pen, and a disposable camera.

If you are involved in an accident you should:

- Stop at the scene if a person or an animal has been injured, or if another vehicle or property has been damaged. It is an offence not to stop.
- Try to stay calm. Ensure the scene of the accident is safe by checking that all engines are switched off, hazard lights are switched on, and oncoming traffic is alerted.
- Call 999 (or 112 from a mobile phone) if anyone is hurt or if the accident has caused a dangerous situation, and alert the police if the other driver leaves without stopping or does not give you their details. Tell the police if you suspect that the other driver's judgement is impaired by alcohol or drugs.
- Get the names, addresses and telephone numbers (home numbers as well as mobile numbers) of all drivers, passengers and pedestrians involved in the accident, **as well as any witnesses.**
- Ask the drivers of any other cars for the name of their insurance company and their policy number – they have to give you this information by law (the Road Traffic Act).
- Take down the registration numbers, makes, models and colours of all vehicles involved.

- If you have a camera or a mobile phone with a camera, take photographs of the vehicles and the damage, but be careful not to put yourself at risk.
- Make a sketch showing the street names, the positions of the vehicles and pedestrians involved both before and after the accident, and where the witnesses were located.
- Make a note of the speeds, distance, road layout, road signs and anything that may have been blocking your view, or the view of other drivers.
- Do not admit blame or liability for the accident or offer to pay for any damage. If any other person admits blame, tell us.
- If anyone was injured or property was damaged, be prepared to show your Certificate of Motor Insurance to the police or anyone else involved in the accident.
- Report the accident to us as soon as possible, even if you do not want to make a claim.
- If your car cannot be driven away after the accident, call us to arrange for your car to be recovered.
- We hope you never need them, but if the worst happens and you do have a road traffic accident, these guidelines can make all the difference when it comes to sorting it all out afterwards.

APPENDIX TWO: Glossary of terms – Conceptual model of commodity business process adoption

Appropriation	Redesigning packages as presented and making them firm specific by blending them with the existing organisational practices.
Articulation	Where fusion of external knowledge/artefacts/methods with internal knowledge/procedures/systems, had changed both in the process phenomenon.
Bounded rationality	Human beings lack the cognitive resources to maximize: we usually do not know the relevant probabilities of outcomes, we can rarely evaluate all outcomes with sufficient precision, and our memories are weak and unreliable. A more realistic approach to rationality takes into account these limitations.
Cognitive dissonance	A discomfort caused by simultaneously holding conflicting cognitions (e.g. ideas, beliefs, values, emotional reactions).
Commodity components	Components that are not specific to any specific process.
Contracts	A contract is an agreement entered into voluntarily by two parties or more with the intention of creating a legal obligation.

Deeper structure	Designers produce designs of business processes based on their perception, explanation, and understanding of organisational reality.
Externalities / overflowing	Externalities: all the connections, relations and effects which are not taken into account when entering a market transaction have an impact on a process. Overflowing: the impossibility of total framing, i.e. where framing is the ability to isolate or cut off a product, service, or actor from externalities.
Feasible decision schemes (and option bars)	A feasible decision scheme is one that would satisfy the criteria of the problem and would not violate any of the option bars. An 'option bar' is where two options from different decision areas are incompatible with each other, thereby ruling it out.
Governance (Hierarchical)	Hierarchical governance is applicable when an exchange is brought within the boundary of the firm.
Governance (Intermediate)	Intermediate governance, the use of complex contracts, strategic alliances, and joint ventures, is applicable when partnering to form a joint venture.
Governance (Market)	Where companies deal at arm's length and rely on market-determined prices to manage an exchange, but they do run the risk of opportunism when a transaction-specific investment is involved.
Information intensive	The degree to which information forms part of a company's technologically and economically distinct activities it performs to do business.
Information threshold	The correlation between data, information and knowledge exchanges within business processes. E.g. a high information threshold would be supportive of a commodity i.e. lots of data but little knowledge is passed.

Innofusion	The process by which an innovation is communicated through certain channels over time among the members of social systems. Innovation and diffusion combined.
Optimising	A decision-making strategy that attempts to meet criteria for optimisation, rather than to identify an adequate solution.
Path dependence	How the set of decisions one faces for any given circumstance is limited by the decisions one has made in the past, even though past circumstances may no longer be relevant.
Satisficing	A decision-making strategy that attempts to meet criteria for adequacy, rather than to identify an optimal solution.
Slow / strategic –fast / tactical	Two contrasting approaches to decision making that are at opposite ends of the decision making continuum.
Tightly-coupled (integrated)	The degree to which processes are connected to other processes and how reliant they are on each other.
Transaction specific investment – Loosely-coupled (stand-alone)	The extent to which the investments made to support a particular transaction have a higher value to that transaction than they would have if they were redeployed for any other purpose.
Trials & pilots	Exploratory studies limited in size and scope that give insight into the operation of a process, project, or mechanism.
Uncertainty 'UR' – Low & High	This refers to the level of uncertainty experienced in a decision area about the related decisions (labelled 'UR') that could impact on the prime decision.
Vanilla software	Vanilla software refers to using the developer's standard product i.e. as in a vanilla ice cream (no additional flavours).

APPENDIX THREE: Multiple Intelligences – Howard Gardner

	intelligence type	description	typical roles	related tasks, activities or tests	preferred learning style clues
1	**Linguistic**	**words and language**, written and spoken; retention, interpretation and explanation of ideas and information via language, understands relationship between communication and meaning	writers, lawyers, journalists, speakers, trainers, copy-writers, English teachers, poets, editors, linguists, translators, PR consultants, media consultants, TV and radio presenters, voice-over artistes	write a set of instructions; speak on a subject; edit a written piece or work; write a speech; commentate on an event; apply positive or negative 'spin' to a story	words and language
2	**Logical-Mathematical**	**logical thinking**, detecting patterns, scientific reasoning and deduction; analyse problems, perform mathematical calculations, understands relationship between cause and effect towards a tangible outcome or result	scientists, engineers, computer experts, accountants, statisticians, researchers, analysts, traders, bankers bookmakers, insurance brokers, negotiators, deal-makers, trouble-shooters, directors	perform a mental arithmetic calculation; create a process to measure something difficult; analyse how a machine works; create a process; devise a strategy to achieve an aim; assess the value of a business or a proposition	numbers and logic
3	**Musical**	**musical ability**, awareness, appreciation and use of sound; recognition of tonal and rhythmic patterns, understands relationship between sound and feeling	musicians, singers, composers, DJ's, music producers, piano tuners, acoustic engineers, entertainers, party-planners, environment and noise advisors, voice coaches	perform a musical piece; sing a song; review a musical work; coach someone to play a musical instrument; specify mood music for telephone systems and receptions	music, sounds, rhythm
4	**Bodily-Kinesthetic**	**body movement control**, manual dexterity, physical agility and	dancers, demonstrators, actors, athletes, divers, sports-	juggle; demonstrate a sports technique; flip a beer-mat;	physical experience and movement, touch and feel

		balance; eye and body coordination	people, soldiers, fire-fighters, PTI's, performance artistes; ergonomists, osteopaths, fishermen, drivers, crafts-people; gardeners, chefs, acupuncturists, healers, adventurers	create a mime to explain something; toss a pancake; fly a kite; coach workplace posture, assess work-station ergonomics	
5	**Spatial-Visual**	**visual and spatial perception**; interpretation and creation of visual images; pictorial imagination and expression; understands relationship between images and meanings, and between space and effect	artists, designers, cartoonists, story-boarders, architects, photographers, sculptors, town-planners, visionaries, inventors, engineers, cosmetics and beauty consultants	design a costume; interpret a painting; create a room layout; create a corporate logo; design a building; pack a suitcase or the boot of a car	pictures, shapes, images, 3D space
6	**Interpersonal**	**perception of other people's feelings**; ability to relate to others; interpretation of behaviour and communications; understands the relationships between people and their situations, including other people	therapists, HR professionals, mediators, leaders, counsellors, politicians, educators, sales-people, clergy, psychologists, teachers, doctors, healers, organisers, carers, advertising professionals, coaches and mentors; (there is clear association between this type of intelligence and what is now termed 'Emotional Intelligence' or EQ)	interpret moods from facial expressions; demonstrate feelings through body language; affect the feelings of others in a planned way; coach or counsel another person	human contact, communications, cooperation, teamwork
7	**Intrapersonal**	**self-awareness**, personal cognisance, personal objectivity, the capability to understand oneself, one's relationship to others and the world, and one's own need for, and reaction to change	arguably anyone (see note below) who is self-aware and involved in the process of changing personal thoughts, beliefs and behaviour in relation to their situation, other people, their purpose and aims	consider and decide one's own aims and personal changes required to achieve them (not necessarily reveal this to others); consider one's own 'Johari Window' and decide options for development; consider and	self-reflection, self-discovery

			- in this respect there is a similarity to Maslow's Self-Actualisation level, and again there is clear association between this type of intelligence and what is now termed 'Emotional Intelligence' or EQ'	decide one's own position in relation to the Emotional Intelligence model	

Source: http://www.businessballs.com/howardgardnermultipleintelligences.htm

Index

Note: Page numbers in **bold** type refer to **figures**
Page numbers in *italic* type refer to *tables*

Lightning Source UK Ltd.
Milton Keynes UK
UKOW04n1955250115

245088UK00003B/41/P

9 780993 057700